365 days of
homegrown
vegetables
& herbs

GROW YOUR OWN VEG
THROUGH THE YEAR

First published in Great Britain in 2024 by Mitchell Beazley,
an imprint of Octopus Publishing Group Ltd
Carmelite House
50 Victoria Embankment
London EC4Y 0DZ
www.octopusbooks.co.uk

An Hachette UK Company
www.hachette.co.uk

Published in association with the Royal Horticultural Society.

Design & layout copyright © Octopus Publishing Group Ltd 2024
Text copyright © The Royal Horticultural Society 2024

Distributed in the US by Hachette Book Group, 1290 Avenue of the Americas,
4th and 5th Floors, New York, NY 10104

Distributed in Canada by Canadian Manda Group, 664 Annette St, Toronto,
Ontario, Canada M6S 2C8

ISBN 978-1-78472-940-0

A CIP catalogue record for this book is available from the British Library.

Printed and bound in China.

10 9 8 7 6 5 4 3 2 1

Publisher Alison Starling
Senior Editor Leanne Bryan
Art Director Juliette Norsworthy
Copyeditor Jo Smith
Designer Lizzie Ballantyne
Illustrator Claire Huntley
Proofreader Catherine Jackson
Picture Researchers Giulia Hetherington & Jennifer Veall
Senior Production Manager Peter Hunt

RHS Publisher Helen Griffin
RHS Consultant Editor Simon Maughan
RHS Head of Editorial Tom Howard

The Royal Horticultural Society is the UK's leading gardening charity dedicated to advancing
horticulture and promoting good gardening. Its charitable work includes providing expert
advice and information in print, online and at its five major gardens and annual shows,
training gardeners of every age, creating hands-on opportunities for children to grow plants,
and sharing research into plants, wildlife, wellbeing and environmental issues affecting
gardeners. For more information, visit: www.rhs.org.uk or call 020 3176 5800.

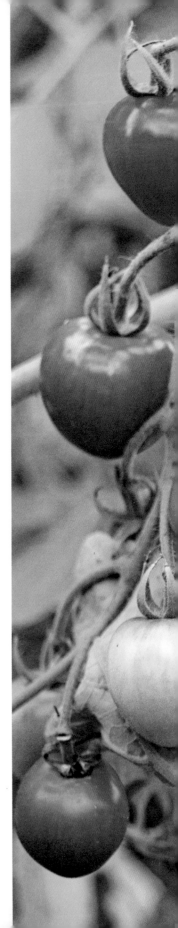

Contents

It all starts with vegetables

Growing food is one of the most powerful ways we can relate to the world around us. It connects us to the seasons, to other people, to our own bodies and minds, and to other lifeforms with whom we share the Earth. It can help us diversify our diets by expanding the range of what we grow and therefore eat, which can help to support a healthy immune system through a well-fed gut microbiome. Our environment will also benefit: for every bit of food we grow ourselves, we ease the burden on a weary food-supply chain that is becoming less and less sustainable.

Most people are not in a position to grow *everything* they need to sustain themselves, but many of us can grow *something*. Every single tomato plant or a herb grown on your windowsill is one less crop to be grown elsewhere, requiring lots of inputs, packaging, transport and often generating waste of all kinds. Seeds are an extremely efficient way to distribute food and, for many crops, if you start collecting your own seeds you could have food for life on your doorstep. Food this fresh tastes amazing.

The range of crops and varieties on offer to homegrowers compared to the limited supply in most supermarkets is staggering, and once you start you can never go back. The pages that follow share the learnings and experience of seven wonderful gardeners at the RHS and will act as a springboard for your own growing journey. We can produce annually and perennially, integrate edibles into our gardens to create beautiful spaces and build dynamic ecosystems where we become part of a food web rather than sitting at the top of a chain.

But whether you sow seeds, buy plants to grow on from nurseries, or nurture seedlings gifted by friends, in the process you will grow yourself. As edible growers, we are continually learning about the complexity of our growing environments as we discover new crops that canoffer some resilience in a changing world, affording us nutritious delights all year round. Growing food is an act full of hope when things around us seem challenging.

Your edible symphony is at your fingertips. Plants, pollinators, predators, prey, a chorus of worms, fungi and billions of microbes are the orchestra – enjoy conducting!

Sheila Das
Garden Manager Edibles, Education,
Seed and Wellbeing
RHS Garden Wisley

Left: When we grow our own, our diet becomes more interesting and diverse.

Right: Growing a mixture of crops is great for biodiversity and makes for a more resilient garden that can cope with climate variability.

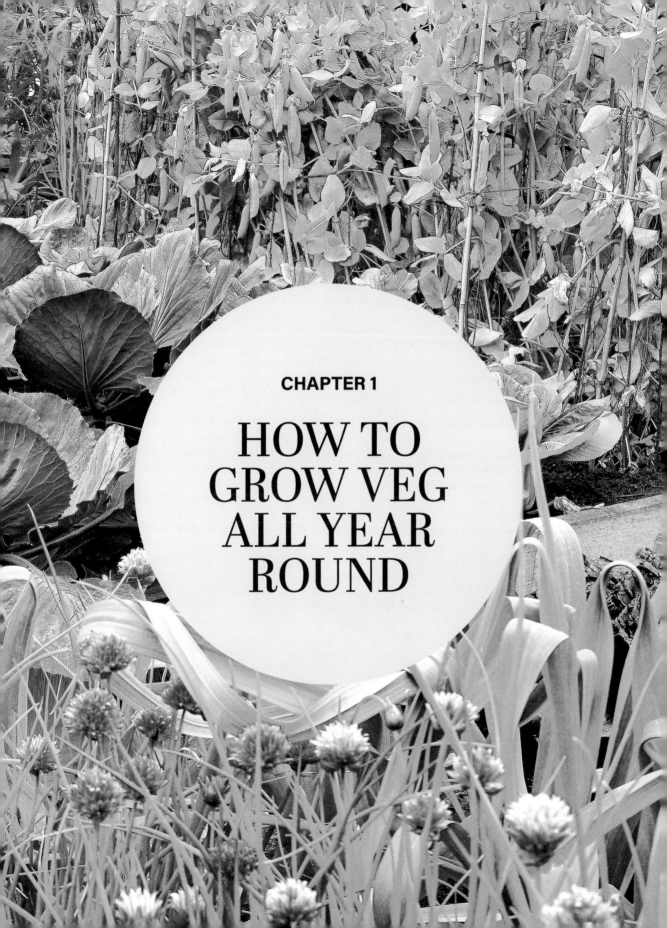

CHAPTER 1

HOW TO GROW VEG ALL YEAR ROUND

What can we grow?

There are two main questions to ask yourself when deciding what to grow: What do you want to eat? And what are your growing conditions? It's important to select crops that you enjoy. Also consider the amount of time you are willing to devote. What will things cost? Do you have somewhere to raise seedlings or will you sow direct? Are you able to store harvests to enjoy at a later date?

We often think of what we want first and look at our circumstances later. As gardeners, this means attempting to manipulate our environment to have whatever we desire. It is, of course, far more sensible and sustainable to think the other way around; instead of trying to change the conditions, we can think about what is suited to the situation and grow accordingly. It saves time and resources, and we can work with what we already have and think about realistic goals.

When thinking of your growing conditions, this chiefly refers to the amount of sun your garden might receive and what the soil is like, or whether you are growing in pots. If your ground is very wet and shady, or dry and baked in sunshine much of the time, this will affect what you can grow. If you have a garden where slugs and snails are prevalent, then you will have to think about how and where you grow lettuces, or whether you should try something different.

Although there must always be an element of experimentation, the key to successful year-round gardening is to research the plants you wish to grow and find out what they like before you begin, as well as any creatures that may enjoy munching on the same things so you can provide protection.

THE VEG CYCLE OF LIFE

Most of the crops you grow will be annuals. That means you'll grow them from seed or young plants and see them through to harvest either later the same year, or early the following year. After this time they die and you will add them to the compost heap and begin again. A year has passed and hopefully you will have personally gained from the experience. Annual crops are usually harvested before they can flower and set seed, but if you want to collect your own seed instead of buying new seed next year, then allow a few to reach maturity. A few crops in this book are perennial, meaning they will grow for many years before dying, going through many harvest cycles along the way. They are great value and worth trying.

Left: Make a plan so that at the end of the day you have a crop that is fulfilling to grow and enjoyable to eat.

Right: Crops such as these sweet potatoes can be grown for their edible leaves and their tubers, and are treated as annuals in cool climates.

How to grow sustainably

Making sustainable choices is complex, but when growing food there are a few rules of thumb that we can bear in mind. Begin by thinking about the materials or resources we use: the 'ingredients' of production. These might include seeds, nursery plants, bottles of fertiliser, potting compost, tap water, containers or insect barriers. Often, we can use materials from our own gardens, or items reused and saved from landfill.

Artificial products, be they 'natural' in their ingredients or synthetic, all require production and transportation, create waste and cost money. Over time, they contaminate our food, damage our health and destroy our environment. Carbon emissions from the energy needed to create and

distribute such products and the plastics used in manufacture are polluting air, land and sea. So, the less we use of such things, the more sustainable our system becomes.

We also need to build resilient systems that can cope with variable, and sometimes unpredictable,

PLASTIC USE

Wherever possible, use natural biodegradable materials instead of plastic. Jute twine, for example, instead of nylon string. Most plastics are unlikely to be reused for other purposes. Left lying around, they will gradually degrade into microplastics. These seep into the environment and become soil contaminants, entering the food chain. Horticultural fleece (composed of polypropylene fibres) is a single-use plastic product that is also energy intensive to produce. Fleece made from sheep's wool is newly available and a far more sustainable option as it can be reused repeatedly until eventually being composted.

weather patterns. Establishing a biodiverse ecosystem in which organisms regulate themselves in natural ways helps to stop us reaching for bottles of chemicals; plants and soil should interact to create a nutrient-rich underground environment which negates the need for expensive fertilisers. Some plants will cope naturally with less nutrient-rich soil (some herbs, for example), so do your research to make best use of available resources.

Our gardens should become more self-contained by making compost from garden waste and kitchen scraps, which can be used to feed our soil and grow healthy and nutritious crops. We can also save our own seeds (see Chapter 9) and share our young plants or produce with the local community. Seed saving can ultimately help with the genetic diversity of our crops, which in turn helps with food security. Quite simply, the more variety we have, the more resilient the system will become.

Left: Restricting yourself to natural or reclaimed materials in the garden can be decorative and fun, as well as sustainable.

TAKING ACTION

- **Reduce the need to buy compost** Raise plants in smaller modules and plant out when younger, or make your own.

- If you can't make your own compost, **consider mixing old compost with new** for potting and seed raising.

- **Ensure compost is peat free**, avoiding those with unnatural additives such as plastic-coated slow-release fertilisers.

- Think about what you can **sow directly into the ground** and sow a little extra to compensate for any losses. You could set up a seedbed where you can sow seedlings densely and then transplant them once they have grown on a little.

- **Avoid single-use plastic** whenever possible by reusing pots, and instead of using plastic ties or disposable module trays, use biodegradable alternatives.

- **Reduce the need to water** by selecting plants suited to your climate. Mulch your soil to help retain moisture.

- **Collect rainwater** in water butts to use for watering when you need it.

- **Minimize the materials you introduce to your growing system** Do you really need to make a raised bed if access or drainage is not a problem? Wooden edges are good hiding places for slugs, snails and woodlice. Consider what resources are needed to make the materials you want to bring in.

- **Avoid the use of synthetic weedkillers, pesticides and fungicides** Instead, suffocate weeds with thick cardboard or paper mats topped with mulch, adopt good gardening hygiene practices to avoid disease and exclude pests with barriers rather than trying to exterminate them.

How to cultivate biodiversity and wildlife

The relationships between the organisms we share our world with are highly complex and fragile. While not all creatures are welcome in the veg plot, maintaining a diverse and healthy balance reduces populations of unwelcome visitors, improves pollination and crop yield, and contributes to healthy soil.

Top: Plants left to go to seed will attract seed-eating birds, such as this coal tit.

Above: Introducing water into your plot will attract a host of beneficial wildlife.

There are some easy ways to make our gardens more biodiverse; it will help us and help our environment, and most importantly it will encourage our veg to flourish.

WELCOMING WILDLIFE

Like us, all creatures share certain basic needs – the first being water. The single biggest wildlife-friendly act in your vegetable plot should be to add a pond or water source, with shallow gravelly edges and marginal planting. This could take the form of a small pond or – at its most basic – a sunken bucket or upturned dustbin lid that can collect rainwater.

Wildlife will also need food. Herbs are particularly good for pollinating insects throughout the season, and around the plot consider planting flowering trees and shrubs. Native plants like ivy, blackthorn, hawthorn and hazel all provide shelter and sustenance for birds, insects, amphibians and mammals. Leaving artichoke and sunflower heads to flower and set seed will attract a range of seed-eating birds like finches, sparrows and tits.

MAKING HOMES

To encourage wildlife to stay, you need to provide habitats. Add dense native hedging or bushes around your veg plot, and hang nest boxes of a suitable design in a position to attract insect-eating birds. Use prunings and dead wood to create log or brush piles, or even 'bug hotels' to provide winter shelter for predatory insects like beetles, centipedes and spiders. Dry stone walls

WHICH ORGANISMS ARE BENEFICIAL?

– Frogs, toads, thrushes, blackbirds, hedgehogs, violet ground beetles and even foxes will help to balance slug and snail populations.

– Wasps, bluetits, robins, blackbirds, wrens, wagtails, centipedes, slowworms, dragonflies and damselflies, lizards, ground beetles, rove beetles, shrews, bats, swallows and swifts will balance populations of grubs, butterflies, caterpillars and other flying insects.

– Parasitic wasps, ladybirds, hoverflies, earwigs, soldier beetles, lacewings, blue tits and goldfinches will keep levels of aphids and other small sap-suckers under control.

– Owls, kestrels, weasels, stoats and foxes will prey on pigeons and rodents.

– Woodlice, earwigs, worms, millipedes, springtails, most of our slug and snail species (of which only three are interested in your crops) and fungi are vital for soil health and aid the decomposition of organic material.

Above: A bug hotel is a step-up from a simple log and brush pile, an attractive statement of intent that gives winter shelter to many insects.

or rock piles are loved by larger organisms like weasels, stoats, hedgehogs, slow worms and other reptiles, as well as all the many other smaller creatures that flourish in the tiny crevices.

It's also important to make sure wildlife can access the space. Leave gaps in your garden boundary to give access to hedgehogs, install pond ramps so creatures can access the water – or get out of it if they fall in – and remove crop mesh and netting when it is no longer in use. Turn compost heaps or leaf piles carefully in case any wildlife is making its home there, especially in winter when animals might be hibernating.

TAKING ROOT

Soil health plays a huge role in biodiversity, and gardeners will certainly benefit as this will result in more vigorous crops and increase the range of crops that can be grown. Add what you can to the soil in the form of biodegradable mulches, leaf mould and home-made compost. Let fallen leaves stay on the soil surface over winter. Feed the soil and it will not only feed you but a whole host of soil-creating microorganisms and fungi, as well as earthworms, which are all part of the food chain.

Growing for taste

When choosing which crops to grow, taste is hugely important as it is the main motivator for growing it in the first place. Everyone will have their preferences, and if you're new to the game then you will have fun trying to grow crops that are better than those you could hope to buy in the shops. Eating tasty food is also great for our mental health – after all, who can say that chewing on bland, watery food gives them any kind of stimulation?

HOW TO EVALUATE CROPS FOR FLAVOUR

The best way to assess crops for their taste is to grow them and eat them. It is the only way to find out what you like best and it certainly applies to learning the subtle differences between varieties. When starting out, however, there are some shortcuts: talk to other growers who can pass on their experience and look at seed packets or websites to get a general idea of what you might expect.

Vegetables you once considered bland and boring can suddenly be full of flavour. Radishes and potatoes are good examples of this. You will probably also find yourself enjoying crops you've never been that keen on before, creatively introducing them into your diet with the help of recipes gleaned from magazines, books or the internet.

Homegrown is so much fresher than shop-bought produce, and therefore more nutritious and better for your gut health. Plus, it is a good idea to constantly try new things. Growing your own opens up a range of taste and flavour possibilities, which you can access through diverse crops and varieties. You may not love the taste of everything you grow, but there is bound to be something to tempt your palate. Once a new favourite is found, saving seed or propagating it will ensure you can grow it for years to come.

OTHER CONSIDERATIONS

When choosing which crops to grow, taste is important, but there are other considerations. These might include yield, ease of cultivation, disease resistance and the chance to grow heritage varieties or those with local pedigree.

The RHS Award of Garden Merit (AGM) is a good indicator of reliable crops. After being trialled, only the best plants are given this award. However, it is worth considering that the AGM does not significantly consider taste, being more focused on reliability and yield.

F1 plants are another category to consider. These are varieties that have been bred to ensure a high degree of uniformity, meaning they produce a reliable and consistent crop. However, there are some questions around the sustainability of F1 crops given the time and effort needed to produce them, and remember that saved seed from these plants will not show the same degree of uniformity.

Choosing crops that are expensive to buy or difficult to get hold of can be a good approach when deciding what to grow. Homegrown carrots and potatoes taste better and are more nutritious than bought ones, but if you don't have space to grow everything, then expensive but easy-to-grow crops, such as lettuce, or hard-to-access crops, such as sea kale, may be more rewarding.

Right: Radishes are a good example of how flavourful homegrown crops can be.

How to plan for a year-round harvest

If you are new to growing, there will be immense pleasure to be had from growing your first crop and eating it – perhaps within minutes of harvesting. Successfully growing even one crop is likely to encourage you to have a go again the following year. It may even inspire you to try to grow a few more things.

As you begin to grow a wider range of crops, some planning will be needed. Think about the space you have and what will fit in it, when different crops need to be sown, and when they will have finished and the ground will be free for other things. You may also start thinking about how different crops can be combined to share the same piece of ground and increase productivity without negatively impacting on each other (see pp44–5).

TIPS FOR YEAR-ROUND VEG

Growing something to eat 365 days of the year is ambitious but, with the right choice of crops, harvests can be extended from late spring/early summer through to late winter. If you have the means to be able to store and preserve harvests by freezing, drying or making jams and chutneys this is another useful way of extending the season and dealing with gluts. For more information, see Chapter 9.

Some late-season crops, such as leeks, parsnips, kale and swede, will stand in the ground in good condition for a long time. Others, such as lettuce and radish, will not keep for long once mature and are best sown frequently in small quantities from early spring through to autumn/winter.

Weave into this summer harvests of sugarsnap peas, mangetout, French and broad beans as seasonal treats that need to be eaten soon after picking (though can be blanched and frozen).

Perennial veg also play a role. These are crops that remain in the soil for many years, providing a long-lasting harvest with minimal effort. Asparagus is a well-known example but, increasingly, gardeners are experimenting with crops like perennial kale (see p194) and perennial broccoli (see p196). Room can also be given to crops that store well, such as winter squash and onions. Stored correctly, these mainstays will see you through lean periods. And if you are good at making preserves and chutneys, then you will be able to stock up the larder with produce that

Left: Increase productivity by planting fairly densely and combining different crops in the same piece of ground.

Right: Grow crops that store well, such as these onions; it is a key component of ensuring a year-round harvest.

FORCING AND BLANCHING

Gardeners can gain early crops by 'forcing' – a term that means to stimulate growth by controlling levels of light and heat. In crops like rhubarb and sea kale, light is almost totally excluded, which also has the effect of 'blanching' the crop, making new growth paler, more tender and less bitter. Blanching can be done year-round on crops like celery, chicory and dandelions. The shanks of leeks are typically long and white; this too is achieved by transplanting seedlings deeply into prepared soil so only their tips are left exposed.

normally has a relatively short season, such as tomatoes, courgettes and aubergines. For more information, see Chapter 9.

Luckily for us, more and more crops that can be grown throughout the winter months are becoming known. Winter is a traditionally lean period, and this 'hungry gap' extends until mid or late spring. Grow a variety of these winter crops to help mitigate against variable weather: if one crop fails, another will survive. Kale and chard,

Below: Cold frames are useful for hardening off plants (see p38) but can also be used to extend the growing season.

for example, stand well over winter and can be harvested continually, as can many herbs, albeit with slower growth rates in the colder months.

Simply having plants in the ground ready to burst into life as the weather warms can also broaden harvesting options, and this can be achieved by a succession of planting all year round (see p44). For example, planting out cabbages in mid- to late summer can bring crops to maturity as the year closes.

Protected growing spaces such as a polytunnels, greenhouses, cold frames or even a windowsill mean that we can usefully extend the growing season. Cloches and fleece used out in the garden can also help. Planting hardy salads such as mustards, rocket, endive and certain varieties of lettuce in early autumn can mean they establish early and can be overwintered with a covering of fleece, raised above the plants with hoops to allow air flow and avoid rotting.

HOW CAN MODULES HELP?

One of the simplest ways of maintaining continuity is to have young plants that have been raised in modules ready to go straight in the ground as the last crop is removed (see p42). It's not the only option, of course, as many crops can be sown directly into the ground where they are wanted, but growing in modules does allow you to raise robust plants in advance and away from the unpredictability of the climate. When planted out, they can better tolerate a brief visit from a slug, for example, which would often be the end of any seedlings newly emerged from direct sowings.

Below: Raising plants in modules enables you to get them underway before the ground is available or while outside conditions are unsuitable.

GREEN MANURES

Year-round veg gardeners rarely leave the ground bare for very long, for the key reason that they want the plot to be as productive for as much of the year as possible. Having plants growing is also the best way to maintain a healthy soil, with the leaves protecting the soil surface from erosion, and the roots improving soil structure, helping to develop good mycorrhizal networks below ground and preventing nutrient leaching.

If you find that you have a bare patch with no crops coming on to fill it, then sow a green manure. As well as the benefits stated above, these plants also nourish the soil in the interim between crops, and they prevent the ground being colonized by weeds. They can also attract and provide homes for beneficial organisms. Common green manures include mustard, field beans, fodder radish, vetches, tares and phacelia. They are all easy to sow and grow, and when they are finished they are useful fodder for the compost heap. As part of your veg-growing arsenal, have a few green manure seeds ready to go.

Where to grow vegetables

All you need to grow veg at home is a small outdoor space, but even if you have just a windowsill, you can still grow something edible. If there is no obvious place to dig a veg patch, then raised beds, large containers or window boxes can all be turned into productive spaces.

There are lots of options when it comes to veg growing, but there are a few things to think about when assessing your growing opportunities. If you are growing in the soil (as opposed to a container) then know your plot and its soil (see pp22–5). Few vegetables thrive in waterlogged soil or compost, and sites that are very exposed to the elements might benefit from a bit of shelter.

With a balcony or a patio, you can have a few things growing in containers, and if you have a shady garden with a big tree with roots going everywhere, you could create a raised planter.

You can even mix your edible crops in with your ornamental borders.

WHAT ABOUT LIGHT AND SHADE?

One of the most important things to think about when growing any plant is how much light it needs, and for veg it is worth thinking of sunlight as a vital nutrient. Most vegetables need plenty of it, but you may find that some will cope with a degree of shade. For example, sweetcorn needs a sunny spot, as do courgettes, squashes and cucumbers. Leafy crops like chard, brassicas (such as kale, cabbage and broccoli) and salad leaves, however, will cope with partial shade, and in situations where summers include long, hot sunny spells, some shade in the hottest part of the day can be very welcome for these plants, especially ones that are prone to running to seed (see p41). Herbs are great in very sunny spots as many of them originate from Mediterranean climates, so think about a good place to grow your herbs, not too far from the kitchen. Herbs that will take a little shade include lovage, lemon balm and chives.

GROWING UPWARDS AND IN TIGHT SPACES

Climbing veg, such as peas and runner beans, can be a great way to produce a good harvest in a small space. These plants should be trained up a wigwam of canes or a support made from hazel branches, all held together with biodegradeable twine or jute netting. Cordon tomatoes and cucumbers can be trained onto a trellis. Remember that this can also be done with veg in containers.

MAKING USE OF CONTAINERS

Growing veg in a container can help to mitigate difficult conditions. So long as planters have drainage, they create a growing opportunity where previously there was none. Pots can be very handy if you are short on space, want to have something close to the house or like to grow something special and keep an eye on it – but, of course, consider the watering that will be required.

THE WONDER OF WINDOWSILLS

If you don't have a garden, but you do have a windowsill, you can grow some herbs such as basil, parsley, coriander or mint. You could grow these outside in a window box too, perhaps including chives, rosemary and thyme. Also consider sprouts and microgreens (see pp72–3).

VEG FOR A SHADY PATCH

The best veg to choose are leafy greens as they have a large surface area to make the most of meagre light. Try loose-leaf lettuce, chard, spinach, rocket and many members of the brassica (cabbage) family. Asian greens such as mizuna, mibuna and mustards also grow well, along with herbs like chervil, coriander and parsley. Runner beans and peas can succeed too, and root veg such as beetroot will produce smaller but worthwhile crops. Plants good for composting, such as comfrey, can also be grown in a shady patch: good for your growing system and for wildlife.

Left: Raised beds will help to contain your veg plot and your ambitions, meaning you can concentrate on a particular area and keep everything maintained.

Above: On a balcony or patio, a raised planter will allow for a varied mix of both herbs and veg.

Looking at your plot

If you could have any land you wanted, the perfect veg plot would be on gently sloping, sunny ground, sheltered from strong winds but otherwise open and bright. It would have a deep, rich soil full of healthy microbial life, which held plenty of moisture but drained well.

The reality for most of us is that we have to make the best of what we have. It's important to remember that, as home gardeners, we don't really need to maximize yield or to grow the perfect crop. Part of the fun lies in the doing, and it may be that by adapting to our conditions we find we can grow something different or unusual, or be forced to diversify. It is certainly possible to grow crops in less-than-perfect conditions and still get a lot of benefits, including something to eat.

CREATING SHELTER

On windy or exposed sites, try to slow the wind down with native hedgerows, which will also provide habitat and food for wildlife. Strong winds not only damage taller plants, but they cool the temperature, slow plant growth and increase moisture loss from both plants and soil. They also reduce insect activity and can lead to poor pollination in crops such as beans and peas.

MAKE THE BEST OF WHAT YOU HAVE

The best thing to do in whatever growing situation you have is to have a go and see what works in your space. Over time you will get to know what works, and you will want to keep experimenting with new things too.

If you have areas that are just too difficult – maybe they sit very wet throughout winter – then consider creating a pond. It's one of the best ways to increase biodiversity. Beyond that, try to put plants where they will be most suited.

Deep, sandy soils can grow fantastic carrots. Shady areas suit many leafy crops and mushroom logs, while some shade from the summer sun is preferred for salad crops and peas. Sunny and sheltered areas will benefit French and runner beans, tomatoes, peppers and aubergines, and vertical spaces can be used to grow annual climbers, such as squashes, peas or beans.

Left: Adapting to conditions, we will certainly find that some crops grow better than others, and this will determine future plantings.

MAKE A START WITH THE SOIL

A good start to understanding your site is to dig some holes and look at the soil (see below), as it's going to be responsible for the success of your plants. You will discover the depth of topsoil and what the underlying conditions are like. Are there many worms in the soil you dig out, or a paltry few? Return to these holes after rain (or fill them with a watering can) to see how well the ground drains (see p41). If it is predominantly clay, it may be poor draining; if it is light and sandy, then it may have difficultly retaining moisture in the warmer months. Adding organic matter, such as home-made compost, is a fantastic way to improve all soil types and will start to build a healthy soil biome that will in turn look after your plants.

Soil can be acidic, neutral or alkaline (also known as soil pH), and while it is worth finding out the pH of your soil – as it affects the availability of soil nutrients to crop roots, and some plants will be better suited to your soil type – in reality, most crops will cope with a wide range of soil types and pH. Soil-testing kits are cheap and readily available and the RHS offers a soil testing service which (at the time of this book's publication) is free to members.

MICROCLIMATES

Lots of gardens have their own peculiarities, which are often to do with quirks of the local climate, surrounding buildings and trees, orientation of the garden and the amount of exposure to the elements. You may find that you have frost pockets (places where cold air collects) or sun traps, for example, and these will all determine what you can grow and where in the garden it is best to grow it.

How to ready your soil

An important first step to building a healthy soil for veg growing is to add plenty of bulky organic matter, such as home-made garden compost, and this should be repeated at least once a year as a surface covering, rather than digging it in.

As we learn more about soil and its complexity, we understand that routine digging is a damaging practice. Healthy soils contain billions of living organisms and networks of fungi that help to make nutrients available for plant growth, create soil structure and regulate the flow of water and air.

We sometimes assume our soil might be compacted or unhealthy when it isn't, and our solution has often been to fork it over or dig to a spade or two's depth. By doing this we disrupt the life systems that are there. Instead, we can allow soil organisms to 'work' the soil for us.

CHOOSING NOT TO DIG

Organic matter is anything that was once living (even if it has passed through another living thing). We often only think of it as compost or manure, but living plants are organic matter too. We can improve our soil simply by growing plants, whether they be crops to harvest or 'cover crops' or 'green manures' (see p20), which veg growers sometimes plant to build and maintain soil health.

Broken down and decaying organic matter (such as home-made compost or leaf mould) should be added as a soil covering to help to conserve moisture and suppress weeds. This is consumed by soil-dwelling organisms, including fungi, which liberate nutrients that plants can use, while also actively feeding the system by drawing down energy from the sun and carbon dioxide from the atmosphere. Soil life thrives on organic matter, and the quality of the soil becomes darker, richer, less prone to drought and waterlogging, and any reliance on artificial fertilisers is removed.

The 'no-dig' system works on the principle that we should feed our soil rather than our plants, and the rest will happen naturally. While it is good to add plenty of well-rotted organic matter regularly, we do not need to do this excessively; on established beds, mulching once a year with a small amount of compost (covering the surface with about 2.5cm/1in of compost) will be ample.

Gardeners will find that when it comes to planting into an established no-dig bed, nothing could be simpler. Soil disturbance will be minimal, requiring much less physical work, making seed drills and planting holes only where they are needed. Water will soak directly into the ground rather than running off, and when it comes to removing harvested crops, they can just be cut at the base, leaving roots in the soil to further strengthen the system.

Left: Home-made compost is great organic matter to add as a mulch to the surface of soil; it feeds soil organisms, which in turn feed plants.

Right: To make a no-dig bed, lay down sheets of cardboard so that they overlap, then dampen the cardboard with water. Cover the cardboard with a generous layer of well-rotted organic matter, such as home-made compost. Veg can be planted into the bed fairly soon after, as their roots will be able to penetrate the softened cardboard with ease.

HOW TO MANAGE POOR DRAINAGE

Soils that drain poorly are not good for veg production, especially during the winter months when standing crops will begin to rot. Air spaces in the soil that are vital for the roots to breathe become filled with water, and the plants will die. Perhaps the simplest solution might be to choose a different site for your veg plot, and to grow instead plants that will tolerate these conditions. An alternative approach would be to create a no-dig bed on top of the soil, possibly one contained within a boundary of wooden boards or sleepers, which will not only raise it above the poorly drained soil but also retain the organic material that has to be added.

HOW TO CREATE A NO-DIG BED

There are a few ways of creating a no-dig bed. If the site is a grassy lawn without many weeds, you may only wish to mow it by way of preparation. Organic matter can go straight onto the area at a depth of about 7.5cm (3in).

In an area with more weed growth, cut it back and then lay down cardboard first as this will prevent weeds emerging by excluding light. This can be done by overlapping the cardboard across the area that you wish to establish for growing. The cardboard should be brown (not printed and glossy) and free from packaging tape. When laid, the cardboard can be wetted. This aids its decomposition, and when plants are planted in the layer of compost above, their roots can penetrate the soft cardboard and get into the soil below.

For a new bed, cover this cardboard with about 7.5cm (3in) of home-made compost, but in situations where the ground is very weedy, this initial covering may be as much as 15cm (6in). You can make a decision about this based on what compost is accessible to you and if you apply a little less, you may just do a little more weeding during the early years of the bed. The beauty of this method is that it is a quick way to get growing straight away.

CROP ROTATION VERSUS MIXED PLANTING

You may be wondering where crop rotation fits into a no-dig system. This is still debated, but the healthier your soil, the less likely is it is that you will need to rotate your crops in the conventional way. In rotational systems, crops are moved around a planted area as part of a four-year system, according to their type: brassicas, legumes, root vegetables and alliums.

Rotation plans (see below) can sometimes create quite a head-scratcher for the gardener, and it also seems to imply that crops must be planted in blocks, in these groupings. In many ways this is not a sensible thing to do as anything wishing to eat your crop can easily locate it in abundance. Mixing up your crops can create resilience. The plan opposite shows just how to do this with a 'squared-up' system, showing how many plants

CONVENTIONAL CROP ROTATION

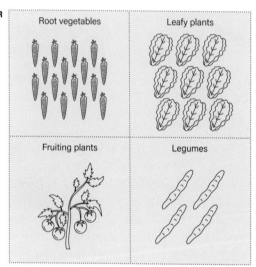

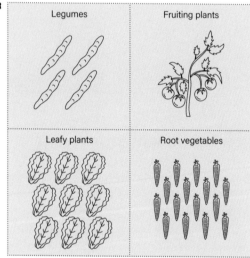

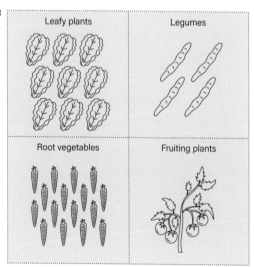

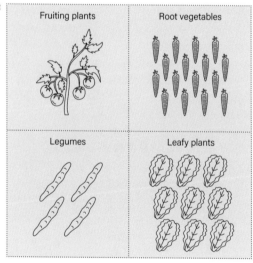

can be grown per block. Individual blocks can be mixed however you like, and blocks can be combined if necessary – sweetcorn, for example, benefits from being in groups of at least eight plants, and it may be more practical to plant all your brassicas under the same mesh net. Paths can be put between the blocks to improve access.

Remember to periodically add well-rotted organic matter to the soil, feeding the soil not the plant. If we spoil our plants with artificial fertilizers and seemingly perfect conditions they can become easy targets for predators and susceptible to disease.

So, vary your plantings but do not worry too much about a strict rotation or planting the same type of crop in the same place one year after another. Mixing crops may bring more benefits than conventional rotation, and it will encourage you to diversify your harvest.

MODERN MIXED PLANTING

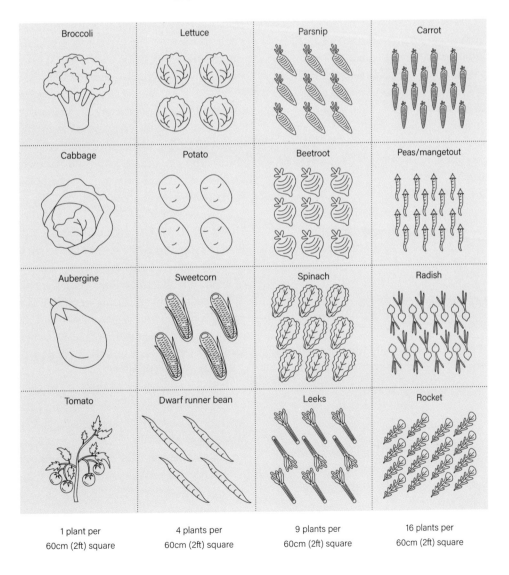

Broccoli	Lettuce	Parsnip	Carrot
Cabbage	Potato	Beetroot	Peas/mangetout
Aubergine	Sweetcorn	Spinach	Radish
Tomato	Dwarf runner bean	Leeks	Rocket

| 1 plant per 60cm (2ft) square | 4 plants per 60cm (2ft) square | 9 plants per 60cm (2ft) square | 16 plants per 60cm (2ft) square |

How to make compost

If there's one secret to good vegetables, it's good, home-made compost. There is no such thing as bad compost, but with care you can make *really good* compost. Compost is all about recycling waste and using what you've got. It all contributes to sustainability, to locking carbon into the soil, and to feeding the organisms that drive healthy soil. With compost you can help build biodiversity and make your soil more hospitable to veg growing. And best of all, it's free.

COMPOST INGREDIENTS

To make compost, you will need a mix of fresh green materials rich in nitrogen and moisture, such as leaves, grass or vegetable scraps; and brown materials rich in carbon, such as twigs, fallen leaves, cardboard or shredded paper, to create air space and bulk. You should aim for around two-thirds green to one-third brown material by volume.

WHAT TO COMPOST

You can, strictly speaking, compost anything organic. But to avoid attracting rodents, keep cooked or processed food, meat or bones away from the compost heap. Excessive amounts of any material can slow the process (it is best to keep things mixed up), but everything will compost eventually. Take care when adding invasive or persistent plants to the heap; their roots are best dried out on a wire rack or thoroughly drowned in a bucket of water first, and only add their seedheads if you can be sure the seed is not ripe. If something is diseased, consider incinerating it and adding the ash, burying it, or disposing of it in the household green waste.

HOW TO CONTAIN COMPOST

From a large three-bay system to a small hot bin or tumbler for smaller spaces – there's loads of choice for the home gardener. Make your own or buy online: just think about what will work for you in terms of your veg plot's size and the amount of green waste you generate. Worm bins are great for just kitchen waste and their exudate makes a good liquid fertiliser.

When you begin to add waste, chuck in a little soil from your garden to bring in the workforce: worms, bacteria and fungi. Chop or shred your material as small as possible to speed up decomposition. Like a lasagne, create your heap with alternate layers of green and brown to encourage airflow.

HEALING YOUR COMPOST

Any problems that occur are easy to fix:

- **Bad smells?** Add brown matter and turn regularly. Check drainage below the heap.

- **Not heating up?** Add green leafy material and turn, cover with cardboard to retain heat and moisture.

- **Too dry and not rotting?** Pour in some water and leave the lid open when it rains.

- **Slugs?** Not a problem: the vast majority of slug and snail species are beneficial as they only eat decaying matter.

HOW TO MANAGE THE HEAP

Although not noticeably, the heap will heat up – this is the bacteria working – and once it cools, turn and mix up the compost. This usually involves shovelling the contents of the heap from one bin to another, but tumbler bins are available to make the job easier.

After turning, the heap may heat up again. Once cooled, the fungi and worms move in to finish the job. Keep it moist in summer and consider covering in winter so the nutrients don't wash away. Once ripe, in as little as four months, sieve it and spread it as a surface mulch between your plants. Bigger pieces or uncomposted material can go back in for another cycle.

Left: Compost should be 'turned over' once a year or more often to help it rot down. It helps to have a system of bins so as one is emptied, another one is filled.

Above: Worm bins work on a tiered system, with the bottom tier filled first and emptied just as the top tier is filled. Mix in a little cardboard to encourage the worms.

If you've followed this process, you'll have free compost, rich in beneficial organisms local to your garden. It'll also probably contain some unexpected seeds, germinating where you have spread the compost. This is normal, and they can be removed – after all, if you didn't have weeds, what would you compost next year?

Crop protection and garden hygiene

Encouraging wildlife into the food garden may seem counter-intuitive, but it's about creating a balance that has been lost through the use of synthetic chemicals and the destruction of habitats. The year-round veg plot, rich in wildflowers, with a small pond or other source of water and a log pile or two, will buzz with insects in summer, providing pollination for crops and protection against plant-eating invertebrates, such as aphids.

CREATING A NATURAL BALANCE

When aphids start to colonise broad beans, which happens from time to time, hold your nerve and trust that the ladybirds will arrive, which they usually do. But without the prey, there wouldn't be sufficient predators – it's about balance.

By growing without chemical sprays or synthetic fertilisers, the focus is instead on soil health and careful choice of crop varieties that grow well in the absence of man-made inputs. Strong, resilient plants produce tasty, nutrient-dense food that is good for our health and for the planet.

CONDITIONS TO THRIVE

To this end, avoid grouping crops in blocks or monocultures, where insect infestations and disease pressures can explode at the complete expense of the crop. Instead, try growing three, four or even five different, unrelated crops in each small bed jostling for space, adding to diversity and generally avoiding problems (see pp26–7).

Most crops are grown out in the open, and small losses are always expected as part of the natural order; take comfort in knowing that you have provided food to support wildlife.

TACKLING PROBLEMS

Many organisms such as asparagus beetle and gooseberry sawfly can be removed by hand. Some especially vulnerable crops, such as many brassicas, can be covered with fine mesh netting (see facing page) to keep hungry birds and insects out, though many gardeners find that birds tend to leave red-leaved brassicas and perennial kale alone. Scarecrows, glittery compact discs and so on may work for you or they may not. It is discoveries like these that will be part of your gardening journey, making you a better, wiser and more environmentally sensitive gardener.

Left: Holding your nerve when aphids first appear provides ladybirds and their larvae with a valuable food source. It's about balance.

Above: Log piles are diverse habitats, supporting a wide range of species over time as they break down.

CLEAN BUT NOT TOO CLEAN

For many years, gardeners have talked about 'good garden hygiene'. This often resulted in removing all fallen leaves and fastidious weeding, but a blurring of these edges can be beneficial. Some detritus in the garden is important for the range of predators and prey that help to maintain a healthy garden. Slugs and snails love decaying material, but remove all of it and you leave them little option but to search for other sources of food – which could include your lettuces.

WHERE TO BUY YOUR CROPS

We must all be vigilant around biosecurity to stop the introduction and spread of potentially harmful non-native biological organisms. This applies particularly to novel tuberous crops such as yacon (see p230) and oca (see p227), which are potential sources of very damaging pathogens with wide host ranges, including many important crops and native plant species. It is important that you ensure all seeds and other plant material that you buy comes from established horticultural businesses and have been locally grown rather than imported. It's vital not to bring any plant material home from overseas travel, as these may include plant pests and diseases, and avoid growing plants from veg imported for eating.

NETTING VERSUS MESH

At the time of writing, most products available to gardeners that are designed to exclude pests from eating our veg are made from plastic. These might be nets to deter birds, or mesh to keep insects away. Where possible, gardeners should either reuse these products year after year, seek out biodegradable alternatives or make permanent caging using chicken wire.

Netting, while it uses less plastic than mesh, can be harmful to birds if they become entangled in it unless the holes are 7mm (⅜in) or less, in which case it may be more useful to use insect-proof mesh as that will have a dual function of excluding small bugs as well as birds and butterflies.

Biodegradable fleece made from sheep's wool is useful for low-lying crops such as carrots. Fleece has the dual function of protecting crops from spring frosts as well as excluding damaging insects.

Below: Raise protective netting or mesh off crop leaves with supports to prevent insects laying eggs onto the plants through the barrier.

When weeding is necessary

While we don't necessarily want to see our veg plots crowded out with plants that are not supposed to be there, these plants that we might call weeds are plants that have wildlife value and should be seen partly as an asset. Docks, for example, are a food plant for the small copper butterfly, and dandelions are an important spring nectar source for many insects.

Weeds do, however, compete with our veg plants for nutrients, light and water. A plot that is not assiduously weeded will almost certainly have lower crop yields, but as a gardener you may tolerate a certain amount of sharing if it increases the wildlife in your garden. Like any other plant, weeds need light to grow. Exclude this and the plant dies. Laying down thick cardboard or paper sheet mulches and covering with a thick layer of loose mulch will suppress many except the most persistent perennial weeds, and annual weeds can be pulled by hand or knocked over with a hoe.

RULES FOR CONTROLLING WEEDS

- An initial layer of cardboard covered by a layer of mulch will control many annual and perennial weeds and should help reduce subsequent weeding.

- For aggressive weeds, such as brambles and docks, slice and dig out the roots and add only to a hot compost heap (not a cool one) to break their life cycle. If adding to a cool heap, dry the roots out first in the sun.

- For perennial weeds, such as dandelion and bindweed, remove with a trowel by hand every week, especially the leaves so they can't take energy from the sun. Repeat as they reappear and you will eventually exhaust the roots.

- Check beds for weeds every week from early spring and try to remove by hand or hoe when they are still tiny seedlings.

- Allow a few weeds to flower for their wildlife value, but try not to let them go to seed.

Below: Remove weeds before they make seeds, which will prevent them from spreading too much.

Feeding crops in pots and planters

If you grow vegetables in pots, supplementary feeding is required to keep crops healthy, as the plants quickly use up the available nutrients. Feeding plants with plants, in the form of seaweed, comfrey or nettle, offers the most sustainable way of keeping your container-grown crops healthy.

Supplementary fertilizers come in many forms, and those derived from organic sources feed the soil over a long period of time. Inorganic feeds may promote a lot of growth, but this will be more prone to damage from predators and disease, and will be less nutritious and tasty to eat.

Mixing in solid organic feeds with the compost when planting is one way to keep your plants well fed. Look for balanced feeds, but leafy crops may benefit from one that is high in nitrogen, such as chicken manure, and root crops one that is high in phosphorous, such as bonemeal. Hungry crops like tomatoes, squash and anything being grown in a container will benefit from liquid organic feeds.

MULCHES

Although they have low nutritional value, organic surface mulches help to keep moisture in the soil, and as they rot down they feed the soil. Organic mulches might include leaf mould, spent coffee grounds or mushroom compost.

LIQUID FEEDS TO MAKE AT HOME

Organic feeds can be made for free from plants you may already have in the garden.

– **Comfrey tea** Comfrey is amazing at extracting deep nutrients from soil with its large tap roots, produces big thick hairy leaves and the flowers are great for pollinators. It makes an amazing liquid feed, which is rich in not only nitrogen and phosphorus, but potassium – ideal for fruiting veg. To make a concentrated feed, fill a bucket with fresh leaves, put a brick or heavy stone on top and leave out of the sun until the material decomposes. Drain the liquid into a bottle (being very careful not to get it on your skin, or in your eyes – it will also smell rather unpleasant) and label and date the bottle. Strength will vary, so dilute one part in ten parts of water, and maybe try on one plant first to see how it responds after a few days.

– **Nettle tea** Repeat this process with stinging nettles to make a more nitrogen-rich feed, great for leafy crops or the early stages of fruiting crops when they're putting on leaf mass. Choose new leaves and young stems – you'll need decent gloves and long sleeves for this.

Use your nettle or comfrey tea within a couple of months of making it. Any surplus makes a great compost heap activator. Always apply the feed around the base of plants, avoid eating crops raw for 2–3 days after the feed is applied, and wash thoroughly to avoid the risk of ingesting harmful bacteria. If handling the liquid or applying as a spray to leaves, wear gloves, a mask and eye protection to reduce the risk of irritation.

How to grow from seed

Most vegetables grow well from seed. It is cheaper than buying young nursery plug plants from a specialist supplier or garden centre and offers a wider choice of varieties. Seed can be sown directly outside – either where it is to grow or in a special nursery seedbed – or sown inside and planted out later. Seed potatoes are not actually seeds, but small spuds that are certified disease free, and it is common to see onions grown from 'sets' rather than from seed.

WHAT EQUIPMENT DO YOU NEED?

For direct sowing, a hoe or hori-hori (Japanese weeding knife) is all that is needed. Inside, module trays (seed trays that are divided into smaller sections), seed trays or pots can be used. Home-made containers, including toilet roll tubes or newspaper pots, are also useful. Peat-free multipurpose compost will usually work well as a substrate for germination, as long as it is fine enough.

WHERE TO SOURCE SEED

Buy seeds from reputable sellers. This helps ensure biosecurity measures are met, and that the seeds are good quality. The number of seeds per packet varies, and specialist retailers are often the most reliable, especially for unusual crops. Seed swaps are useful for obtaining different varieties. Keep seeds cool to prolong their life. Seeds past their use-by date will often germinate, but it is sensible to sow a few extra just in case.

SOWING THE SEED

Timing, depth and spacing varies depending on the crop and variety, so checking the seed packet is vital. Many crops benefit from sowing little and often to encourage successional harvests instead of gluts. Also check how much water the seed needs to germinate.

Temperature will also affect how quickly seed germinates. Carrots, for example, sown in cold soil in early spring may take up to three weeks to germinate, but just two weeks if the soil is warmed with horticultural fleece or the sowing is made later. Covering with fleece can really bring the season forward for direct sowing.

Station sowings are made by sowing two or three seeds in each location where the plants are to grow, at the correct spacing, and thinning the seedlings to one healthy one after germination.

Drills involve drawing out a little furrow in the soil, about 1–2cm (1/2–3/4in) deep depending on the type of seed being sown, sprinkling seeds along the bottom of the drill and covering with soil.

Broadcast sowing is where the seed is scattered across the soil in an evenly random fashion and lightly raked in.

A nursery seedbed is an outside area where seeds are sown before they are transplanted into their final position.

HOW TO 'MULTI-SOW'

Plants grow well in company, and multi-sowing promotes this. Instead of thinning seedlings to one, multi-sowing involves growing crops, such as beetroot, spring onions and pea shoots, in clusters of 4–10, depending on the crop. As they grow, the seedlings push apart. To harvest successively from a single sowing, twist out the largest plant in the cluster, leaving the rest undisturbed and able to keep growing.

Right: If small seeds are sown in drills, they will need to be thinned out. The thinnings of these lettuce plants can be eaten.

Above: A heated propagator is very useful for germinating seeds of tender veg, such as tomatoes and pumpkins.

STARTING SEEDS EARLY

Many crops can be started off early by germinating seeds on a sunny windowsill, in a propagator (which is like a mini-greenhouse), or in an actual greenhouse. Unheated propagators can be improvised out of recycled plastic pots with clear lids, and are suitable for most veg seeds. Tender veg like tomatoes and chillies will benefit from electrically heated propagators. Avoid sowing so early that seedlings have to stay on the windowsill for a long time, as the seedlings can become quite stretched out and leggy as they search for the sun.

TINY SEEDS AND THINNINGS

If the seeds are small, you can expect small seedlings, and this can make for fiddly transplanting if they are sown into pots or modules for later planting. To avoid this, sow thinly. Leeks are a good example. For those that are sown directly where they are to grow, such as carrots or parsnips, the same advice can be followed. As the crops grow, they will need to be 'thinned out' so that the larger ones have space to grow. The thinnings of veg crops are often edible.

Starting seeds indoors enables earlier sowings, and allows tender plants to be started before the last frost. Modules, with different sizes available for different seeds, allow for minimal root disturbance when thinning and planting. Seeds sown in seed trays will need transplanting or 'pricking out' into individual pots once they are large enough and have at least two sets of leaves: always hold the leaves not the stem when doing this. Larger seeds (such as broad beans) are easy to sow directly into large modules or 9cm (3¾in) pots.

Hardening off and planting out

Regardless of whether you have germinated the seed yourself or bought from a nursery, young plants will get to a stage where they need to be planted into their final growing positions. Take care not to plant out too early, and check they are not tender to frost. A sudden cold spell in late spring can be enough to wipe out a newly planted crop.

PLUG PLANTS AND PERENNIALS

Many vegetables are available to purchase as plug plants. These small rooted seedlings can either be potted up and grown on, or planted straight out where they are to grow. Perennial vegetables can also be bought as larger plants. Buying crops this way saves space and time compared to growing from seed, but usually restricts the choice of varieties. Most garden centres and online retailers sell a range, although online is generally better for more unusual crops. Be sure to buy from reputable sellers, and try to avoid purchasing from overseas because of biosecurity risks.

Below: Use a cold frame to acclimatize plants when moving them from indoors to outdoors.

HOW TO HARDEN OFF

Once plants are of a size to be planted, most people will advise hardening them off because if the environment around plants changes too suddenly, the shock can check their growth. This involves gradually acclimatizing plants to being outside after having been grown in a protected environment until that point. Plants can be put outside during the day and brought back in at night, or placed into a slightly less sheltered location. For example, plants in an open cold frame will harden off much more reliably compared to those in a greenhouse.

However, hardening off is usually not necessary. If care is taken with the time of planting – for example, not planting just before a frost – then plants will adapt quickly. If necessary, plants can be covered with horticultural fleece or a cloche when planted. If this is removed after a few weeks the plants were essentially hardened off in situ without having to be relocated more than once.

HOW TO PLANT OUT

When planting out any crop, ensure that it is being planted at a suitable time for that plant. Once planted, all crops should be watered, and then kept well-watered until they start growing, which indicates they are established.

A lot of plants are best positioned at the same depth they were in their modules or pots. However, many annuals can be planted up to the first leaves, especially brassicas, tomatoes and most salads. This helps to ensure the plants are firmed well into the ground and can correct any leggy tendencies that previously developed.

Spacing varies a lot between crops, so ensure the final size is known. Ensure that there is a good distance between the plants to aid weeding and air circulation, and if you are mixing different types of crops together take care that taller plants do not overshadow smaller ones. A matrix style of planting can work well for single crops, where all plants are equidistant from each other, allowing more to be fitted into the same space.

Top: A covering of horticultural fleece will protect young plants, allowing them to be brought on a little earlier than if left unprotected.

Above: Plant at the correct spacing for the crop; closer spacing may reduce weeding but could affect yield and plant health.

How to water wisely

Plants need water to grow. However, with rainfall patterns becoming ever more erratic, water is an increasingly scarce resource and often most needed when it is in limited supply. Gardeners need to be aware of these issues and adopt practices that ensure plants stay hydrated and grow more resilient.

SAVING WATER

It is said that the Earth's soils can store eight times as much water as the Earth's rivers, but for this to happen we need healthy soils that are ready to receive it. You can promote this by adding organic matter as a mulch to improve water absorption and retention. Mulches will also reduce evaporation and soil cracking.

Harvesting water from rooftops is also a great idea, as the best thing to water veg with is rainwater. Install and use a water butt on as many drainpipes as possible, including sheds and greenhouses, and leave buckets or trugs outside when rain is due. Store rainwater in a shady place, with a lid or cover, and keep containers clean.

If you are growing veg in containers, then put drip trays under them in summer so that any water that tries to drain away is captured. Also available are self-watering pots, which contain a reservoir from which the plants can draw moisture.

Most grey water (water that has been saved from baths, showers and washing up) is unsuitable to use for watering edible plants as there is a risk of contamination from pathogens and chemicals in the water, but you can reuse detergent-free water previously used for simple rinsing.

Left: Plants much prefer rainwater over water from the tap, so collect what you can in storage containers connected to any available gutters. Stored water is also a great resource during drought.

Right: Watering with a watering can may seem like a chore compared to using a hose, but it will stop you wasting precious water.

KNOW YOUR SOIL

Different soils drain at different rates, and too much water can be a bad thing. Dig a 30cm (12in) square drainage hole and fill with water. Measure the depth hourly until empty, then calculate the average. Optimum drainage is 2.5–7.5 cm (1–3in) per hour. Adding organic matter as a mulch will, over time, improve both drainage and retention for both poorly and free-draining soils.

HOW TO RECOGNIZE WATER STRESS

Plants show water stress in many ways. Reduced flowers or fruit, drooping leaves or new leaves with browning at the tips or edges can all indicate drought. Some leafy crops like spinach or lettuce can run to seed or bolt (see box). Likewise, slow growth and pale, yellowing older leaves can indicate overwatering. On really hot days, some foliage can droop or curl to preserve water, so always check the soil. Electric moisture meters for container plants are surprisingly affordable.

WHEN AND HOW TO WATER

Always water with a can rather than a hose. It prevents wastage, saves water, and a watering can ensures water is directed to where it is needed: the root zone. Watering cans are generally a more efficient way to apply water, and they encourage us to use water more judiciously. As time goes on, you get to really understand the amount of water your soil and plants need.

Make a habit of pushing your hand into the soil before and after you water to assess moisture and to see how your soil is responding. Watering little and often encourages shallow root systems that are susceptible to drought, whereas watering thoroughly but less often encourages deep root systems and resilient plants. It's best to water plants in the morning or the evening when they'll benefit most, and less will be lost to evaporation. Remember that not all plants need the same amount of water.

BOLTING OR RUNNING TO SEED

Under normal conditions, all veg will eventually flower and set seed but most are harvested and used in their immature state before they can flower. Some veg, such as lettuce, pak choi and spinach, however, will often flower prematurely (known as 'bolting' or 'running to seed') in hot, dry weather, producing flower spikes but no harvestable leaves. Prone crops should be grown in a cooler, moister position – out of direct sun, for example – or grown only during the cooler months of spring and autumn.

How to combine crops for maximum production

Choosing the correct crop combinations will help ensure the vegetable garden is productive for as long as possible. This can be done by mixing crops, growing them one after another, or squeezing them between harvests so that there is always something to eat. Many combinations are tried and tested; others you will have fun experimenting with.

Growing multiple crops in the same bed also ensures better soil protection, keeping the soil surface mostly covered and nutrients and water locked in. Harvested crops are simply cut off at ground level once finished and new crops planted amongst them to minimize disturbance to the soil. Some plants can even be left to flower as they provide an important food source for insects. In this way, your plot will nourish much more than just the people who visit.

SUCCESSION PLANTING

With careful planning, an area of soil can provide harvests from three or four different crops a year. When one crop finishes, another can be planted – a regime that will maximize productivity. Starting crops indoors often helps as the next crop is ready to plant as soon as the previous one is harvested.

Above: Experiment with mixing crops and varying planting times so that there is always something to eat.

CATCH CROPPING

Catch crops fill a bed before the main crop for that year is planted, enabling an extra crop to be harvested from the soil. For example, many overwintering brassicas are not planted until late summer. Instead of leaving the ground fallow early in the season, fast-growing crops, such as lettuce and beetroot, can be grown and will be out of the way by the time the brassicas are due to be planted.

INTERCROPPING

When a second crop is grown in the gaps between a first crop, this is known as intercropping. For example, rows of radishes sown between rows of parsnips will grow and be harvested before the parsnips get too large and fill the space. The intercrop will be a fast-growing vegetable that fills the space not yet used by the slower-growing crop nearby. Intercropping allows for two harvests from the space instead of one.

Many crops can be intercropped close to harvest time, giving new intercrops a head start. For example, onions close to harvest can be undersown with a salad crop. A few weeks later, the onions are then twisted out of the ground, leaving the salad to keep growing.

COMPANION PLANTING

This involves intermingling different plants to provide benefits for all. Companion plants are commonly flowers, such as marigolds and nasturtiums, which are often edible themselves and will attract pollinators and beneficial insects into the garden. Beneficial insects, including ladybirds and hoverflies, can then prey on pests such as aphids, helping to control them without the use of chemicals. Some flowers also have more specific benefits, for example there is some evidence *Tagetes patula* can help control eelworms in the soil.

Companion planting can also refer to the mixing of compatible crops. A classic example is the three sisters combination, where climbing beans grow up sweetcorn, using them as a support, and squashes cover the ground underneath, helping suppress weeds and hold in moisture. Many specific plant combinations said to bring benefits are often based on garden folklore rather than actual evidence. However, mixed plantings are generally more resilient and can help to camouflage certain crops from insects. Some combinations do have supporting evidence: for example, parsley gives increased vigour to crops such as asparagus.

Below: Radishes make an excellent catch crop as they can be started early and are fast to mature.

Below: Spring onions here make an intercrop between lettuce, which still have a way to go before harvest.

How to grow crops in pots

The beauty of growing crops in pots is that you create an adaptable and moveable feast, which can be really close to the kitchen door. Most herbs are suited to this, but think of large containers planted with tomatoes, peppers and chillies all soaking up the sunshine in summer, with leafy crops, chives and microgreens on the windowsill for the easiest harvests.

Most seed producers stock mini varieties of crops that are suited to container-growing, or you may find specialist suppliers offering nursery plants. The usual, full-size varieties often work just as well, however, provided they are given enough space to grow. If you have a covered or sheltered area in which to site the containers, more tender crops such as sweet potato and coriander can be grown in autumn to extend the season. If the pots are close to the house, the ornamental qualities of the veg will probably be something to think about as well – try growing purple-leaved sage, for example, instead of the plain green variety.

If containers are the only growing space you have, it helps to have several containers on the go at once to ensure a continuous supply. If the pots are large, then think about how you might move them: perhaps you have a trolley or they are on a set of castors? Containers can be moved around so that only the ones that are ready for harvest are on display and closest to the kitchen. When the crop is spent, the container can be moved away for replanting.

YEAR-ROUND PLANNING

In **spring**, pretty leafy crops, such as lettuce, spinach, rocket, chard and taller-flowering crops, including peas and broad beans, provide a good display and a short enough cropping season to be replaced for summer. Potatoes, especially red varieties, have attractive foliage. Onions, shallots and garlic are good gap-fillers, but don't expect huge yields, so grow something special.

By **summer**, squash, cucumbers and beans can climb and trail and flower enthusiastically. Beetroot has interesting foliage, and herbs like thyme, sage and rosemary are attractive, compact if trimmed regularly, and flower as well as lasting long into winter. Unusual edibles like sweet potato and shiso, a Japanese culinary herb, have stunning purple-leaved varieties and are ornamental in their own right. Peppers, aubergines and tomatoes look good when fruiting and flowering.

For **autumn**, brassicas such as kale, cavolo nero and cool-season salads like lamb's lettuce,

---

LOW-FUSS CROPS IN POTS

These veg and herbs usually thrive and are the first choice for beginners.

- Carrots, radishes and beetroot: sow thinly into a well-drained loamy compost mix and keep moist.

- Woody herbs such as thyme, oregano and rosemary: grow in a sunny spot in a gritty well-drained mix. Avoid overfeeding and watering to concentrate flavour.

- Spring onions, chives, garlic chives and leeks prefer moist well-drained compost, much like garden bulbs.

Right: Many containers, each planted with different crops, provide an extended and varied harvest.

THIRSTY CROPS IN POTS

These crops all need a reliable supply of water, and when growing in pots you should allow them a little bit of shade.

- Lettuce, salad leaves and pea shoots: grow these in a seed tray as cut-and-come-again crops.

- Beans and peas will need deeper pots with good stability, as well as support from string or mesh to climb.

- Kale, chard and mustard: grow in a semi-shade location and don't allow to overheat or dry out as bolting (see p41) can occur.

Below: Carrots make a low-fuss container crop, but the pot needs to be a deep one for the roots.

pak choi, radicchio and endive are a good option. Alliums such as leeks, chives and spring onions can add a reliably frost-hardy splash of green and the promise of early spring flavour.

Winter is a challenge, but more rewarding for it. Kale, sage, rosemary, thyme and brassicas, including kalettes and Brussels sprouts, all last well in frost, as do autumn-sown turnips and swede; sow these densely as baby veg for Christmas.

HOW TO CHOOSE CONTAINERS

Start with large containers. A common mistake that is made is selecting too small a container, and no amount of watering and feeding will remedy overcrowded roots. Generally, vegetables need good amounts of space to grow well. Larger, thirsty plants use up water stores quickly, and self-watering pots with built-in reservoirs are a good choice in these instances.

Naturally, there is a huge choice of sizes, shapes and materials when it comes to containers. Not all are suitable, and the first thing to check is that they have holes in the bottom for drainage and airflow. If the only holes are in the flat bottom, raise the pot with feet or a gravel tray to prevent them from becoming blocked.

The most sustainable pots are those that are repurposed, reused, recycled or salvaged. These include sturdy plastic, cement and fiberglass containers if that means extending their useful life. It is possible to get quite creative. Stone, clay and terracotta is long-lasting and easier to reuse – but can chip, crack or shatter, and terracotta loses water in hot weather if not lined. Thin plastic and metal can get very hot and scorch roots, making them fairly unsuitable, and they also tend to degrade quickly.

Growbags are available and commonly used, but be aware of what's in the compost. Often peat is used, and the plastic sack is non-recyclable, although this is true of all bagged composts. The bags also tend to leave marks on porous surfaces, so take care when placing them on patios and decking, or use a growbag tray.

HUNGRY CROPS IN POTS

When grown in pots, these crops will require feeding. Use a feed derived from a natural substance, such as seaweed or comfrey, rather than something artificial.

– Tomatoes, peppers, aubergines and chillies: plant these in a large pot in a sunny location and support as needed.

– Squash, cucumbers and courgettes: plant in a deep, wide pot and plan to add support or allow them to trail. Limit winter squash to one fruit per vine and no more than three or four fruits in total.

– Potatoes and sweet potatoes: grow in a large trug, or even a sack or old compost bag in very rich compost or even manure.

Above: Peppers are fairly easy to grow, but need a warm sunny location and regular feeding and watering.

CHOOSING POTTING COMPOST

Potting compost (as distinct from home-made compost, see pp28–9) is nutrient-rich and holds water, but can dry out and shrink. It also varies a lot in consistency and quality. Always buy peat-free compost, be aware of synthetic feed additives, and look for a loam-based compost for longer-term planting to reduce shrinking and settling, and to stabilize taller plants.

For some plants, such as herbs, you may want to improve the drainage of the potting compost. Mix in some horticultural grit with the compost, or choose a product that is advertised as being well-drained. It is not necessary to put crocks or lightweight expanded polystyrene in the bottom of pots to stop the drain holes becoming blocked, but it can be useful for filling redundant space in particularly large planters or to reduce overall weight and the amount of potting compost required. If using expanded polystyrene, keep it contained in a bag to stop small fragments from breaking off and getting into the environment.

The prime location for most container crops will be somewhere that receives afternoon sunlight as well as shelter from breezes. A position adjacent to a wall or fence that stores and reflects heat is ideal, reserving more shady spots for salad crops and leafy veg.

Below: Potatoes need plenty of room to bulk up – use any large container, or even an old sack or compost bag.

The veg plot for a healthy gut

'Grow and eat a rainbow' is a golden rule for gut-health gardeners, and you can start simply by sowing red onions, yellow courgettes, ruby chard and purple sprouting broccoli. Find space also for strong-tasting varieties of high-fibre crops, such as beetroot and kale, and if you grow them hard (without too much feeding or watering) they will develop super-concentrated phytonutrients.

To harvest the 30-plus plants per week that food experts advise, you'll require multiple crop seeds and a well-planned system. Ideally, you'll also have a growing space at least 3 × 3m (10 × 10ft), a cool, dry store cupboard and a large freezer. You could also use an airy space for Kilner jars to ferment probiotic pickles, sauerkrauts and kimchis to protect your gut health into winter.

NEED TO KNOW
– Use herbs and spices to ramp up to the 30-plus weekly plant target, harvesting your crops fresh just before eating.

– Invest in perennial crops such as Jerusalem artichokes (see p227), asparagus (see p224), kale (see p194) and skirret (see p234).
– Eat gut-healthy crops fresh or fermented as a first choice, and rely on freezing for next-best nutrients (see p282).
– Combine healthier preparation methods such as steaming or eating raw (julienning or grating can be useful here) rather than frying or overboiling.
– Boost gut heath further by eliminating ultra-processed foods.

Below: A rainbow harvest for a healthy gut might include cabbages, beetroots, beans and carrots.

VEG TO TRY

Beetroot (see p202), beans (see pp116–19), cabbages (see p190), carrots (see p204), garlic (see p132), kale (see p186), leeks (see p136), onions and shallots (see p132), peas (see p112), sprouts and microgreens (see p72).

If you've got space and suitable growing conditions also try ginger (see p266), turmeric (see p246), edible flowers (see p104), squash (see pp150–5) and edamame (see p120).

The budget veg plot

Talk is cheap... and when it comes to saving cash, one of the best things you can do is get chatting to your gardening neighbours. More often than not they'll be willing not just to share knowledge but spare plants and seeds too. Seed packets often contain more than you can grow in a season, and if you order online together you can share seeds and postage costs.

If money is tight, take into account the value of what you're growing too. For example, a recent study showed that a courgette plant can produce courgettes worth 40 times the cost of a good-quality seed.

NEED TO KNOW
- Store cupboard essentials can be a great source of microgreens – try sprouting mung beans, pea shoots and coriander from dry seeds. Buying them from local grocery stores is much cheaper than buying from seed merchants.
- Gardening clubs or allotment societies often have deals with seed suppliers, giving members access to lower prices, and are a great way to meet other growers. Seed swaps are great fun as well as saving you money.
- Timing is everything. For example, herbs are often sold cheaply in small 9cm (3¾in) pots in garden centres in early spring. Later on in the season, the same plants will be in much larger pots for at least three times the price.
- Don't be tempted by ultra-bargain tools and equipment; the cheapest plastic tools may break within a year.

- Make your own compost – every scrap of green waste is worth something, even in monetary terms (see p28).
- Grow from seed rather than buying plants, and save your own seeds (see p280).

Right: Grow from seed if you can – a single seed has the potential to give a lot of value and a lot of veg.

The quick and easy veg plot

Almost all of us wish we had more time for our hobbies, and growing your own is no exception. It can be useful to think of your veg patch as a club or class, with set times for activities, like you'd have for tennis practice or yoga classes. Building a routine is key, whether that's visiting your allotment on the way to work, or spending 20 minutes in the garden every Saturday morning.

It is not necessary to try to grow everything. Just start off with crops you know you'll love and expand your repertoire if time allows. And while there's no such thing as a 'no maintenance' garden, there are plenty of things you can do to make your veg growing as quick and easy as possible.

NEED TO KNOW
- Picking the right crops for your conditions (see p9) means you'll get maximum crops for minimum effort.
- Mulch, mulch, mulch! This not only saves time watering and weeding, using a no-dig system saves you time turning over the soil in the first place (see pp24–5).

- Be aware that growing in containers might save on soil prep, but will cost in terms of watering.
- Grow the thirstiest crops (especially anything in pots) nearest to your water supply.
- Select low-input varieties. For example, consider bush tomatoes rather than cordon varieties, which need tying in and training. Generally, perennial veg, such as asparagus and Jerusalem artichokes, are less work than annual veg, such as cauliflowers and traditional leeks.
- Little and often is key – it's much better to spend 10 minutes every day than two hours every fortnight.

Below: Raised beds positioned on top of soil are a quick and easy way to get a veg plot going.

The greenhouse veg plot

It is said that by simply having a pane of glass or plastic overhead, your plants will have conditions similar to growing 500 miles south. So growers in cool regions who fancy the taste of a warmer climate, with its abundant melons, peppers and tomatoes, can transport themselves with a greenhouse or polytunnel.

You'll also get a month extra growing time in both spring and autumn. Depending on your space and budget, undercover growing can be as basic as a cold frame made of old windows, or as elaborate as a tailor-made greenhouse.

NEED TO KNOW

- It is not necessary to provide heating. The extra protection from rain, wind and snow makes all the difference, allowing you to grow salads from late autumn right through to spring. Try lamb's lettuce, spinach, mizuna, mustard greens and herbs such as coriander and parsley.
- The extra summer heat under cover is perfect for warmth-loving crops such as tomatoes, aubergines and chillies.
- Growing under cover is the perfect way to get seedlings ready for planting out as soon as other crops have finished – brilliant for ensuring continual harvests.
- Remember, plants under cover are totally dependent on you for their water needs, so install as many water butts as possible alongside greenhouses for an easily accessible water supply.
- You'll need to water crops under cover every day in the summer months, especially if they're in pots or growbags rather than in the ground.
- Polytunnels are much cheaper to put up than greenhouses, but be aware that the plastic covers will need replacing every decade or so.
- It can get very hot under glass or plastic. Make sure there is plenty of opportunity for ventilation on warm days.

Above: Shelving in a greenhouse allows for a lot of warmth-loving plants to be packed into a small space, but pay attention to watering and ventilation.

The family veg plot

From making mud pies, to eating their first delicious pea straight from the plant, veg gardening with children is gloriously messy but lots of fun. Many children have no idea where their food comes from and it's hugely rewarding to watch them make the connections in real time. There's growing evidence to suggest that connecting with nature early in life is hugely beneficial for children's mental and physical health. In a recent survey of RHS members, a key finding was that the majority of today's keen gardeners started gardening as children, usually with a parent or grandparent. So it's vital that to produce the gardeners of tomorrow, we garden with the children of today.

Inspiring children to enjoy plants and grow their own food can give them a healthy hobby for the whole of their lives. Capture their interest by making it fun and allowing them to make some of their own decisions, such as what to grow when choosing seeds at the garden centre.

NEED TO KNOW
- Get kids interested in grow your own by growing things they enjoy eating.
- Children's tastebuds can be quite different to adults. They can often enjoy sour flavours that might make adults' faces screw up, so crops like cucamelons (see p170) can be a hit with toddlers. However, their tolerance of bitter flavours can be much lower (broccoli, anyone?).
- Try quick-growing crops to grab their attention, like germinating runner bean seeds (see p118) in toilet roll tubes filled with compost.
- Saving seed (see Chapter 9) is a great way to teach children about the life cycle of plants.
- Give children a goal, such as growing a pumpkin for Halloween, or guessing when their runner bean plant will be taller than they are.

THINGS TO GROW
Peas (see p114)

Runner beans (see p118)

Microgreens (especially pea shoots – see p99)

Cucamelons (see p170)

Potatoes (see p214)

Pumpkins (see p152)

Sweetcorn (see p148)

Left: It's hugely rewarding to involve children in growing food and see them make connections in real time.

The gourmet veg plot

One of the most profound pleasures of growing your own fruit and veg is the incredible depth and range of flavours you can experience.

No shop-bought pea will ever compare to the sublime sweetness of one eaten just seconds after picking, and supermarket veg represent just a tiny fraction of the varieties of edible plants that adventurous gourmet gardeners can choose from.

Many unusual types of common vegetables also exist, and you never see these in the shops. Beetroot, for example, is available in a rainbow of colours from deep burgundy through to golden orange, and even ring-patterned in beautiful pink and white. Each has its own distinctive flavour, from earthy through to nutty and sweet.

UNUSUAL VEG TO TRY

- American groundnut (see p236) looks like a wisteria crossed with a runner bean. Grow it for its delicious roots – they're sold as a delicacy in Japan.
- Chickpeas (see p120) are easily germinated and grow into attractive, lacy-looking bushes. Eat the immature pods like edamame beans.
- Yacon and dahlia (see p230) will surprise and delight your friends if you serve these ornamental edibles as an autumn feast.

NEED TO KNOW

- Adding unusual edibles to your diet is a great way to boost the number and diversity of plants you are consuming, which is good for gut health (see p48).
- Introduce new foods slowly into your diet in case of allergies and intolerances.
- Shop around for maximum choice – there are lots of small independent nurseries dedicated to unusual edibles. Beware of buying from online auction sites as quality isn't guaranteed.

VEG TO TRY

Kalettes – roast until crispy

Cavolo nero – lightly sauté this kale

Sweetcorn – unbeatable sweetness when fresh or if frozen immediately after picking

Peas – delicious straight from the pod

Mangetout – eat straight from the plant

Asparagus – lightly steam soon after harvesting for an unbeatable flavour

'Red Drumhead' cabbage – eat raw in a coleslaw with other cabbage and grated beetroot, or lightly fry in butter with cumin

Sprouts – sauté in butter with walnuts, leeks and pine nuts

Baby leeks – sauté with sprouts or cabbage or serve in a leek crumble

Beetroot – use in hummus and serve with home-made gram flour crackers

Parsnip – make into crisps

Potatoes – best simply roasted ('Pink Fir Apple' is ideal) or cut up small and toss in herbs and olive oil and bake until crispy

Oca – try growing in a container

Kohlrabi or yacon – serve both thinly sliced in a salad

Beefsteak tomatoes – slice ripe and juicy into a Greek salad; 'Yellow Oxheart' and 'Brandywine' are good varieties

'Sungold' tomatoes – drizzled with olive oil and scattered with salt and basil, still warm from the sun. 'Shimmer' is almost as tasty.

The intensive veg plot

Intensive, small-scale horticulture is the most productive form of farming – and you can practise it in your own garden. If you've got the time to do it, you can easily get two, if not three, harvests from the same piece of ground within a year. There are several ways to do this, but the key idea is to plan ahead and think about what your different crops will be doing at different times of year. Think also what spaces they'll be growing in. To simplify it even further, the goal is to avoid bare soil – it's wasted ground.

Intercropping Sow rows of a quick-growing crop such as radishes between rows of a slow-growing one like parsnips (see p43). By the time the parsnips need the space, you'll have harvested all the radishes. Trailing squashes work well underneath tall, slender sweetcorn plants as they occupy different growing spaces.

Catch cropping Make use of any gaps in the veg-growing calendar to grow speedy crops. For example, you could grow salads over summer in the space left after you've finished picking broad beans in early summer. The salads will be over in time for you to plant garlic in autumn.

Some kind of **undercover space** is vital for the intensive grower – not only do you get bigger yields, you also have somewhere to raise seedlings and young plants. Think of your greenhouse, cold frames or polytunnel as the engine room of your veg-growing factory.

Extend the season with a greenhouse or polytunnel to grow salads in the space left by tomatoes from late winter to late spring (see p51). Optimum conditions in greenhouses mean you can pack lots of warmth-loving plants in too, such as climbing cucumbers or gherkins on the ends and tomatoes along the sides.

Use **raised beds** and try out a **'square-foot' growing system** (see p27), which involves growing well-defined patches of crops intensively on a smaller area. This makes it easy to grow lots of different crops, minimizes competition from weeds and helps to fit a productive veg patch into even tiny spaces.

NEED TO KNOW

– If you're aiming for maximum yields, you've got to be generous to your plants, so give them plenty of compost, mulch them and keep them well watered.

– It is not necessary to use lots of fertiliser to get maximum yields. Nowadays gardeners are looking to feed the soil, not the plant, which means making and using as much garden compost as you can.

– Using green manures and cover crops is another great way to improve your soil in an eco-friendly way. If you choose leguminous plants such as clovers, they'll even add extra fertility to your soil, making the crops listed in the box below even more productive.

– Plan ahead. Once you learn to predict when crops will have finished, you can work backwards and ensure that you have seeds or seedlings ready to plant as soon as space becomes available.

Left: A square-foot growing system will allow veg to be grown in well-defined patches in an intensive way.

Right: Make use of any gaps in your growing calendar to grow speedy veg, such as these salad crops.

SUPER-PRODUCTIVE CROPS

Runner beans (see p118)

Potatoes (see p214)

Courgettes (see p150)

French beans (see p118)

Lettuce (see p78)

Spring action plan

Spring can sometimes feel a long time coming. While it may take coaxing, preparation and sunshine to get most gardeners out of the house, the veg plot doesn't hang around, and new crops – if planted ahead of the game – will be taking advantage of any bit of favourable weather to get growing. You may be surprised as you step out into your garden in early to mid spring to see rhubarb already producing red stems under a forcing pot, and broad beans well on their way to flowering.

The period between late winter and early spring, however, is not called the hungry gap for nothing. It is a time of year that holds the greatest challenge for year-round veg growers, as the winter harvests are running out and the spring crops have a time to go before they start to produce in earnest. Crops in storage, whether frozen, preserved or kept in the larder, will pay dividends at this time of year, and it is a good opportunity to use everything up, clear shelves and get ready for the coming year. Windowsill salads, microgreens and sprouts are quick to harvest and will provide much-needed fresh greens.

Out in the veg plot there will be plenty to organize. Many crops sown in late winter can be planted out now, such as spring cabbages and hardy lettuce. More tender crops, such as tomatoes and chillies, will need a bit more time indoors. Potatoes that have been chitted will be ready to go in the ground, and you will no longer have to wait to sow the coming year's crops. The only problem will be managing all the plants you want to grow, as pots and seed trays all take space, so plan carefully and be realistic about your capabilities.

You may only want to grow a few plants of each crop, in which case rather than trying to sow everything from seed, you can opt to buy young plants online or from your local nursery. It will save time and space and hopefully reduce waste. Perennial crops such as asparagus, herbs or globe artichokes may have to be bought this way, and onions and sweet potatoes can be bought as sets or slips, which really saves a lot of bother.

If you have made a lovely bed for your veg plants to grow in, there is a good chance that weed seeds will have already, or will be about to, make their home there too. When the weather warms up this can happen at an alarming rate. A hoe is a good tool for removing these seedlings, and if they get a bit larger you can pull them out by hand, making use of them by adding them to the compost heap. Perennial weeds may also be showing up and these should be dealt with as described on p32. Large containers can also be prepared now, for planting as soon as the weather is amenable, or for immediate sowing.

Late spring can begin to feel a lot like summer, but for one important detail: temperatures can still dip low at night, which is enough to kill frost-tender seedlings like tomatoes and courgettes. It may seem like an eternity, but if you can wait until right at the end of spring then you will have much happier plants. In the meantime, start to put up supports for your climbing veg like beans and peas, and cover any borderline or newly planted veg with layers of horticultural fleece on cold nights.

Right: Many crops sown directly in late winter or the previous autumn will be bounding ahead by spring, giving you a head start and minimising the hungry gap.

Summer action plan

The year-round veg grower will seize summer's bounty and make the most of the warmth and sunlight it has to offer. Over-producing crops will be saved and stored, use will be made of vertical as well as horizontal surfaces, and as soon as one crop is cleared away, another one is waiting to fill its space. Every bit of space will be used, including patios and windowsills for container growing. Weeds will also be growing strongly and should be removed before they set seed.

Early summer will also give time for sowing more crops: carrots, chard, chicory, courgettes, cucumbers, beans, kohlrabi, lettuce, parsley, spring onions... to name just a few. This will allow for successional harvesting, if sowing and planting are at staged intervals, so that gluts are avoided. Tender crops that were brought on in late winter or spring can safely be planted out now, although they may not really start to flourish until midsummer when night temperatures are much warmer with no hint of a chill. Savvy year-round gardeners may have already preceded them with an early crop in the same space.

More importantly, harvesting can begin. Early potatoes, fresh sprigs of herbs, asparagus, broad beans, sweet spring cabbages, radishes and salad onions usher in the new season, with later crops of tomatoes, cauliflowers, aubergines, beetroot, garlic, carrots and many other things to follow. The year-round grower will be busy in the kitchen, thinking ahead to winter and the coming hungry gap, saving and storing, pickling and freezing what is not needed for immediate use.

Crops growing in a protected environment, such as a greenhouse or polytunnel, will need particular care and attention, because temperatures can rise very quickly. On all but the coolest summer days, keep the doors and windows wide open to allow for ventilation, and make sure everything is getting enough food and water.

Managed well, crop yields can be high, and as well as regular feeding and watering, these can be sustained by regular harvesting. Most crops taste best when they are young and tender, and if the emerging bounty keeps being removed, the plants often respond by producing more, whether that is leaves, flowers or fruit. Late-season crops like sweetcorn and winter squash need to be left alone to develop to their full size and ripen properly. With pumpkins, this can stretch well into autumn, in anticipation for a Halloween harvest.

By the end of summer, many crops will have already been lifted and stored; maincrop onions, for example, and some root veg. Be prepared for this with seeds of autumn salads, or seedlings of winter veg like winter and spring cabbages, leeks and Brussels sprouts, that were sown into pots earlier in the summer. Use cold frames and horticultural fleece to extend the season and keep things growing for as long as possible.

Left: If a veg plot is managed well, summer yields can be high. With this bounty can come gluts, which either need to be avoided or planned for, so that harvests can be stored and not wasted.

Autumn action plan

Autumn is the changeover season. Summer ends, and with it comes a final harvest and then preparation for the year ahead. It may seem early to be thinking of the new season when the old one isn't even over, but the cycle is constantly turning and we must turn with it. Climate change, however, is extending the growing season by up to a month with much longer, warmer autumns than were experienced just 30 years ago.

Much of what is harvested in autumn can be prepared for store. Lift maincrop potatoes, cure the skin of pumpkins and winter squash in the sun, and take in any beans left out to dry. Any remaining root crops like beetroot, carrots, swedes and turnips can also be lifted, although some gardeners leave them in the ground and dig them as required through the winter. The ground can then be cleared and waste vegetation added to the compost heap.

Continue to harvest autumn brassicas and any summer crops that might be still growing if fine weather prolongs the growing season. Chicory plants can be lifted and forced for late crops under cover. Once the harvest is over and the ground cleared, and plant supports and netting stored away for next year, it is the perfect opportunity to feed the soil well with a thick mulch of well-rotted compost, leafmould or manure. Consider also sowing a winter green manure, such as field beans, to lock nutrients in the soil over winter.

Spring cabbages that were sown in later summer can be planted out now into the newly prepared soil, and winter cabbages and other brassicas that are already in place should be earthed up to prevent them toppling over and their heads rotting in the winter wet. Any brassica material affected by club root should be removed immediately and disposed of off-site.

When it comes to sowing seed, autumn is the perfect time to get ahead while the soil is still warm. With the protection of a cloche, late crops of Oriental salad leaves and spinach can be brought on, and sowings made now of calabrese, carrots, early summer cauliflower and peas will promise an early harvest next year – just check that the variety chosen is appropriate for autumn sowing. Japanese onion sets can be planted out as well as garlic and autumn-sown broad beans such as 'Aquadulce'. Seedlings of biennial herbs like parsley can be planted out now too. Protect seedlings over winter with cloches.

Last of all, cut down old stems of perennial crops such as Jerusalem artichoke and asparagus, and lightly trim back any woody herbs like lavender, rosemary and sage. This is also a good time to plant new perennial crops, such as rhubarb and oca. Be on the lookout for any fallen leaves, which can be stacked to make leaf mould.

Right: Colourful winter squashes are emblematic of the autumn veg patch, reminding us that much of what is harvested at this time of year can be prepared for winter storage.

Winter action plan

Gone are the days when we might think of 'putting the veg garden to bed' in the winter, a lean period that traditionally extends until mid or late spring. Luckily for us, more and more crops that can be grown throughout the winter months are becoming known, and growing a wide variety of them can help to mitigate against variable weather – if one crop fails, another will survive.

Increasingly mild winters can make it feel as though autumn is stretching on indefinitely. There is an opportunity here to make use of the borrowed time and continue with late autumn jobs: more time to sow broad beans, plant garlic and protect tender plants from the coming frosts. But as the hours of daylight shorten, and the evenings close in, the certainty of winter brings the growing year to a close.

Our bodies also seem to respond to this seasonal shift. It seems natural to switch to a diet that consists of more hearty fare, making use of stored crops like potatoes and winter squashes, and going out into the cold to harvest winter vegetables like kale, leeks, parsnips and Brussels sprouts. This is the time to really enjoy and benefit from the fruits of your labour, but remember to keep your eye on that stored veg, to make sure it's keeping okay.

It is also the time to reflect on what you have achieved over the past year, and to think about how you might want to do things differently or what you might want to grow in the year ahead. Browse for ideas online, in seed catalogues or in magazines, and read books so that you can become more of an expert.

Once you have ushered in the new year, plans for the coming year can be put into practice. Vegetable seeds and seed potatoes can be ordered, as well as any tools and equipment you might need, and the ground can start to be prepared for spring planting. Clear away any dead or unwanted vegetation, adding it to the compost heap, pulling up any wild plants that are growing in the way with their roots intact so they don't continue to grow and spread.

A good job to keep you warm on a cold winter's day is to turn the compost heap. Well-rotted compost that is ready to be used can be added in bucket loads to the veg plot and spread as a mulch. A layer of carboard can be added beforehand (with any plastic tape removed first), which will have the added benefit of smothering and preventing the regrowth of unwanted plants.

You will notice, as the days begin to lengthen in late winter, plants beginning to emerge from their dormancy. Bulbs will be pushing their way through the soil and some early wildflowers, like red deadnettle, may already be in bloom. This is a signal for gardeners to begin their own seed sowing: early summer cabbages, leeks, onions and shallots, radishes, spinach, turnips, tomatoes and chillies can all be started under cover. On the windowsill, seed potatoes can be 'chitted' (started early) in repurposed egg boxes, and sprouts and microgreens will provide quick harvests of high nutritional value.

Right: Winter is naturally a quiet time in the garden, but that doesn't mean it can't be productive. With a little planning, harvests of leeks, brassicas, rainbow chard, parsnips and other root crops can be made.

Year-round planner chart

This quick reference chart pulls together all the information provided throughout chapters 2 to 8. Once you have chosen what to grow, you can use this chart to make a plan so that you are growing your own veg 365 days of the year.

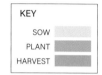

KEY
SOW
PLANT
HARVEST

CROP	PAGE	mid-winter	late winter	early spring	mid-spring	late spring	early summer	mid-summer	late summer	early autumn	mid-autumn	late autumn	early winter
Sprouts and microgreens	72												
Spinach	74												
Swiss chard	76												
Lettuce	78												
Watercress	81												
Amaranth and callaloo	82												
Caucasian spinach	84												
Salad rocket	85												
Orach	86												
Celtuce or stem lettuce	87												
Perilla or shiso	88												
American landcress	89												
Lamb's lettuce	90												
Endive	91												
Chicory and radicchio	92												
Mizuna and mibuna	94												
Winter purslane	98												
Pea shoots	99												
Mustard greens	100												
Wild rocket	102												
Garlic cress	103												
Peas	112												
Broad beans	116												
Climbing beans	118												

CROP	PAGE	mid-winter	late winter	early spring	mid-spring	late spring	early summer	mid-summer	late summer	early autumn	mid-autumn	late autumn	early winter
Chickpeas	120												
Lentils	121												
Soya and mung beans	122												
Peanuts	124												
Edible lupins	125												
Spring onions	130												
Onions and shallots	132												
Garlic	134												
Leeks	136												
Chives	138												
Elephant garlic	140												
Wild garlic	141												
Society garlic	142												
Egyptian walking onion	143												
Sweetcorn	148												
Courgettes, marrows and summer squashes	150												
Winter squashes	152												
Cucumbers	156												
Chilli peppers	158												
Sweet peppers	160												
Aubergines	162												
Okra	164												
Chayote	165												
Tomatoes	166												
Melons	170												
Gourds and luffa	172												
Cauliflower	178												
Calabrese broccoli	180												
Sprouting broccoli	182												
Pak choi	184												

CROP	PAGE	mid-winter	late winter	early spring	mid-spring	late spring	early summer	mid-summer	late summer	early autumn	mid-autumn	late autumn	early winter
Kale	186	▓	▓	▓	▓	▓		▓	▓	▓			
Brussels sprouts	188	▓	▓	▓		▓	▓	▓				▓	▓
Cabbages	190	▓	▓	▓	▓	▓	▓	▓	▓	▓	▓	▓	▓
Perennial kale	194	▓	▓	▓	▓	▓	▓	▓	▓	▓	▓	▓	▓
Perennial broccoli	196		▓	▓	▓	▓							
Sea kale	197			▓	▓	▓	▓						
Beetroot	202			▓	▓	▓	▓	▓	▓	▓	▓		
Carrots	204		▓	▓	▓	▓	▓	▓	▓	▓	▓	▓	
Celery	206				▓	▓	▓	▓					
Celeriac	207									▓	▓	▓	
Florence fennel	208	▓	▓					▓	▓				
Parsnips	210								▓	▓	▓	▓	▓
Sweet potatoes	212	▓	▓										
Potatoes	214			▓	▓	▓	▓						
Radishes	218	▓	▓	▓	▓	▓	▓	▓	▓	▓		▓	▓
Kohlrabi	220		▓	▓	▓	▓	▓	▓	▓	▓	▓		
Turnips	222				▓	▓	▓	▓	▓	▓	▓	▓	
Swede	223				▓	▓	▓					▓	▓
Asparagus	224			▓	▓	▓	▓						
Globe artichokes	226					▓	▓	▓	▓	▓			
Jerusalem artichokes	227			▓									
Rhubarb	228	▓	▓	▓	▓	▓	▓	▓	▓			▓	▓
Yacon and dahlia	230			▓							▓	▓	
Agretti and samphire	232		▓	▓	▓	▓	▓	▓					
Skirret	234	▓	▓	▓	▓	▓	▓	▓	▓	▓		▓	▓
Scorzonera and salsify	235	▓	▓	▓	▓	▓						▓	▓
American groundnut	236	▓	▓	▓	▓							▓	▓
Dill	242			▓	▓	▓	▓	▓	▓	▓	▓		
Caraway	243				▓	▓	▓	▓	▓	▓	▓		
Tarragon	244						▓	▓					
Coriander	245				▓	▓	▓	▓	▓	▓	▓		
Turmeric	246	▓	▓				▓	▓			▓	▓	

CROP	PAGE	mid-winter	late winter	early spring	mid-spring	late spring	early summer	mid-summer	late summer	early autumn	mid-autumn	late autumn	early winter
Lemon grass	247												
Herb fennel	248												
Angelica	249												
Chervil	250												
Lovage	251												
Oregano and marjoram	252												
Lemon verbena	253												
Mint	254												
Szechuan pepper	256												
Cumin	257												
Basil	258												
Parsley	260												
Rosemary	262												
Bay	263												
Sage	264												
Thyme	265												
Ginger	266												
Horseradish	268												
Black caraway	269												
Fenugreek	270												
Chamomile	271												
Lavender	272												

CHAPTER 2

SALADS
AND LEAVES

Growing salads and leaves sustainably

Growing your own salads and leafy crops is incredibly rewarding and can give you the quickest results in the vegetable garden, as microgreens can be ready to harvest in as little as two weeks. The range of flavours and colours available in homegrown salads far surpasses anything that can be bought.

The number of salad crops we can grow has expanded over recent years, enabling us to have a more interesting and diverse diet. As well as the old favourites, such as lettuce and salad rocket, why not branch out and try crops such as celtuce and chrysanthemum greens?

With a little planning, it is possible to produce your own salad crops all year, greatly enhancing the sustainability of your meals and allowing you to grow without the use of synthetic chemicals or fertilisers. Through the winter, crops such as winter purslane and mustard greens can be added to the staples of Swiss chard and spinach.

There are salad crops for most soils and situations, and you can grow quick crops in containers outdoors and on the windowsill, providing quick access for the hurried cook.

It's also worth considering growing perennial leafy crops. These have a sustainability advantage over annuals because they can put down deeper roots to access water and nutrients, and the constant presence of roots helps to bind the soil together. Potential perennial crops include garlic cress and wild rocket, but don't overlook the edible leaves you may already be growing without even knowing it, such as nettles, dandelions and hosta. So, why not give growing salads and leaves a go and see what new flavours you can discover?

Left: The diversity of salad crops available to grow is huge, allowing for unlimited experimentation.

Right: The beauty of leafy crops is that they are generally easy to grow and give a quick bounty. Some, like nasturtiums, also give edible flowers.

Sprouts and microgreens

Sprouts and microgreens are salad leaves grown to harvest quickly when they are still young. Crops suitable for harvesting this way include cress, mustard and bean sprouts. They are packed with flavour.

WHAT YOU NEED

These crops are best grown in containers with peat-free, multipurpose compost. They can be grown in the smallest spaces such as a windowsill, and should be grown indoors in an area of bright light, but not direct sunlight.

SOWING AND PLANTING

The wonderful thing about sprouts and microgreens is that they can be grown all year – sow regularly for continuous harvests. They are grown in small, shallow containers and virtually anything – for example a fruit punnet – can be used so long as it has drainage holes. Nearly fill the container with peat-free, multipurpose compost, sprinkle the seeds on top and then lightly cover

with a little more compost. The seeds can be sown relatively densely as they are to be harvested young. The soil can be reused for multiple harvests because the plants do not use all the nutrition within it as they are harvested so quickly.

Alternatively, it is possible to grow these crops without soil. Line the base of a container with kitchen paper and thoroughly wet it. Sprinkle the seeds on top and place somewhere warm and bright to germinate.

Mung beans (bean sprouts) are slightly different. The seeds will need soaking in cold water overnight before sowing. Rinse again the following day and sow in the same way as other crops. If growing without soil, cover the seeds with newspaper to prevent light from reaching them.

Left: Cress is a classic windowsill crop. Sprouting from seeds in just a matter of days, it can be grown any time of year.

HOW TO GROW THE CROP

Besides keeping the kitchen paper or soil moist, but not wet, these crops are low maintenance. Sometimes the young seedlings can be prone to damping off, in which case they need to be removed and the process started again. It is best to replace any soil, or thoroughly wash or replace any containers, if disease does occur.

WHEN THE CROP IS READY

Sprouts and microgreens are harvested in as little as two weeks. When they start to show their first true leaves, the whole plant can be cut off at the base using scissors.

STORING AND COOKING TIPS

These crops do not store well as they are so small. They are best cut as needed to use the same day, although they will store for a day or two in the fridge. Sprouts and microgreens are used as a garnish on salads, or in a range of other dishes. Suitable combinations will depend on which crops are grown. For example, egg and cress sandwiches, mustard as a finishing touch to a curry, or bean sprouts in a stir-fry.

Above: Microgreens are allowed to grow a little more than sprouts, so that there is generally a bit more leaf – these are especially nice if the leaves are a pretty colour.

AT A GLANCE:

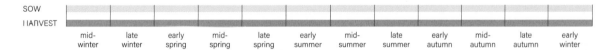

SOW											
HARVEST											
mid-winter	late winter	early spring	mid-spring	late spring	early summer	mid-summer	late summer	early autumn	mid-autumn	late autumn	early winter

Planting Overview: Can be grown without soil; try growing on a windowsill; sow regularly for continuous harvests.

Varieties to Try: Cress, amaranth, coriander, purple basil, rocket, mustard, mung beans (bean sprouts).

Amaranth

Mustard

Spinach

This easy-to-grow crop is highly nutritious and provides tasty harvests through much of the year. True spinach is an annual crop, distinct from spinach beet or perpetual spinach, which is actually a type of chard (see p76).

WHAT YOU NEED

Grow spinach in full sun, except if plants are growing in summer, then choose a lightly shaded location instead. Spinach prefers fertile, moisture-retentive soil.

SOWING AND PLANTING

Spinach can be sown from late winter to early autumn, but it is best to avoid sowing in summer as spinach rises to flower too fast. Sowing more than once allows for successional harvests. Ensure later sowings are established before winter.

It is good to sow spinach inside in modules, which enables the earliest sowings. Sow two or three seeds per module, thinning to one. Germination should occur in a fortnight, but may take longer earlier in the year. Plant out once the seedlings have their first true leaves, aiming for 20cm (8in) spacing, or closer if growing baby leaves.

For sowing spinach outdoors, wait until spring when the soil has warmed up a little. Create drills 2.5cm (1in) deep and 20cm (8in) apart and sow the seeds along the base. Cover the seeds and thin after germination.

HOW TO GROW THE CROP

Water well, especially in hot, dry weather, to try to slow down flowering. This crop is good for pots, but these will need regular watering and fortnightly balanced feeds. Try to avoid evening watering as damp leaves overnight make plants more susceptible to downy mildew, although resistant varieties are available. Remove yellow leaves as they appear.

If plants start to flower, it's best to replace the whole plant. This usually occurs from late spring through summer, depending on the sowing time. Spinach plants are generally hardy, but may need

Left: Spinach grown in modules allows for the earliest harvests; later sowings can be made direct in drills.

protection in colder areas; some varieties are more reliable over winter.

WHEN THE CROP IS READY

Once plants are established with several leaves, they can be harvested. Early sowings are harvestable from mid spring, and later sowings in mid to late autumn, and again in the spring. Small harvests can be taken through the winter in milder areas. Leaves can be picked as baby leaves, or as larger and more mature leaves. Harvest by carefully removing individual leaves. Only take a few leaves from each plant so the crop can keep growing. If all leaves are removed, the plant should regrow but there will be a gap in harvesting.

STORING AND COOKING TIPS

Spinach is tastiest when fresh, but can be blanched and kept in the freezer for a few months. Baby leaves can be eaten raw but mature leaves are best wilted down and added to dishes such as stir-fries and curries. The leaves reduce in volume with cooking so ensure plenty is picked.

Above: Best eaten fresh, harvest leaves as needed, but ensure plenty are picked if they are to be cooked.

AT A GLANCE:

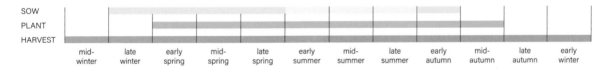

mid-winter	late winter	early spring	mid-spring	late spring	early summer	mid-summer	late summer	early autumn	mid-autumn	late autumn	early winter

Planting Overview: Start seeds inside or out; water well; sowing in summer is often unrewarding as plants flower too quickly.

Varieties to Try: 'Giant Winter' (reliable over winter, large leaves), 'Apollo' AGM (good resistance to downy mildew, slow to bolt), 'Trombone' (good for overwintering, smooth, rounded leaves), 'Missouri' AGM (fast growing, good for containers).

'Apollo' AGM

'Giant Winter'

Swiss chard

This crop adds a multicoloured splash to the garden. It is simple to grow and provides harvests all year in milder areas.

WHAT YOU NEED

Grow in fertile, moisture-retentive soil. Does best in full sun but will grow in partial shade, especially in summer.

SOWING AND PLANTING

Sow from early spring to late summer. Later sowings can provide a harvest of baby leaves, but will not establish enough to overwinter. Spring sowings can overwinter, but a second sowing in summer ensures the plants keep going for that long. Sow more frequently for baby leaves. Avoid sowing if the weather is too cold, or too hot and dry, as these can both trigger bolting (flowering).

Inside, sow 2–3 seeds per module and thin to one on germination. Once they have developed true leaves, the seedlings can be planted out at 25cm (10in) spacing, or closer for baby leaves. Starting the seeds inside protects the seedlings from slugs and snails.

Alternatively, sow direct outside. Either station sow 3–4 seeds at 20–25cm (8–10in) spacing and then thin to one, or sow in drills 2cm (3/4 in) deep and 25cm (10in) apart, thinning after germination.

PERPETUAL SPINACH/SPINACH BEET

Perpetual spinach, also known as spinach beet, is closely related to chard – the same species but a different variety – and is grown in the same way. It is more similar to chard than spinach as it produces the same large leaves. Spinach beet leaves are green with a pale green mid rib.

HOW TO GROW THE CROP

Swiss chard flowers in spring the year after it is sown, but can be prone to flowering earlier. Provide plenty of water to help prevent this. If flowering occurs the leaves turn bitter, but cutting off the initial flower spike will temporarily delay this. Anecdotally, red and white varieties bolt quicker than others, although they still provide a harvest beforehand.

Swiss chard in pots needs regular watering and a regular balanced feed to keep cropping well. Remove any leaves that turn yellow or develop powdery mildew to maintain good air circulation. This crop is mostly hardy in winter and will not need protection in mild areas. It withstands some frost, but is killed by prolonged or particularly hard frosts, therefore cloches or horticultural fleece are useful.

WHEN THE CROP IS READY

Swiss chard leaves can be harvested either as baby leaves, or larger ones after 6–8 weeks.

Left: Swiss chard can be started out in modules indoors for planting out in spring.

Above: Harvest the leaves as soon as they are large enough, leaving a few so the plant can continue to grow.

Right: The colourful stems of some Swiss chard varieties make them ideal for container growing.

Light harvests continue through winter in mild areas with last year's crop flowering just as next year's early sowings are ready, providing a year-round harvest. Pick off individual leaves by hand using the cut-and-come-again method, taking leaves from the outside and leaving those in the centre to keep growing.

STORING AND COOKING TIPS

Swiss chard is best eaten fresh, but it will store in the fridge for around a week. Baby leaves can be eaten raw, but mature leaves and stems should be lightly cooked. Try adding to stir-fries, stews or salads. Chard can also be blanched and frozen for several months.

AT A GLANCE:

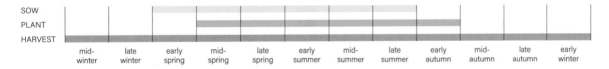

	SOW	PLANT	HARVEST

mid-winter	late winter	early spring	mid-spring	late spring	early summer	mid-summer	late summer	early autumn	mid-autumn	late autumn	early winter

Planting Overview: A colourful crop with year-round harvests; sow inside to protect against slugs; may need winter protection in some areas.

Varieties to Try: 'Bright Lights' AGM (multi-coloured stems with deep purple and green leaves), 'Bright Yellow' AGM (golden yellow stems, mid-green leaves), 'Vulcan' (less prone to bolting than other red varieties, especially if sown later).

'Bright Lights' AGM

'Vulcan'

Lettuce

Lettuce is a staple food crop in the vegetable garden. It comes in many different colours and leaf shapes, and can be either loose leaf (producing rosettes of foliage) or hearting (forming a centre). There are varieties of lettuce that are slightly hardier and can be grown in the winter months.

WHAT YOU NEED

Grows best in full sun but will grow in light shade, particularly in the hotter summer months. Free-draining fertile soil enriched with organic matter is ideal.

SOWING AND PLANTING

This crop can be sown from late winter to mid autumn. Use winter varieties for later sowings. Be aware that lettuce germination is inhibited if the temperature gets too high so try to avoid sowing in really hot weather. Also, lettuce seeds need light to germinate so, however they are sown, ensure that they are only covered with a thin layer of soil or compost. It is easy to sow too much lettuce and end up with a glut, so smaller repeated sowings are better for prolonging the harvest.

Lettuce is suitable for starting inside and out. Inside, sow into modules and then thin to one on germination, which usually takes 7–14 days, with the slower germination occurring in the cooler months. Plant out once the plants have developed a few true leaves. Space at 15–30cm (6–12in), depending on the variety – information may be on the seed packet. Earlier sowings may need protection when planted. Winter types should be sown in early or mid autumn.

If sowing outside, wait until the soil has warmed up a little in the spring, and don't sow after late summer. Take extra precautions against slugs and snails as the young seedling stage is when the plants are most vulnerable. Create drills that are about 1cm (½in) deep and 15–30cm (6–12in) apart, depending on the variety. Sow the seed along the base of the drill and then lightly cover, thinning the resulting seedlings as they appear. Thinnings can be eaten.

Below left: Lettuce is easy to start inside in modules and will also grow well in containers.

Below: Water lettuces well when they start to grow, preferably in the morning.

HOW TO GROW THE CROP

Water well when establishing, and then try not to let the plants dry out. This crop is great for pots, but they will need extra water and occasional feeds. Avoid watering in the evening if possible as damp foliage overnight can encourage fungal diseases such as grey mould. Keep lettuces well watered to help deter cutworms, which can cause plants to wilt and die. If root aphids occur, grow future crops in a different location.

Winter varieties will keep cropping through winter in mild areas, especially if grown under cover. Those outside will be killed by hard frosts. Even light frosts will cause frost burn on the leaves, so plants are best protected by cloches or horticultural fleece, or grown in pots so they can be moved inside if frost is forecast.

Lettuce will eventually rise to flower, at which point the leaves turn bitter. This happens quickest in hot, dry weather. The first indication that a plant is starting to flower is the centre of the plant getting taller than would otherwise be expected. Leave the plant in situ to save the seed, or remove to create space for a new crop.

WHEN THE CROP IS READY

The harvest method will depend on the type of lettuce being grown. Loose leaf lettuces can be harvested after 4–6 weeks of growing. The whole plant can be cut back, and may reshoot if a short stump is left behind, but it is best to harvest using the cut-and-come-again method. This is where individual leaves are picked off, leaving the plant to keep growing. The lower leaves should always be harvested first, leaving the youngest leaves at the centre. The plant can be picked quite hard, as long as the central cluster remains, and can usually be harvested in this manner about once a week in the summer. By picking in this way, it is possible to achieve several harvests from one sowing, meaning fewer repeat sowings are needed for a continuous harvest.

Hearting varieties are best left until the heart has formed and then the whole plant can be

Top: Early or late crops may need the protection of horticultural fleece, which can be suspended over the crops using hoops.

Above: Loose leaf lettuces can be harvested by picking off individual stems, leaving the plant to keep growing. Hearting varieties should be left until the whole plant is ready to be harvested.

harvested. Cos lettuces (upright with a crisp mid rib) and crisphead lettuces (large hearts with curled leaves) take about three months from sowing to harvest. Butterhead lettuces (soft leaves with a slightly open shape) will mature a bit quicker. Once the heart has formed, the plants should be harvested promptly before they start to flower. To harvest, cut through the stem above the soil and it should reshoot to provide another small harvest. Some Cos types can also be harvested using the cut-and-come-again method, and the outer, loose leaves of crispheads and butterheads can be picked off in advance of the main harvest.

Winter lettuces will crop from late autumn through to early spring if protected well enough.

STORING AND COOKING TIPS
Lettuce is best eaten fresh, although it will store in the fridge for a few days. The flavour of homegrown lettuce is incomparable to bought plants, and really livens up salads or sandwiches. In order to store lettuce, it should first be processed into something like soup and then frozen. It should then keep for 3–4 months.

AT A GLANCE:

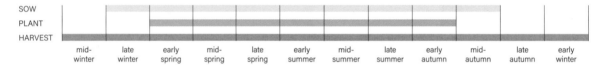

| | mid-winter | late winter | early spring | mid-spring | late spring | early summer | mid-summer | late summer | early autumn | mid-autumn | late autumn | early winter |

Planting Overview: Sow inside or out but avoid sowing in really hot weather; harvest loose leaf types as a cut-and-come-again crop and hearting varieties as a whole plant; winter varieties benefit from some protection.

Varieties to Try: 'Lobjoit's Green Cos' AGM (hearting Cos but can be cut-and-come-again, winter type, deep green, upright leaves), 'Winter Density' AGM (hearting Cos but can be cut-and-come-again, winter type, mid-green leaves), 'Little Gem' AGM (hearting Cos, sweet and crisp leaves), 'All the Year Round' (hearting butterhead, suitable for sowing every season), 'Marvel of Four Seasons' (hearting butterhead, leaves tinged deep red), 'Sioux' AGM (hearting crisphead, tinted leaves get redder in warmer weather), 'Iceberg' (hearting crisphead, classic, reliable variety), 'Lollo Rossa' (loose leaf, frizzy, purple-tinged leaves, great flavour), 'Salad Bowl' AGM (loose leaf, oak-leaved variety, comes in red or green, high yielding).

'Little Gem' AGM

'Lollo Rossa'

'Marvel of Four Seasons'

'Lobjoit's Green Cos' AGM

Watercress

This easy-to-grow perennial is a shallow-water plant, cultivated for its peppery leaves which are rich in vitamins. Native to Europe, it thrives near moving water, but will grow successfully in moist, rich soil in the garden or in a container.

WHAT YOU NEED

Best grown near running water in dappled shade. Watercress will also succeed in free-draining but moisture-retentive soil rich in organic matter.

SOWING AND PLANTING

Sow direct or in modules from early spring to early autumn. Final spacing is 15cm (6in) apart. Watercress can also be propagated by stem cuttings.

HOW TO GROW THE CROP

Watercress requires constant moisture. It is prone to frost damage so protect with horticultural fleece in cooler months for a prolonged harvest.

It will grow well in a container standing in a tray of water. Refresh the water in the tray regularly to avoid stagnation. If left to flower, it will self-seed readily.

WHEN THE CROP IS READY

Harvest when the plants are big enough and start spreading. It is a good cut-and-come-again crop. Harvesting will encourage new growth.

Above: Watercress grows happily in containers as long as the soil is kept moist.

STORING AND COOKING TIPS

The vibrant, peppery leaves are best used fresh in salads, smoothies and as an addition to sandwiches. It can also be cooked into delicious soup. Wash the leaves in plenty of water before using, and they will stay fresh if kept in a plastic bag in the fridge for a few days.

AT A GLANCE:

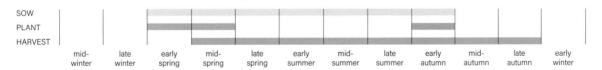

	mid-winter	late winter	early spring	mid-spring	late spring	early summer	mid-summer	late summer	early autumn	mid-autumn	late autumn	early winter
SOW												
PLANT												
HARVEST												

Planting Overview: Propagate by seed or cuttings; plants need permanent moisture; suitable for container growing; good cut-and-come-again crop.

Varieties to Try: 'Aqua' (delicious strong flavour and a crisp texture).

Amaranth and callaloo

This edible and highly ornamental tender crop is native to the Americas. The seeds and leaves are edible and rich in protein, vitamins and minerals. The leaves are used in Caribbean cuisine and called 'callaloo' after the traditional dish.

WHAT YOU NEED
Suitable to grow in any soil in full sun. It is drought-tolerant.

SOWING AND PLANTING
Best to sow outdoors after the last frost. Sow approximately 2mm (1/8in) deep in rows 40cm (16in) apart. Thin seedlings to 30cm (12in) apart.

Alternatively, sow earlier indoors in modules and plant out 30cm (12in) apart when the danger of frost passes.

HOW TO GROW THE CROP
Amaranth is a low-maintenance and problem-free crop. Water after planting. Plants might need support as the seedheads get heavy towards harvest time.

WHEN THE CROP IS READY
For harvesting leaves, cut the stems to a leaf node. The plant will then bush up and provide a continuous harvest.

When the seeds fall out of seedheads after a light shake, they are ready to harvest. Cut the seedheads, place them in large paper bags and let them dry. When dried, rub the seedheads off the stems; the seeds will fall out freely. Winnow the debris from the seeds and store the clean seeds in an airtight container.

STORING AND COOKING TIPS
Young leaves are used fresh in salads. Mature leaves are steamed and used the same way as spinach. To freeze, blanch leaves, cool down in icy water and drain. Frozen leaves will last up to six months in the freezer.

Seeds can be used as an alternative to couscous or porridge.

Left: Amaranth self-seeds readily, providing free plants that transplant easily. These are great for filling gaps in your garden. Water well after transplanting.

Above: Rub dried amaranth flowers to release their seeds in your palm. Seeds vary in colour and size.

AT A GLANCE:

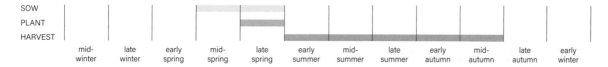

SOW											
PLANT											
HARVEST											
mid-winter	late winter	early spring	mid-spring	late spring	early summer	mid-summer	late summer	early autumn	mid-autumn	late autumn	early winter

Planting Overview: Easy-to-grow tender annual; after initial establishment, the plant is drought-tolerant; suitable for container growing; provide support to tall plants when the seedheads become heavy.

Varieties to Try: For leaves, callaloo types, 'Red Army' (red leaves and flowerheads), *Amaranthus* species, 'Blondie' (pale green leaves on an upright stem). For seeds, *Amaranthus cruentus* 'Oeschberg' (red leaves and flowerheads), *Amaranthus cruentus* 'Hot Biscuits' (green leaves, biscuit-coloured flowerheads), *Amaranthus caudatus* 'Viridis' (green tassel-like flowerheads), *Amaranthus caudatus* 'Coral Fountain' (dusky pink tassel-like flowerheads).

'Coral Fountain'

'Red Army'

'Hot Biscuits'

'Oeschberg'

Caucasian spinach

Caucasian spinach (*Hablitzia tamnoides*) is a hardy perennial climbing plant native to the Caucasus and is cultivated for its edible leaves. It can be harvested from early spring and resembles spinach.

WHAT YOU NEED
This woodland plant is happy in shade or semi-shade in rich, moisture-retentive soil.

SOWING AND PLANTING
Sow fresh seeds in the autumn in a container. Leave outdoors over winter in a sheltered place, or a cool greenhouse, until the seeds germinate. To germinate successfully, the seeds need a period of cold. The seeds can also be exposed to cold by placing them in the fridge in fine, damp compost or sand for 7–10 days. After that, place them in a pot of compost and this will trigger germination. The seedlings should appear within a couple of weeks. When the plants are big enough, with a good rootball, plant out 30cm (12in) apart.

Below: Caucasian spinach can be used as a vertical green screen throughout the growing season.

HOW TO GROW THE CROP
Water well after planting and don't let the plant dry out. Caucasian spinach can grow over 3m (10ft) tall and will need support such as an arch or trellis. Plants can be grown in large pots but will need more water and regular feed. Slugs and snails can be a problem for young plants.

WHEN THE CROP IS READY
Harvest leaves from early spring to midsummer.

STORING AND COOKING TIPS
It is used like spinach in salads, or can be steamed or sautéed in butter. It is best used fresh but can be lightly cooked and frozen.

AT A GLANCE:

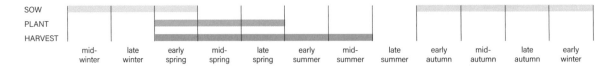

	mid-winter	late winter	early spring	mid-spring	late spring	early summer	mid-summer	late summer	early autumn	mid-autumn	late autumn	early winter
SOW												
PLANT												
HARVEST												

Planting Overview: Hardy perennial climber; plant in shade or partial shade and provide with plenty of moisture; best trained on an arch or other tall support.

Salad rocket

This annual crop adds a peppery, spicy taste to salads. For perennial wild rocket, see p102. The edible yellow flowers can also attract beneficial insects.

WHAT YOU NEED
Grow in sun, or light shade during the summer, in fertile, moisture-retentive soil.

SOWING AND PLANTING
Start seed indoors in early spring to late summer, or outdoors from mid spring to early autumn. Spring and autumn sowings are more reliable as this crop is prone to running to seed. Sow regularly for continuous harvests.

Inside, sow 2–3 seeds into each module and thin to one seed after germination. Plant out at 15cm (6in) spacing once the first true leaves have developed. Outside, sow in drills 1cm (½in) deep and 15cm (6in) apart. This crop can also be sown into pots.

HOW TO GROW THE CROP
Salad rocket often flowers prematurely. Grow in the cooler months or, if growing in the warmer months, avoid overcrowding and provide plenty of water. Remove any plants that flower, unless self-seeding is desired. Crops in pots will also need fortnightly balanced feeds. Cover plants with horticultural fleece to protect them from flea beetles.

Above: Young wild rocket leaves are good raw in salads.

WHEN THE CROP IS READY
Harvest once the leaves are large enough, from late spring to late autumn, depending on sowing time. Carefully remove individual leaves using the cut-and-come-again method.

STORING AND COOKING TIPS
Salad rocket is best used fresh but will store in the fridge for a few days. The flowers are also edible. Young leaves are milder and good raw, whereas older leaves are best lightly cooked.

AT A GLANCE:

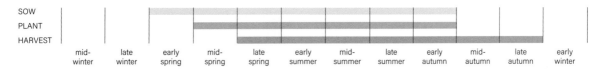

SOW											
PLANT											
HARVEST											
mid-winter	late winter	early spring	mid-spring	late spring	early summer	mid-summer	late summer	early autumn	mid-autumn	late autumn	early winter

Planting Overview: Start seed inside or out; water well; grow in light shade in summer to try to delay flowering.

Varieties to Try: 'Runway' (fast growing, reliable), 'Sky Rocket' (stronger flavour than some other varieties), 'Buzz' (slow to flower).

Orach

Orach (*Atriplex hortensis*) is a fast-growing hardy annual with succulent edible leaves that are high in nutrients. The red-leaved variety is a striking plant often used in ornamental gardens. Orach can be grown as a microgreen all year round.

WHAT YOU NEED
Orach will grow happily in any soil, in full sun or partial shade.

SOWING AND PLANTING
For an early crop, start indoors in modules and plant out after the danger of frost passes. Alternatively, sow directly after the last frost in drills 2cm (¾in) deep and 30cm (12in) apart. For mature plants, thin to 30cm (12in) apart. If the aim is to harvest young plants, thin to 5–10cm (2–4in) apart. For continuous harvest of young leaves, sow every three weeks.

HOW TO GROW THE CROP
Keep well watered for a supply of large succulent leaves. Plants will easily grow to over 1m (3ft) tall and might need staking. Orach self-seeds very easily and is generally problem-free.

WHEN THE CROP IS READY
Start harvesting leaves when plants are 30cm (12in) tall. Harvest by cutting the growing tips to encourage bushier growth and continuous harvest. For young leaves and stems, start harvesting when plants are about 10–15cm (4–6in) tall. Leaves are of the best quality before flowering.

STORING AND COOKING TIPS
The leaves are best used fresh but will last in the fridge for a few days. Blanched leaves can be stored in the freezer. Young leaves add colour to salads. Mature leaves are used like spinach, in soups, pasta or side dishes, or can be substituted for vine leaves.

AT A GLANCE:

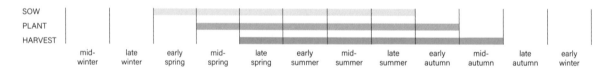

	mid-winter	late winter	early spring	mid-spring	late spring	early summer	mid-summer	late summer	early autumn	mid-autumn	late autumn	early winter
SOW												
PLANT												
HARVEST												

Planting Overview: Extremely easy to grow; plant out after the last frost; stake tall plants in windy conditions; if self-seeding is not desirable, cut seedheads before the seeds are ripe.

Varieties to Try: *Atriplex hortensis* (green leaves), *A. h.* var. *rubra* (striking red leaves and stems), 'Scarlet Emperor' (deep scarlet leaves).

Atriplex hortensis

A. h. var. *rubra*

Celtuce or stem lettuce

This hardy, leafy vegetable (*Lactuca sativa* var. *angustana*) is an unusual type of lettuce cultivated for its crisp and tender central stem. With its mild flavour, celtuce is great to eat raw or cooked. It is a popular vegetable in Asian cuisine.

WHAT YOU NEED
Grow in fertile, moisture-retentive soil in full sun or partial shade.

SOWING AND PLANTING
For good germination, the seeds need cool conditions. Sow in early spring or summer in trays or modules. Keep in a cool greenhouse or cold frame. Plant out in clumps when the seedlings have a few true leaves about 30cm (12in) apart. Thin the clumps to one plant before the stem starts elongating. Alternatively, sow 1–2cm (½–¾in) deep outdoors in rows 30cm (12in) apart.

Above: Celtuce stems, leaves cleared and ready to use.

HOW TO GROW THE CROP
Celtuce is grown in the same way as lettuce. It prefers the cool conditions of spring and autumn. Water regularly for a good-quality stem. Clear the stem of older leaves when about 30cm (12in) tall to allow air flow around the plant, reducing the chance of disease. Young plants are prone to slug and snail damage.

WHEN THE CROP IS READY
Cut the stem when it is over 30cm (12in) tall. Stems get woody and bitter if left in the ground too long.

STORING AND COOKING TIPS
It is best eaten fresh but will store in the fridge for a week. It can also be pickled. Use raw in salads, or cooked in stir-fries, soups or stews. Peel the skin before use. The leaves are also edible.

AT A GLANCE:

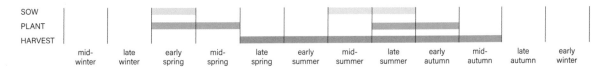

	SOW	PLANT	HARVEST
mid-winter			
late winter			
early spring			
mid-spring			
late spring			
early summer			
mid-summer			
late summer			
early autumn			
mid-autumn			
late autumn			
early winter			

Planting Overview: Celtuce needs cool conditions for germination; grow it in the same way as you do lettuce; water regularly for a good-quality stem.

Varieties to Try: *Lactuca sativa* var. *angustana* (green leaves), 'Cracoviensis' (red leaves).

Perilla or shiso

Perilla (*Perilla frutescens*) is a tender leafy vegetable from the mint family, which looks beautiful in a kitchen or ornamental garden. Its fragrant leaves are used frequently in Asian cuisines. The flowers and seeds are also edible.

WHAT YOU NEED
Grow in moist, well-drained soils rich in organic matter, in full sun.

SOWING AND PLANTING
Sow seeds indoors in trays from mid spring, ideally in a propagator at 20°C (68°F). Cover seeds only lightly, as they need light to germinate. Transplant seedlings to 9cm (3¾in) pots when they have a few true leaves. Plant out after the danger of frost has passed. Alternatively, sow direct in June in shallow drills 30cm (12in) apart. Ideally perilla should be spaced 30cm (12in) apart within the drills.

HOW TO GROW THE CROP
After planting, protect the seedlings against strong winds and cold weather with horticultural fleece.

When established, perilla is fairly drought-tolerant; however, for better-quality leaves, water in dry spells. It is a good plant to grow in containers, with regular watering and occasional feed.

WHEN THE CROP IS READY
Start harvesting when plants are about 30cm (12in) tall by cutting the growing tips to encourage bushier plants. Flowers are also edible.

STORING AND COOKING TIPS
Perilla leaves add a complex flavour of mint, cinnamon and basil, with a hint of citrus and aniseed, to stir-fries and other dishes. The leaves can be used as wraps. The red-leaved form is used in pickling to add flavour and colour to pickles such as Korean kimchi.

AT A GLANCE:

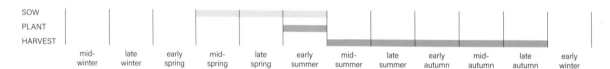

	SOW	PLANT	HARVEST

mid-winter · late winter · early spring · mid-spring · late spring · early summer · mid-summer · late summer · early autumn · mid-autumn · late autumn · early winter

Planting Overview: Plant out or sow after last frost; water in dry spells; pick regularly for a continuous harvest.

Varieties to Try: 'Britton' (reliable variety, green leaves with red undersides, very attractive), *Perilla frutescens* (green and red forms), *P. f.* var. *crispa* (curly leaves in green or red).

'Britton'

P. f. var. *crispa*

American landcress

This hardy, cold-season vegetable (*Barbarea verna*) is a source of salad leaves in the winter months. Its strongly flavoured spicy leaves are a good substitute for watercress and can be used in the same way.

WHAT YOU NEED
It will grow well in any position and enjoys rich, moisture-retentive but free-draining soil.

SOWING AND PLANTING
Best sown direct in early spring, or in late summer to autumn. Sow in drills 1cm (½in) deep and 30cm (12in) apart. Thin the seedlings to 20cm (8in) apart. Can be sown up to mid autumn.

HOW TO GROW THE CROP
Keep the plants moist, especially those sown in spring. Landcress is prone to bolting in hot weather. It is easy to grow in containers. Harvest regularly for a continuous supply of leaves. It is suitable to grow as a cut-and-come-again crop.

WHEN THE CROP IS READY
Leaves are ready to harvest about eight weeks after sowing. Late sowings will produce leaves through the winter up until late spring. Start picking the outer leaves first. When harvested regularly, the plant will keep producing leaves, although regrowth is likely to be slow during winter.

STORING AND COOKING TIPS
The peppery leaves are rich in vitamin C and are best used fresh in salads or cooked in soups. Leaves will store for a few days in the fridge.

Below: Landcress is a tough plant that withstands severe cold and provides salad leaves in the winter.

AT A GLANCE:

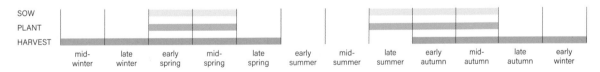

SOW
PLANT
HARVEST

mid-winter | late winter | early spring | mid-spring | late spring | early summer | mid-summer | late summer | early autumn | mid-autumn | late autumn | early winter

Planting Overview: Suitable to grow in shade; water well; easy to grow in containers; harvest regularly for a continuous supply; useful as a cut-and-come-again crop with a long season.

Varieties to Try: *B. vulgaris* 'Variegata' (attractive variegated leaves).

Lamb's lettuce

Lamb's lettuce or corn salad is a low-growing, hardy annual salad crop with a nutty flavour. It is fast growing and great in salads and stir-fries.

WHAT YOU NEED
Grow in full sun, in fertile, free-draining soil.

SOWING AND PLANTING
Sow from early spring, but ideally in late summer or early autumn otherwise flowering often occurs before a significant crop of leaves. Inside, sow 2–3 seeds in each module and thin to one after germination. Plant out at 20cm (8in) spacing, ensuring all seedlings are planted before mid

Below: Lamb's lettuce plants are ready to harvest when they are about the size shown.

autumn. To sow outside, wait until mid spring and sow in drills 1.5cm (5/8in) deep and 20cm (8in) apart, thinning after germination.

HOW TO GROW THE CROP
Water well until established and during dry spells. More water is needed when grown in pots. Flowering occurs in spring and early summer, at which point the leaves turn bitter. The plant can be removed immediately, or left to flower. The lower leaves sometimes develop grey mould, especially in damp soil or if planted too close, and these should be removed. This crop may need protection from severe weather.

WHEN THE CROP IS READY
Harvest from about six weeks after planting, all year round with regular sowing. Removing individual leaves using the cut-and-come-again method prolongs the harvest, although the whole rosette can also be cut. Harvest lightly in winter.

STORING AND COOKING TIPS
This crop will store for a few days but is best eaten fresh. Try adding to salads or stir-fries.

AT A GLANCE:

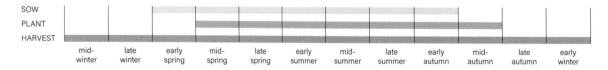

	mid-winter	late winter	early spring	mid-spring	late spring	early summer	mid-summer	late summer	early autumn	mid-autumn	late autumn	early winter
SOW												
PLANT												
HARVEST												

Planting Overview: Start seeds inside or out; leaves turn bitter once the plant starts to flower; harvest using the cut-and-come-again method.

Varieties to Try: 'Favor' (more upright habit reduces risk of disease).

Endive

Endive is an annual from the lettuce family and produces crunchy bitter leaves which can be harvested into winter. There are two main types – curly or frisée with frilly leaves, and broadleaved (escarole or Batavian) with large flat leaves.

WHAT YOU NEED
Endives enjoy full sun or partial shade and well-drained soil rich in organic matter.

SOWING AND PLANTING
Best sown in summer to early autumn. Start in modules, plant out when seedlings have at least two true leaves. Alternatively, sow direct in rows 30cm (12in) apart and 1cm (½in) deep. Thin seedlings to 30cm (12in) apart for mature heads; spacing can be closer for individual leaf harvest.

HOW TO GROW THE CROP
Keep plants well watered in hot weather. Protect them under cloches in the autumn in order to prolong the cropping season. Endive is well suited to container growing.

Slugs and snails can be a problem and wet weather in the winter might cause rotting.

WHEN THE CROP IS READY
Start to harvest one month after sowing. Pick the outer leaves first and harvest regularly.

Above: The crunchy, bitter leaves of endive may be curly or frilled, or broad like this Batavian variety.

Alternatively, cut the mature plants at ground level about three months after sowing.

STORING AND COOKING TIPS
It will store for over a week in the fridge in a plastic bag. The young leaves are a good addition to salads. More bitter mature leaves are tasty in stir-fries or can be sautéed with garlic.

AT A GLANCE:

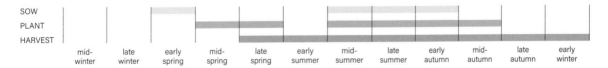

SOW													
PLANT													
HARVEST													
	mid-winter	late winter	early spring	mid-spring	late spring	early summer	mid-summer	late summer	early autumn	mid-autumn	late autumn	early winter	

Planting Overview: Protect from cold temperatures in early spring or late autumn; water well in hot weather; a good cut-and-come-again crop suitable for container growing.

Varieties to Try: 'Riccia Romanesca da Taglio' (bred as a cut-and-come-again crop, with bright green leaves), 'Fine de Louviers' (reliable frisée type), 'Natacha' AGM (broadleaved Batavian type).

Chicory and radicchio

Chicory is an annual leafy vegetable from the same family as endive and lettuce, grown for its bitter leaves. They come in various shapes and colours, and make an attractive addition to autumn and winter gardens.

There are several different types of chicory, including radicchio, witloof, sugarloaf and loose leaf. Radicchio produces tight red heads of leaves. The leaves in the centre of the head self-blanch, so they are lighter in colour and less bitter.

The sugarloaf type produces large green heads of bittersweet leaves, while witloof types are used for forcing – over winter, they produce chicons, smaller heads grown with the exclusion of light. These are sweeter and tender.

WHAT YOU NEED
Will grow well in free-draining soil rich in organic matter, in full sun or partial shade.

SOWING AND PLANTING
Sow forcing types in late spring or early summer. Non-forcing varieties are best sown in early to midsummer. Sow indoors in modules, two seeds per module, and thin to one plant. Plant out seedlings when they have two or more true leaves.

Alternatively, sow outdoors in drills 30cm (12in) apart. Plant out or thin according to harvesting method – for mature head harvest or forcing chicory, space plants 30cm (12in) apart. For baby leaves, space 10–15cm (4–6in) apart. Water well after planting.

HOW TO GROW THE CROP
Chicory is cultivated in a similar way to lettuce, just with different timings. Water well in dry spells. Slugs and snails can damage young plants. If rabbits and deer are a problem, cover with bird netting. Chicory is suitable for growing in containers. Non-forcing varieties can be grown for baby leaves as a cut-and-come-again crop.

To produce chicons, dig up plants with roots in autumn. Cut the crowns down to 2.5cm (1in), pot the biggest up in moist compost and place indoors in the dark at 10–15°C (50–59°F). The crowns will start producing new shoots. Thin these to achieve good-sized chicons.

Above: Plant chicory and radicchio 30cm (12in) apart for mature heads or 10–15cm (4–6in) apart for baby leaves.

Left: For baby leaves, harvest continually.

WHEN THE CROP IS READY

Radicchio and sugarloaf heads are ready to harvest when firm and enclosed with outer leaves. Cut at ground level or twist the plant out with roots. Clean the outer leaves and store the heads. If the plants are cut at ground level, secondary smaller heads might regrow.

Harvest chicons when the blanched shoots reach 15cm (6in). Harvest baby leaves continuously.

STORING AND COOKING TIPS

Radicchio heads and chicons will store well for a few weeks in a dark, cool place. With the bittersweet flavour, they are great additions to winter salads, or can be grilled, baked or sautéed. Chicory is also grown for its roots, which can be dried and ground as a coffee substitute.

Right: To harvest radicchio, cut the mature head at ground level. Plants will produce a second harvest of smaller heads.

AT A GLANCE:

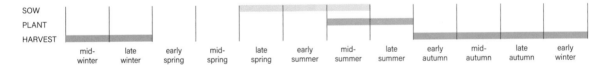

	mid-winter	late winter	early spring	mid-spring	late spring	early summer	mid-summer	late summer	early autumn	mid-autumn	late autumn	early winter
SOW												
PLANT												
HARVEST												

Planting Overview: Grows in a similar way to lettuce; water well in dry spells; suitable for container growing and forcing; grow as a cut-and-come-again crop for baby leaves.

Varieties to Try: 'Zucharina di Trieste' (loose leaf), 'Palla Rossa' AGM (radicchio), 'Rossa di Treviso Precoce' (columnar red heads with white veins), 'Variegata di Castelfranco' (red freckles), 'Pan di Zucchero' AGM (leafy sugarloaf, reliable), 'Totem' and 'Witloof Zoom' F1 (good for forcing), 'Magdeburg' and 'Cicoria di Chiavari' (root chicories).

'Palla Rossa' AGM

'Totem'

Mizuna and mibuna

Mizuna and mibuna are easy-to-grow Asian vegetables from the cabbage family. They both produce leaves with a mild spicy mustard flavour and are a great addition to winter salads or stir-fries.

Mizuna has deeply serrated, green or red leaves, while mibuna has thin green smooth leaves that grow in clumps. They are both cold-weather plants and will supply leaves over a long period of time.

WHAT YOU NEED

Will grow well in rich, free-draining soil, in sun or partial shade.

SOWING AND PLANTING

As cold-season plants, they are best sown in the spring or after midsummer to avoid bolting in hot weather. Sow direct in early to mid spring or in late summer to early autumn in drills 1cm ($^{1}/_{2}$in) deep and 30cm (12in) apart. Thin seedlings to 15cm (6in) apart for continuous leaf picking, or to 30cm (12in) apart to harvest as mature plants. Alternatively, sow from late winter indoors in modules and plant out after the true leaves appear. Protect seedlings from frost with fleece in early spring.

HOW TO GROW THE CROP

These crops are very easy to grow and can be cultivated throughout the season if protected in temperatures below −3°C (27°F). Water well during dry spells to avoid bolting. Slugs and snails might cause damage. Cover plants with fine mesh to prevent flea beetle damage.

Below left: If sowing mizuna and mibuna direct, cover sown seeds with fleece or Enviromesh to protect seedlings from flea beetle damage.

Below: Mature plants can be uncovered as they are more resilient to pest damage.

These compact plants are ideal for container growing. They are both good cut-and-come-again crops and can be used as gap fillers between plants with longer growing seasons.

Mibuna and mizuna are easy plants from which to collect seeds. Leave a few plants to flower and collect the flowerheads when dried, as at this point the seeds are ready. Save the seeds for the following year.

WHEN THE CROP IS READY

Start harvesting the outer leaves when the plants are about 15cm (6in) tall. For a continuous supply, harvest regularly. As cut-and-come-again crops, harvest the plants by cutting all the leaves a few centimetres above the crown. The plant will regrow from the crown and supply more leaves. Alternatively, harvest mature plants when 30cm (12in) high.

STORING AND COOKING TIPS

Mizuna and mibuna leaves are best used fresh butwill store for a few days in the fridge. They are used in salads but are also good in stir-fries or can be added to stews and soups. They can also be grown as microgreens for salad additions and decorative garnishes.

Above: Harvest the outer leaves first to encourage further leaf production and a continuous harvest.

AT A GLANCE:

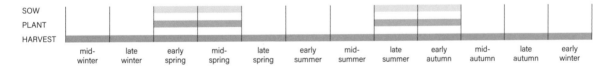

	mid-winter	late winter	early spring	mid-spring	late spring	early summer	mid-summer	late summer	early autumn	mid-autumn	late autumn	early winter
SOW												
PLANT												
HARVEST												

Planting Overview: Mibuna and mizuna are low-maintenance, cold-season crops; water well to prevent bolting; ideal for container growing; harvest regularly for a continuous supply.

Varieties to Try: 'Red Knight', 'Red Empire' F1, 'Waido'.

'Red Knight'

'Waido'

Asian salad greens

There are many different types of Asian vegetables that are all worth trying for their surprising textures, flavours and different periods of harvest. Here are a few lesser-known crops which are easy to grow and useful in the kitchen.

EDIBLE CHRYSANTHEMUM/SHUNGIKU

Glebionis coronaria is an attractive leafy green, popular in Asian cooking. Flavoursome leaves and shoots can be used in salads, stir-fries or sautéed with garlic. It is easy to grow from seed sown directly in spring or late summer. Start harvesting when plants are 20cm (8in) tall, picking the tips of the shoots to encourage bushier growth and further harvests. Leaves, stems, young shoots and flowers are edible. Note: do not use ornamental chrysanthemums for consumption.

CHINESE MALLOW

Malva verticillata is a leafy green with a long history in Asian cooking and medicine. It is mainly grown for its large edible leaves, but the young shoots, flowers and seeds are also edible.

It can provide tasty leaves from late spring into late autumn. Sow in spring, direct or in modules to prevent slug damage on young plants. The plants are tall and attractive. The leaves are harvested when hand-sized and are used in the same way as spinach. Young shoots and stems are made into tempuras while the young leaves and flowers are a good addition to salads. Chinese mallow 'Crispa' is an attractive, reliable variety with crinkly leaves.

Far left: A seedling of edible chrysanthemum, also known as Chop Suey greens. Cut the tips of seedlings to encourage bushier growth.

Left: These attractive leaves of the 'Crispa' variety of Chinese mallow are ready to harvest.

Above: Flowering shoots of choy sum can be used as a substitute for sprouting broccoli.

Right: Komatsuna leaves can be picked as a baby leaf.

CHOY SUM/FLOWERING CHINESE CABBAGE

Brassica parachinensis is a fast-growing, cool-weather vegetable from the cabbage family. It is best sown direct in spring or after midsummer, in drills 30cm (12in) apart. The final plant spacing should be 25cm (10in), closer if harvesting as baby leaves. Harvest when plants start flowering. Cut the edible flowering shoots down to a leaf bud and the plant will produce more shoots. Sow every few weeks for a continuous harvest. As a cold-tolerant plant, choy sum will produce well into winter. It is prone to the usual brassica problems, such as flea beetle, caterpillars and bird damage.

The advantage of choy sum is that, unlike other brassicas, it retains good flavour and tenderness after it starts flowering. With its mild cabbage flavour, choy sum is popular in Asian cooking and is used in stir-fries and soups or can be steamed.

'Gunscho' has green stems and leaves, '70 D Improved' is fast growing and green, and purple-stemmed varieties might be available.

KOMATSUNA

Brassica rapa var. *periviridis* is a leafy vegetable plant from the brassica family that produces mild mustard-flavoured leaves. It is a quick-growing, cold-season vegetable that comes in a variety of colours and leaf shapes and is cultivated in a similar way to choy sum. It is a good cut-and-come-again crop and suitable to grow in containers. It has similar problems as other brassicas.

The tasty leaves provide greens in the winter months and can be added to salads, stir-fries and soups.

'Comred' F1 is a red-leaved, attractive variety, while 'Carlton' F1 has green leaves.

Winter purslane

Also known as miner's lettuce, this salad crop has succulent leaves and is great for overwintering. Its pretty spring flowers are also edible.

WHAT YOU NEED
Grow in full sun or light shade, in fertile, well-drained soil.

SOWING AND PLANTING
Sow from early spring, but be aware early sowings are prone to flowering prematurely. Outside, create drills 1.5cm (5/8in) deep and 20cm (8in) apart. Thin germinated seedlings to 10cm (4in) spacing. Inside, sow into modules, thinning to one inch.

Below: Winter purslane can be grown in pots with a bit of extra care.

HOW TO GROW THE CROP
Water well until germination and during dry spells. Plants in pots will need more water and occasional feeds. This crop is generally hardy and needs no winter protection unless it is exceptionally cold. If desired, remove plants before flowering to prevent self-seeding. Overwintered plants flower in mid spring.

WHEN THE CROP IS READY
The plants form low mounds and are best harvested as a cut-and-come-again crop. Remove the leaves to 1–2cm (½–¾in) above the ground using secateurs and tidy away any remaining yellow leaves. The plant will reshoot, providing two or three harvests. Regrowth is slowest in winter, so avoid harvesting in midwinter when the cold will prevent regrowth. The flowers are also edible.

STORING AND COOKING TIPS
Eat fresh – leaves will store in the fridge for up to a week. Try adding to salads, or using as a garnish for soups and stews.

AT A GLANCE:

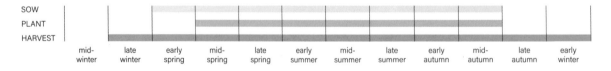

	mid-winter	late winter	early spring	mid-spring	late spring	early summer	mid-summer	late summer	early autumn	mid-autumn	late autumn	early winter
SOW												
PLANT												
HARVEST												

Planting Overview: Easy to direct sow; harvest using the cut-and-come-again method; best sown for harvests over winter and in the spring.

Pea shoots

The young growing tips of pea plants are a quick and tasty crop with a sweet, pea-like flavour. Any pea variety can be grown this way.

WHAT YOU NEED

Grow in full sun, and in fertile, well-drained soil. Inside, use a peat-free multipurpose compost and position on a bright windowsill away from direct sun.

SOWING AND PLANTING

Seed can be sown any time inside, or outside from early spring to early autumn. Inside, try multi-sowing into large modules with 4–5 seedlings per cluster. Plant out once the first true leaves appear at 10cm (4in) spacing. If sowing outside, sow in drills 2.5cm (1in) deep and 10cm (4in) apart. In mild areas, with protection, this crop can survive outside over winter, but it is safer to grow in pots that can be moved inside if needed.

HOW TO GROW THE CROP

This crop needs regular watering, especially when grown in pots. Feed plants in pots fortnightly. There is no need for a support structure but some protection from pigeons, such as netting or horticultural fleece, may be necessary (see also Peas, pp112–15).

Above: Rows of pea shoots are easy to germinate and are usually ready to eat within a month.

WHEN THE CROP IS READY

Harvest occurs within 3–4 weeks of sowing when the plants are around 10cm (4in) tall. Pinch out the tips back to a leaf and they will carry on growing. Plants usually provide two or three harvests.

STORING AND COOKING TIPS

This crop will store in the fridge for a few days but is best eaten fresh in salads, or used as a garnish on dishes such as soup.

AT A GLANCE:

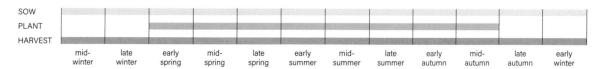

	SOW	PLANT	HARVEST

mid-winter | late winter | early spring | mid-spring | late spring | early summer | mid-summer | late summer | early autumn | mid-autumn | late autumn | early winter

Planting Overview: Good for sowing in pots; harvest within a month; may need protection from pigeons.

Varieties to Try: All peas can be grown for shoots instead of pods.

Mustard greens

This easy-to-grow salad crop provides a spicy kick to dishes, and can overwinter for harvests during the hungry gap. The leaves come in a range of colours and shapes to add interest to the veg garden throughout the year.

WHAT YOU NEED

Grow in full sun or partial shade, particularly in the summer. Fertile, moisture-retentive soil in a sheltered location is best.

SOWING AND PLANTING

Sow from early spring through to mid autumn; it is usually best sown later in the season so the plants can overwinter and provide an early crop the following year. For overwintering, try not to sow too early as larger plants are more susceptible to being killed by winter frosts. Conversely, sowing too late means that the plants will not be established before winter. An early autumn sowing is usually best, although seed can be sown into mid autumn if the plants are under cover, or in pots that can be moved when cold weather is forecast. This crop can be started outside but is often sown inside to protect young seedlings from slugs and snails. Inside, sow into modules and thin to one plant per module after germination. Mustard germinates quickly, usually in under a week, and can be planted out once some true leaves have developed. Space at 20–25cm (8–10in). Outside, sow directly in drills 1.5cm (5/8in) deep and 25cm (10in) apart, thinning after germination.

HOW TO GROW THE CROP

Water plants well when establishing, and then again in hot and dry weather. Plants in pots will need extra water and occasional balanced feeds. The plants will flower in the spring and summer, and watering well helps to delay this. The flowers are edible, as are the seeds. If plants are overwintering, they should be fine in a greenhouse and can survive some frost outside, particularly when they are small. However, they

Right: The leaves of mustard greens are quite varied, even ornamental, like these of the slightly tender variety 'Red Frills', grown here in a greenhouse.

are best protected with cloches or horticultural fleece if a prolonged or particularly hard frost is forecast. Plants in pots should be moved inside or to sheltered locations. Plants grown in the spring and summer may need covering to keep off the flea beetle, while those grown in winter can need protection from pigeons.

WHEN THE CROP IS READY

Mustard greens can be cropped all season, with lighter harvests in winter; the flowers and seeds are ready in late spring and early summer. Harvest using the cut-and-come-again method by individually picking leaves when they are the desired size. Older leaves have a hotter flavour.

STORING AND COOKING TIPS

The leaves and flowers are best eaten fresh, but will store in the fridge for a few days. The seeds can be dried and stored in an airtight jar for up to a year. Try using this crop in salads, or adding to dishes such as stir-fries.

Above: Pick tender baby leaves as and when they are ready, allowing the plant to regrow.

AT A GLANCE:

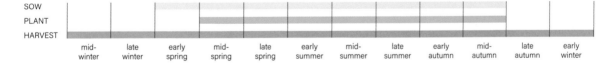

	SOW	PLANT	HARVEST

mid-winter · late winter · early spring · mid-spring · late spring · early summer · mid-summer · late summer · early autumn · mid-autumn · late autumn · early winter

Planting Overview: Start inside to protect from slugs; water well when establishing; may need some winter protection.

Varieties to Try: 'Red Giant' (large red-purple leaves, ornamental), 'Dragon Tongue' (red-purple fringed leaves, strong flavour), 'Green in Snow' (long, mid-green leaves, fairly mild flavour), 'Red Frills' (red-purple with delicate, frizzy leaves, slightly less winter hardy than some).

'Green in Snow'

'Dragon Tongue'

Wild rocket

This perennial plant provides rocket leaves with a stronger flavour than annual salad rocket (see p85) and it makes an easy-to-grow alternative.

WHAT YOU NEED
Grow in well-drained soil in full sun or light shade, in a sheltered location.

SOWING AND PLANTING
Sow seed from early spring to late summer inside, or mid spring to early autumn outside. Inside, sow in module trays, thinning to one after germination, and plant once the seedlings have decent roots. Outside, sow in drills 1cm (½in) deep and 20cm (8in) apart. Wild rocket can also be grown in pots.

HOW TO GROW THE CROP
Wild rocket produces attractive yellow flowers in the summer. It can then be cut down and it will reshoot. Provide plenty of water when establishing, after cutting back and in dry spells. This crop is hardy but will need protection in particularly cold weather. Covering plants with horticultural fleece in spring and summer will protect against flea beetles. Mulch in winter.

WHEN THE CROP IS READY
Harvest all year, including light harvests through winter and early spring if the crop is given protection. Harvest using the cut-and-come-again method by picking off individual leaves, or cut back to near ground level.

STORING AND COOKING TIPS
The leaves and flowers are edible, and are best eaten fresh, although they will store for a few days in the fridge. Add to salads for a peppery taste.

Left: Wild rocket leaves harvested in summer tend to have the hottest flavour.

AT A GLANCE:

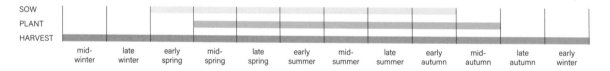

SOW											
PLANT											
HARVEST											
mid-winter	late winter	early spring	mid-spring	late spring	early summer	mid-summer	late summer	early autumn	mid-autumn	late autumn	early winter

Planting Overview: Perennial crop with a spicy flavour; sow inside or out; cut back after flowering and keep moist.

Garlic cress

A handsome hardy perennial, garlic cress (*Peltaria alliacea*) has tasty, edible leaves and flowers that add all-year colour to the veg garden.

WHAT YOU NEED
Grow in moist soil in sun or partial shade.

SOWING AND PLANTING
This crop can be grown from seed, but is often bought as small plants. Sow seeds from spring to early autumn, allowing time for them to establish before winter. Garlic cress can also be divided in spring or autumn as it produces numerous sideshoots. Plant at 25cm (10in) spacing, or as underplanting around other perennials.

HOW TO GROW THE CROP
Water well when establishing, and try to prevent the crop drying out, although garlic cress tolerates periods of dry weather fairly well. The small white flower stems reach 45–60cm (18–24in) tall in late spring and early summer. Cut back hard after flowering to encourage an autumnal flush of leaves. This crop will spread via lateral sideshoots: it grows well in pots which will prevent this. Mulch with organic matter in winter.

Right: Being a perennial crop, garlic cress leaves are simply harvested as and when they are needed.

WHEN THE CROP IS READY
Leaves can be picked all year, although the main harvest is from autumn to spring when the plant is not flowering. Harvest using the cut-and-come-again method by picking off individual leaves. The flowers can be harvested when they appear.

STORING AND COOKING TIPS
This crop is best fresh but will store for a few days. The flavour is comparable to a cross between garlic and mustard. The flowers and green-purple leaves make attractive additions to a salad.

AT A GLANCE:

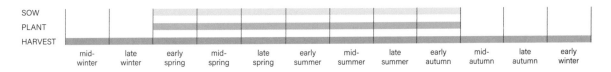

SOW											
PLANT											
HARVEST											
mid-winter	late winter	early spring	mid-spring	late spring	early summer	mid-summer	late summer	early autumn	mid-autumn	late autumn	early winter

Planting Overview: Can propagate by division or seed; harvest the leaves and flowers; grows well in pots or in moist soil.

Extraordinary edible flowers

Many herbaceous or woody plants in our gardens have edible flowers that can be used in different ways to enrich our diets. These flowers can be colourful and flavoursome and can be collected as they flower throughout the year.

Above: Nasturtiums are highly ornamental additions to salads, with a strong peppery taste.

Edible flowers are used to add colour and flavour in cooking, baking, salads and herb butters. Frozen in ice cubes, they are beautiful and add zing to cocktails. They can be dried and stored in an airtight container to use later for infusions and tisanes. Adding flowers to salt or sugar can bring an interesting twist – try lavender-flavoured sugar, for example. The petals are the main part of the flowers used for culinary purposes.

ORNAMENTAL PLANTS WITH EDIBLE FLOWERS

Nasturtium is an easy-to-grow annual plant with edible flowers, leaves and seeds. Propagated by seed, the trailing types are good ground cover or can be trained onto supports. Flowers and leaves are a peppery addition to salads. Green seeds can be pickled as a caper substitute.

The flowers of the annual pot marigold (*Calendula officinalis*) are a bright addition to salads,

with a slight peppery flavour. The orange petals can be used as a food colouring, instead of costly saffron.

Rose petals have a delicate flavour and are used in drinks, fruit dishes or jams. Crystallized rose petals are used for cake decoration.

Well-loved sunflowers are an ornamental annual known for their edible seeds. The flowers are also edible. Lightly steamed sunflower buds, dressed with butter and garlic, resemble artichokes. Remove the green base of the flower before cooking. The petals have a slightly nutty flavour and are good in salads.

Consider the elder, a deciduous tree, native to the UK and Europe. The fragrant flowers are commonly used in cordials and wines, but they can also be dipped in batter and deep-fried as a tempura. The flowers are traditionally foraged from wild growing trees or can be harvested from many varieties that are cultivated in our gardens.

FRUIT AND VEGETABLES WITH EDIBLE FLOWERS

From the cucumber family, the large flowers of courgettes (see p150), pumpkins and winter squash (p152) are edible, and used in stir-fries, stuffed with soft cheese and baked, battered and deep fried, or cut fresh into salads. Pick only male flowers for cooking, as the female flowers will produce the pumpkin and courgette fruit. Female flowers have small fruit forming at the base.

From the allium family you can eat the flowers of chives (see p138), onions (see p132) and garlic (see p134). They add colour and a mild garlic or onion flavour to dishes. The flowers, separated in individual florets, can be used in salads, omelettes, or as a decorative garnish. Garlic flower buds with stems, known as 'scapes', are delicious lightly steamed and tossed in butter.

Plants from the brassica family also have edible flowers, so if cabbage (see p190), rocket (see p85), radish (see p218) or pak choi (see p184) runs to flower too early, just add their blooms to salads and other dishes. Rocket or mustard flowers have a spicy peppery flavour.

The flowers of some fruit, such as strawberry, apple, pear, plum and citrus blossom, can also be used for culinary purposes. These are used as garnishes, cake decorations or steeped in hot water to make tea. Honey can be infused with citrus flowers to add flavour to it.

HERBS WITH EDIBLE FLOWERS

Borage has blue, white or pink, star-shaped edible flowers. They have a distinct cucumber flavour with a hint of honey. They are great in salads or can be added to cocktails. The flowers are attractive to bees and other insects.

The flowers of perilla (see p88) are also edible. The stalks are made into tempura or can be added to salads and stir-fries.

Lavender flowers (see p272) can be used in sweet or savoury dishes. Use them sparingly as the strong lavender flavour can easily overpower other flavours.

Flowers of most common herbs, such as mint (see p254), basil (see p258), dill (see p242), coriander (see p245) and rosemary (see p262) are edible. They have similar flavours to the herb leaf and can be added to salads and savoury or sweet dishes. They are also used to make flavoured salts or sugars.

Above: Courgette flowers are best picked just before they open and used fresh, the same day.

Right: Ice cubes made with borage flowers refresh and beautify any summer drinks. Let borage self-seed to have a supply of flowers year after year.

RULES FOR COLLECTING

There are a few basic rules to follow when collecting edible flowers.

- Only collect the edible flowers you can identify correctly. The flowers of many plants are poisonous.
- Some of the flowers will have medicinal properties and might not be suitable to eat for everyone, particularly if pregnant or nursing. People with severe allergies, or asthma sufferers, should test a small amount before using flowers in their food.
- Edible flowers are best when picked in the morning.
- Ensure pesticides have not been used on flowers that are picked for eating.

Extraordinary edible leaves

Apart from the traditional leafy vegetables we are familiar with, there are many plants we know of that have edible leaves. These could be leaves from trees, climbing plants, ferns or plants that are considered 'weeds'. They may have been eaten in the past, across different cultures, and some are still popular today.

A common tree we grow in gardens that has edible leaves is the lime tree (*Tilia*). The young leaves are a crisp, tasty addition to salads, and can also be cooked and used as spinach. They are rich in protein. One of the best lime tree leaves to eat is *Tilia × europaea* with smooth non-hairy foliage. Harvest young leaves with stems, as this will encourage new growth, allowing further picking.

The beef and onion tree (*Toona sinensis*) is named for the flavour of its leaves. The shoots and leaves are best harvested young to add to salads or stir-fries. They can also be pickled or roasted and used as a tea. The plant was traditionally used for medicinal and culinary purposes in China.

Sorrel is a plant worth growing in the edible garden for its flavoursome acidic leaves. These are a tangy addition to salads, and can be used in soups, or cooked with fish. Sorrel is an easy-to-grow hardy perennial and cut-and-come-again crop that will produce leaves throughout the year. There are different types of sorrel, but they all have sour lemon-tasting leaves.

EDIBLE WEEDS

Plants that we usually consider weeds in our gardens, such as plantains, ground elder (a quick-spreading plant that was introduced to England by the Romans as a food source), dandelion, nettle and many others all have edible leaves. Use them in salads, soups or pesto. They can also be cooked and added to a variety of dishes as a substitute for spinach. Ensure that the plants were not treated with pesticides and are correctly identified before you eat them.

Many also have edible flowers, including dandelion, clover and nettles. Dandelion flowers are delicious raw, or can be dipped in batter and fried. They can be made into syrup or wine. The flowers of these plants are also great for insects and support biodiversity in our gardens.

Above: The young leaves of the beef and onion plant, (*Toona sinensis*), taste like beef and onion crisps.

Above: Hosta leaves are best used as they are just emerging as shoots in spring, when the leaves are still rolled up.

Right: The baby leaves of red-veined sorrel bring a lemony flavour to salads all year round.

Shade-loving hosta is an ornamental hardy perennial plant with edible foliage. The leaves are best harvested young when still rolled up. They can be used raw in salads, steamed and tossed with garlic and butter, stir-fried, made into tempura or pickled. All the hosta species are edible but *Hosta fortunei* is the species traditionally eaten in Japan.

Another cut-and-come-again crop is the hardy perennial buck's horn plantain (*Plantago coronopus*), also known as minutina or erba stella. This is a traditional salad vegetable in Italian cuisine. The crisp leaves are best picked when young. They have a mild nutty flavour and are great in salads. Mature leaves can be cooked and used as spinach. It readily self-seeds.

YOU MIGHT ALSO LIKE TO TRY:

- Mulberry, fig and beech leaves.
- Oyster leaf plant (*Mertensia maritima*), native to Scotland – the edible fleshy leaves have a salty flavour.
- Other sorrels, such as French or buckler-leaved sorrel (*Rumex scutatus*), broad-leaved sorrel (*Rumex acetosa*) or red-veined sorrel (*Rumex sanguineus*).
- Chickweed (*Stellaria media*) – the leaves, stems, flowers and seeds are all edible.
- Hairy bittercress (*Cardamine hirsuta*) – all parts are edible and it makes a good substitute for cress.
- Garlic mustard (*Alliaria petiolata*), a hairy garlic-flavoured biennial – all parts are edible.

CHAPTER 3

PODS, PEAS AND BEANS

Growing pods, peas and beans sustainably

Peas and beans are a staple of the veg plot almost all year round, and they are probably the most significant group of crops to consider. Many have flowers, some are fragrant and pretty, and when trained up their wigwams and support frames they make the veg patch a brighter and more attractive place.

Their freshly picked flavour is a highlight of the growing year, although be aware that some, such as soya beans, will need cooking first to make them edible. The sweetness of homegrown peas means they often do not make it as far as the kitchen.

Peas and broad beans provide the earliest harvests, runner beans are the most productive and great for beginners, and peanuts and chickpeas follow later – though with frequent sowings you can harvest lots of crops over many weeks. French beans are good for smaller plots or large containers, while sugarsnaps and mangetout are expensive in the shops and much cheaper to grow at home.

As well as the familiar crops of mangetout and French beans, you could try growing soya beans or edible lupins. The latter provide a small and delicate crop that is fun to try and rewarding when mastered.

By growing your own, you can be sure you're growing in a sustainable way, avoiding the cost and carbon footprint of imported crops. With careful planning you can be eating some crops earlier or later, and well-stored crops will still be providing when the shops have long run out.

Many pods, peas and beans will store for months when needed. Peas, broad beans, French and runner beans can be frozen for storage right through the year, while dried beans – such as borlotti, chickpeas and lentils – can be stored for many months with the taste unaffected. Go on, give peas and beans a chance.

Left: Runner beans were introduced to Europe as an ornamental plant for their bright flowers, but their culinary uses were soon appreciated.

Right: Colourful mangetout peas like 'Shiraz' make veg growing a joy, and you would never find anything like them in the shops.

Peas

There are a number of different types of pea that can be grown in the garden – they are all grown in the same way, just harvested at different stages.

Shelling peas produce the classic garden pea, while sugarsnaps are eaten as whole pods and are sweeter in flavour. Mangetout are also eaten whole but at an earlier stage than sugarsnaps. They are not quite as sweet and come in a range of colours. Marrowfat peas are left on the plant to dry before harvesting and shelling.

WHAT YOU NEED

Grow in full sun and in fertile, well-drained soil. A sheltered location with a neutral to alkaline pH is best.

SOWING AND PLANTING

Peas can be sown inside from late winter onwards, or outside from early spring to early summer. A mid to late autumn sowing indoors can be made for an early spring planting, and a couple of extra sowings throughout summer will extend the season of harvest. There are early and maincrop varieties available, especially of shelling peas, with maincrops taking longer to come to harvest.

Starting plants inside helps to prevent mice eating the seeds, and it provides an earlier start if the soil is too wet for direct sowing. Peas can be multi-sown, aiming for 3–4 seedlings per large module. Cardboard toilet roll tubes are also good for sowing in, and peas are sometimes sown into a length of guttering, in a double row at 5–10cm (2–4in) spacing; the compost in the guttering can later be slid into a trench outside. Sow the seeds 3–5cm (1–2in) deep; they should germinate within a fortnight. Plant the seedlings outside from early to mid spring once they have developed some true leaves. Do it without delay as the young plants can become straggly quite quickly.

Plant multi-sown clumps 10–15cm (4–6in) apart, and individual plants at 5–10cm (2–4in). Ideally position them in a double row with pea sticks around the outside as support. These can be

Above: Save your old toilet rolls: they make perfect starting pots for peas.

Left: Seedlings can be planted outside from early spring, once they have true leaves.

twiggy pieces of hazel, or a support can be made out of netting or chicken wire. The necessary height will depend on the variety, but they can reach over 1.5m (5ft) in height. Leave 1m (3ft) between double rows, or more for taller varieties, to enable access for harvesting. Early sowings will be helped by wrapping horticultural fleece around them. This provides extra warmth, and some protection from pigeons.

Peas can also be sown directly outside. Create a drill about 15cm (6in) wide and 5cm (2in) deep, and scatter seeds along the base at 5–10cm (2–4in) intervals. Cover them with soil and then position your support structure around the outside. There are dwarf pea varieties that will not need supporting, and these are good for growing in pots at least 30–40cm (12–16in) in diameter.

HOW TO GROW THE CROP

Peas need plenty of water when they are establishing, and when flowering and setting pods, but besides that they are fairly low maintenance. Peas grown in pots will need more regular watering, as well as a fortnightly balanced feed. The support structure should provide some protection from pigeon damage, but netting can also help. Powdery mildew can sometimes occur – wider spacing will improve air circulation and help to prevent this.

Pea moth can be an issue with these crops. Mangetout are unaffected as they are harvested before the caterpillars cause damage, and early pea varieties will usually escape major harm. Pheromones can be used to disrupt the mating patterns of the insect, and insect-proof mesh can be used if the threat is particularly bad. Traps are also available.

WHEN THE CROP IS READY

With all types of peas, regular harvests will encourage the setting of more pods. Early sown, early varieties should be ready within 12–14 weeks of sowing, which can be as early as late spring. Maincrops take 14–16 weeks to harvest and they, and later sowings, should be harvestable through the summer into early autumn. Shelling peas are harvested when the pods have swollen and are firm to the touch, sugarsnaps when the pods are

Right: Twiggy branches make excellent natural supports for peas; they don't grow very high but they keep them from sprawling on the ground.

Far right: Harvest peas once the pods have swollen and are firm to the touch. The peas can be enjoyed both raw and cooked.

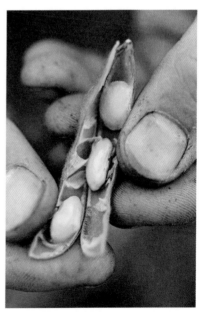

just starting to swell, and mangetout when the pods are flat before the peas start to swell. To harvest, carefully snap the pods from the plant with your hands. Marrowfat peas are left to dry on the plant before being harvested.

STORING AND COOKING TIPS

All crops, besides marrowfat peas, are great raw. Shelling peas will freeze well – remove the peas from the pods before freezing and they should store for 8–10 months.

Sugarsnaps and mangetout are eaten whole. Sugarsnaps are sweeter, but both make tasty snacks in their own right, or can be added to dishes such as salads and stir-fries. As well as eating straight from the plant, peas can be used in a wide range of dishes including stews. Once fully dried, marrowfat peas can be stored in an airtight jar in a cool location for a whole year. They can be soaked for a couple of hours before being added to dishes such as casseroles.

Right: Taller varieties of pea will need more substantial support, such as this jute netting. Check the seed packet to find out how tall they are likely to grow.

AT A GLANCE:

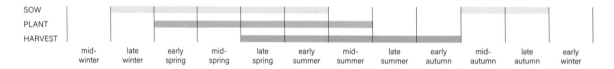

| | SOW | PLANT | HARVEST |

mid-winter | late winter | early spring | mid-spring | late spring | early summer | mid-summer | late summer | early autumn | mid-autumn | late autumn | early winter

Planting Overview: Starting seed inside helps to avoid issues with mice; provide a support structure for all but dwarf varieties; growing a range of varieties increases the harvest window.

Varieties to Try: 'Kelvedon Wonder' AGM (shelling pea, early variety, excellent flavour), 'Hurst Green Shaft' AGM (shelling pea, maincrop variety, uniform, long pods), 'Delikata' (mangetout, crisp, dark green pods) , 'Shiraz' (mangetout, purple pods), 'Golden Sweet' (mangetout, yellow pods), 'Sugar Bon' (sugarsnap, great flavour), 'Sugar Ann' (sugarsnap, early cropping, good yield), 'Maro' (marrowfat variety, reliable cropping), 'Meteor' (dwarf early pea, well-filled pods).

'Kelvedon Wonder' AGM

'Golden Sweet'

'Sugar Ann'

'Shiraz'

Broad beans

Broad beans make a really great, easy crop. The hardy varieties, sown in autumn, just take care of themselves, overwintering without complaint and producing a bounty of pods in spring for little effort. The beans come in red or green and store well once frozen.

WHAT YOU NEED

Grow in full sun, although light shade also works, and in a sheltered location, preferably with well-drained, fertile soil that does not sit wet over winter.

SOWING AND PLANTING

Sow in mid to late autumn or late winter to mid spring – only certain varieties are good for overwintering, so check before buying. Sowing too early in the autumn results in plants with too much vulnerable leafy growth, but sowing too late can mean sowings do not establish.

Starting seeds indoors prevents mice eating them. Sow two seeds per large module and thin to one after germination. Plant out once they have developed a reasonable root system, usually within 4–6 weeks. Ensure autumn sowings are planted well before winter, at roughly 20cm (8in) spacing.

If sowing directly, take care that the soil is not too damp and station sow two seeds per location, thinning to one. Spares can be transplanted. Create a slit in the ground and push the seeds in, sowing 5cm (2in) deep.

HOW TO GROW THE CROP

Autumn sowings overwinter as small plants that may need protection during particularly cold spells. Autumn sowings help to avoid blackfly because the plants are mostly mature before this insect arrives. If blackfly occurs in late spring, then pinch out the growing tips, because that is where they aim for, and squish any others. Shoot tips can be pinched out pre-emptively once the first pods have set, which also encourages plants to focus on pod production rather than leaves.

Left: The shoot tips of broad beans are an unexpectedly delicious crop. Remove them as soon as the first pods have begun to set.

Water well when establishing and when the plants are setting fruit. Taller plants may need staking; simply put a stake at each corner of a group and tie string in between. Dwarf varieties in pots will need fortnightly feeds through the growing season. Chocolate spot fungus can occur, but correct spacing and avoiding damp growing areas helps its control.

WHEN THE CROP IS READY

Broad beans should be ready in late spring from an autumn sowing, and summer from a spring sowing. The beans should be almost touching inside the pods, although the immature pods can also be harvested. Remove the pods from the plant by hand, or with secateurs. Regular picking encourages more pods to form. The shoot tips are also edible, if unaffected by blackfly.

Right: The mature pods can become quite sizeable and may be harvested by hand or with secateurs.

STORING AND COOKING TIPS

Pythagoras forbade eating broad beans because he believed they contained the souls of the dead, but thankfully this is no longer a common concern. Immature pods can be cooked whole, but older beans need removing from their pods. They freeze well and can store this way for 8–10 months. They can be added to a variety of dishes. Try eating the beans lightly steamed; the shoot tips, also steamed, are good in stir-fries.

AT A GLANCE:

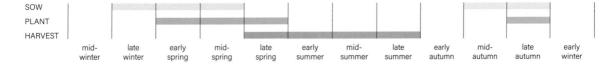

	mid-winter	late winter	early spring	mid-spring	late spring	early summer	mid-summer	late summer	early autumn	mid-autumn	late autumn	early winter
SOW												
PLANT												
HARVEST												

Planting Overview: Start inside or outside; taller plants will need staking; pinch out tips to avoid blackfly.

Varieties to Try: 'Aquadulce Claudia' AGM (good for overwintering, reliable crop), 'Red Epicure' (red beans, uniform pods), 'Masterpiece Green Longpod' AGM (extra-long pods, great flavour), 'The Sutton' AGM (dwarf variety, good for pots).

'Masterpiece Green Longpod'

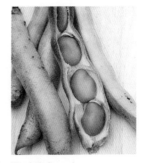

'Red Epicure'

Climbing beans

There are several types of climbing beans. French beans are satisfying to grow, with their long, cylindrical or flat pods in a range of colours. Dried beans are varieties of French bean that are harvested later. Runner beans also climb and produce long, flat pods. They are all grown in similar ways. Non-climbing French beans, known as dwarf beans, are also popular for containers and small spaces.

WHAT YOU NEED
Grow in full sun in a sheltered location and in fertile, moisture-retentive soil.

SOWING AND PLANTING
These beans are frost tender and so are best started indoors in mid to late spring. Beans for drying, in particular, need a long season to mature, so start them early. Sow two seeds per 9cm (3¾in) pot and thin to one on germination. Plant out in early to midsummer, 20cm (8in) apart at the base of a structure for climbing, one plant per leg. This can be a teepee, arch or A-frame, and needs to be about 1.8m (6ft) high.

The beans can also be sown directly outside in late spring or early summer once the soil has warmed up. Sow two seeds per station, thinning to one on germination.

HOW TO GROW THE CROP
These plants sometimes need help to start climbing, so loosely tie them in until they start

Below left: Delay planting until the last frost has passed, as climbing beans are frost tender.

Below: Robust supports are important for climbing beans as they can become top heavy.

twining themselves. Once they reach the top of the structure, the tops can be pinched out. Water well until established, and then again when plants are flowering and setting pods.

Sometimes climbing beans – runner beans in particular – do not set pods well and struggle in changeable or hot weather. French beans are more reliable as they are self-fertile. Ensure the soil is constantly moist to aid fruit set.

WHEN THE CROP IS READY

French beans and runner beans should be ready from midsummer, and keep cropping until mid autumn. Harvest the beans when they are relatively small, about 10cm (4in) long for French beans and 15cm (6in) for runners. Runner beans are prone to becoming tough and stringy if left too long. Picking regularly ensures more beans keep being produced.

With drying beans, the young pods can be eaten, but they need to be left until mature and starting to dry in order to harvest the dried beans. This occurs in late summer to early autumn. Ideally, harvest after a period of dry weather.

DWARF BEANS

These are perfect for pots, with the bushy plants reaching only 45cm (18in) tall. Sow from late spring through to midsummer and plant with 20–25cm (8–10in) spacing. Water well as they grow, and feed those in pots. They do not crop for quite as long as climbing beans. Try varieties 'Safari', 'Purple Teepee', 'Hestia', or 'Yin Yang' (for drying).

STORING AND COOKING TIPS

French and runner beans can be eaten fresh but also freeze well. Top and tail the beans before freezing and they should store for 6–8 months. Dried beans store for up to a year – shell the beans and then dry thoroughly before storing in an airtight jar. They need to be soaked for 1–2 hours before being used in cooking. Cook before eating. Try lightly steaming French and runner beans, or adding to dishes including stir-fries. Dried beans make a good addition to curries and stews.

AT A GLANCE:

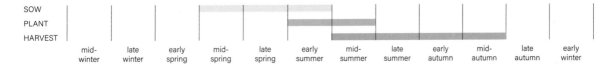

	mid-winter	late winter	early spring	mid-spring	late spring	early summer	mid-summer	late summer	early autumn	mid-autumn	late autumn	early winter
SOW												
PLANT												
HARVEST												

Planting Overview: Start seed inside or out; grow up a supporting structure; harvest regularly to prolong cropping; choose dwarf varieties for pots.

Varieties to Try: 'Hunter' AGM (French, flat pods, prolific), 'Violet Podded' (French, purple beans), 'Cobra' AGM (French, great flavour), 'Firelight' (runner, reliable in hot weather), 'Borlotto Lingua di Fuoco 2' (dried, attractive speckled pods), 'Greek Gigantes' (runner typically grown for drying).

'Hunter' AGM

'Borlotto Lingua di Fuoco 2'

Chickpeas

One of the oldest cultivated crops in the world, chickpeas are widely used in Mediterranean, East Asian and Indian cuisines. They grow two or three per pod and are packed with protein, fibre and healthy oils.

WHAT YOU NEED
Chickpeas grow well in full sun or partial shade, in free-draining soil. Overly rich soils encourage leafy growth, rather than fruiting.

SOWING AND PLANTING
Chickpeas are best started in spring, indoors in modules. Soak seeds overnight before sowing for

Below: Chickpeas are a versatile pulse that helps regulate blood sugar levels and blood pressure.

faster germination. Sow two seeds per module, then thin to one seedling. Plant out 30cm (12in) apart and protect with fleece during cold spells. Alternatively, sow direct in late spring, two seeds per station, thinning to one plant.

HOW TO GROW THE CROP
Cultivation is simply a matter of watering in dry spells and when pods are forming. It is a low-maintenance crop, but rodents can be a problem.

WHEN THE CROP IS READY
For fresh chickpeas, pick the pods when green and swollen. Harvest these regularly for continuous supply. For mature chickpeas, harvest when the pods are beige and dry. Wear gloves when harvesting, as the plant contains a skin irritant.

STORING AND COOKING TIPS
Mature chickpeas can be dried and stored in an airtight container. Soak them for a few hours before cooking and use in curries, dhals, salads or to make hummus.

AT A GLANCE:

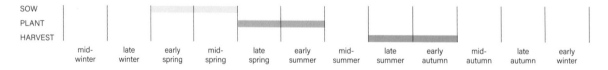

	SOW	PLANT	HARVEST

mid-winter | late winter | early spring | mid-spring | late spring | early summer | mid-summer | late summer | early autumn | mid-autumn | late autumn | early winter

Planting Overview: Watch for cold weather after planting and protect crop with fleece if needed; water in dry spells and when pods are forming; rodents can be a problem.

Varieties to Try: 'Principe' (easy-to-grow, heavy-yielding variety; the crop can be eaten when young, as with petit pois).

Lentils

Lentils are an important food crop. They are eaten worldwide and form a part of many different cuisines. They are not hard to grow, but it takes lots of effort for a home gardener to collect a good number of lentils for a meal.

WHAT YOU NEED
Lentils will grow in any well-drained soil rich in organic matter, in a sunny position.

SOWING AND PLANTING
Sow directly outside 2–3cm (¾–1in) deep, a couple of weeks before the last frost, in rows 30cm (12in) apart. Thin seedlings to 15cm (6in) apart. Alternatively, start indoors, sowing two seeds in each small pot, thinning to one plant on germination. When seedlings are 10–15cm (4–6in) tall, plant out.

HOW TO GROW THE CROP
This annual plant is easy to grow and will cope well with drought. Water well after planting and during hot spells. To keep plants upright, place pea sticks between them. Mice can be a problem.

WHEN THE CROP IS READY
The lentils are ready when the foliage dies down and the lower pods are dry. Cut a whole plant at the base and complete the drying process indoors

Above: Lentils are valued for their nutritious qualities and used in stews, dhals and soups.

or out. When dried, remove the pods from plants and shell the seeds.

STORING AND COOKING TIPS
Store dried lentils in an airtight container, or cooked lentils in the freezer for up to six months. They will only keep for a few days in the fridge. Cook lentils before eating.

AT A GLANCE:

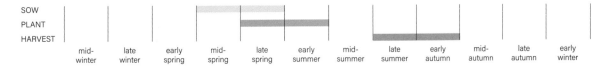

SOW											
PLANT											
HARVEST											
mid-winter	late winter	early spring	mid-spring	late spring	early summer	mid-summer	late summer	early autumn	mid-autumn	late autumn	early winter

Planting Overview: Easy-to-grow plant with low watering requirements; best grown in full sun; the harvesting is labour intensive.

Purchase seeds from reputable suppliers for best results. Small green Italian lentils bought from food retailers can also be used for seeds.

Soya and mung beans

The soya bean is one of the world's most important food crops, cultivated for its protein-rich seeds. Eaten when green and immature, they are referred to as edamame beans; soya beans are the mature beans that can be dried and stored. All soya beans need to be cooked before consumption. Mung beans are similar but darker and longer. They are cultivated in the same way as soya beans.

WHAT YOU NEED

Soya beans grow well in full sun, in free-draining soil rich in organic matter.

SOWING AND PLANTING

Sow indoors in mid spring, with two seeds per pot or module. A propagator will help, as the beans need warmth to germinate. Plant out seedlings 20cm (8in) apart after the danger of frost passes. Alternatively, sow directly outdoors in late spring and early summer. Water the young plants well. If the weather is cold, protect the young plants with fleece to ensure good growth.

Below left: Mature soya bean pods turn brown. Collect dried pods and shell the dried beans, making sure they are fully dry before storing.

Below: Sprouted mung beans are packed with nutrition. Repeatedly soak and drain the mung beans in water. After a few days, edible sprouts will appear.

HOW TO GROW THE CROP

Soya beans require heat and it is good to mulch around the plant to help retain moisture. They will produce a better yield if grown under cover and are suitable to grow in containers supplied with plenty of water and the occasional feed.

WHEN THE CROP IS READY

For edamame, harvest when the pods are green and swollen with the immature beans. For mature soya beans or mung beans, harvest when the pods are dry and brown.

STORING AND COOKING TIPS

All soya beans need to be cooked before eating. Edamame can be boiled or steamed until the seeds are tender. After this, they can be kept in a freezer for a few months. The dried mature seeds should be stored in an airtight container. Before these are used, soak them overnight, then cook them for a few hours until they are tender. A pressure cooker will speed up cooking.

Use the beans in curries or roast them as a snack. Many other foods are made from soya beans, such as tofu and soya milk. From fermented beans, miso and soya sauce are made. Mung beans can be sprouted and used raw in salads or cooked in stir-fries.

Above: Mung bean seed pods are longer and darker than soya beans. Each pod has 10–15 beans.

AT A GLANCE:

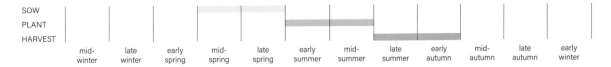

	SOW	PLANT	HARVEST

mid-winter | late winter | early spring | mid-spring | late spring | early summer | mid-summer | late summer | early autumn | mid-autumn | late autumn | early winter

Planting Overview: Fast-growing plants that need plenty of water and heat; mulch around the plants to keep moisture in the soil; yields are better if grown under cover.

Varieties to Try: 'Fiskeby V' (Swedish heirloom variety, suitable for cooler climates), 'Green Shell' (suitable for cooler climates).

'Fiskeby V'

'Green Shell'

Peanuts

This is a fun crop to grow at home, popular with children, and the seeds are a good source of protein. It is a frost-tender, heat-loving plant that has a curious habit of burying its seedpods, which contain the edible peanuts, underground.

WHAT YOU NEED
Best grown in full sun, in free-draining soil rich in organic matter. It prefers a sheltered spot and will not thrive in waterlogged soil.

SOWING AND PLANTING
Sow indoors in early spring in small pots 5cm (2in) deep. When the plants fill the pot, transplant to a bigger container or plant out in a greenhouse or polytunnel. Alternatively, plant outdoors 30cm (12in) apart after the danger of frost, or sow direct in early summer.

Below: Peanuts grow underground and can be eaten raw or roasted as a delicious snack.

HOW TO GROW THE CROP
Grow in a warm, sheltered place with plenty of sun, and water well. Mulch around the plants to keep the soil moist. 'Pegs' will begin to form around the base of the plants, pushing into the soil. From these, the seedpods will form underground.

Peanuts will grow in large containers with adequate watering and feeding. To avoid fungal disease, avoid watering overhead. Mice and squirrels may eat the buried peanuts.

WHEN THE CROP IS READY
When the foliage dies down, lift the plants by pulling them out by hand. Shake off excess soil and allow the entire plant to dry for about one week. After this, remove the seedpods and allow them to cure in a cool, dry place for about three weeks.

STORING AND COOKING TIPS
Store in an airtight container in the fridge. Use raw or roasted as a nutritious snack, in salads and in stir-fries, or blend to make peanut butter.

AT A GLANCE:

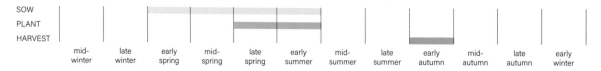

	SOW	PLANT	HARVEST

mid-winter · late winter · early spring · mid-spring · late spring · early summer · mid-summer · late summer · early autumn · mid-autumn · late autumn · early winter

Planting Overview: This is a sun-loving plant that needs plenty of water and heat; it is best grown under cover and is suitable for container growing.

Edible lupins

Lupins are known as ornamental plants, but the seeds of edible and sweet lupins (*Lupinus albus* and *L. angustifolius*) have been grown as food crops for thousands of years. They are high in protein and fibre and are good for storing.

The edible lupin is a hardy annual plant that will grow well in cool temperate climates, but here is a very firm warning: do not consume the seeds from ornamental lupins as they are toxic and can cause an allergic reaction similar to peanuts.

WHAT YOU NEED
Grow in sun or partial shade, in any free-draining soil rich in organic matter.

SOWING AND PLANTING
Start the seeds indoors in the spring, as this will help to reduce slug damage to the seedlings. Sow in small pots, with two seeds per pot, thinning to one plant. When ready, plant the seedlings out 30cm (12in) apart.

HOW TO GROW THE CROP
Lupin is low maintenance. Water in dry spells. Plants are tall and sprawly and will need support. If saving seeds from edible lupins, make sure no other lupin species are cultivated within 50m (165ft). Slugs and mildew can be a problem.

Above: Lupins are pretty plants to grow, but stick to the edible varieties as all the others are poisonous.

WHEN THE CROP IS READY
Harvest the mature seedpods as soon as they become dry and brown.

STORING AND COOKING TIPS
Store dried seeds in an airtight container. Soak seeds in advance, then cook until tender. They can be used in stews, soups or salads.

AT A GLANCE:

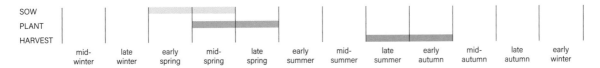

mid-winter	late winter	early spring	mid-spring	late spring	early summer	mid-summer	late summer	early autumn	mid-autumn	late autumn	early winter

Planting Overview: Easy-to-grow plant; slugs can be a problem for young plants; water in dry spells; do not eat seeds of other lupin species as they are toxic.

Varieties to Try: As well as the two species forms *Lupinus albus* and *L. angustifolius*, try also the variety 'Dieta'.

CHAPTER 4

ALLIUMS

Growing alliums sustainably

With their distinctive upright foliage, alliums are unmistakable in the vegetable garden. Ranging from diminutive spring onions to the larger elephant garlic, there is space for alliums in any vegetable garden and at any time of year – winter-harvested leeks, for example, spring onions, summer garlic and an autumn supply of maincrop onions.

Once you have discovered how easy it is grow alliums at home then you will never want to pay for them again. Thankfully, with a bit of planning, these crops can provide you with harvests through every month of the year. Many of these crops, including leeks and garlic, are fully winter hardy while others, including onions, will store well.

You could also branch away from these allotment staples to grow some of the more unusual alliums that have started to become readily available over the last few years. Crops such as wild garlic and Egyptian walking onions are perennial, meaning their roots help to bind the soil together all year, providing a more sustainable growing environment. Society garlic is a must-have because it provides garlicky flavour without making your breath smell, hence the name! It has beautiful flowers as well.

Growing alliums can provide a sustainable, year-round, tasty and very healthy addition to your menus, making them a central part of your diet and vegetable-growing year. A garden without alliums is lacking; a kitchen without them is almost unthinkable.

Left: Maincrop onions are a staple veg and fun to grow if you have the room, but as they are cheap to buy in the shops you may choose to grow a more unusual allium instead.

Right: Onions need to be left out in the sun to dry before they are stored away. Another crop can quickly follow in the space they leave behind.

Spring onions

Fresh spring onions provide an extra flavour for salads and come in white or red. They can provide fresh produce in the 'hungry gap', before most other crops get going, as well as at other times of year.

WHAT YOU NEED
Grow in full sun and in free-draining, fertile soil.

SOWING AND PLANTING
Sow this crop at intervals to provide successional harvests. If sowing outside, sow from early spring to early autumn. Early sowings will benefit from being covered with horticultural fleece. Certain varieties are more reliable for early and late sowings. Create drills 1cm (½in) deep and 10cm (4in) apart. Scatter the seeds thinly along the base to minimize the need for thinning and then cover. Alternatively, grow in pots.

Spring onions grow well if started indoors, where they can be sown from late winter for an early crop. Using modules makes it easier to multi-sow; aim for 8–10 seeds per module. They should germinate in a fortnight and be ready to plant out within 4–5 weeks. Plant the clumps at 15cm (6in) spacing, burying the lower parts of the stems in the ground.

HOW TO GROW THE CROP
Water regularly to avoid the spring onions drying out. The plants should not need feeding unless being grown in pots, in which case a fortnightly feed can be beneficial. In most areas spring onions

Left: Drill-sown spring onions make for tasty thinnings as the crop grows.

Below: Spring onions can be sown in winter indoors for an early crop.

should not need winter protection unless the weather is particularly harsh.

Spring onions are fairly trouble free but can be affected by downy mildew, in which case affected leaves should be removed. Onion white rot, which causes the decay of roots, is more serious and plants should be removed. Onion fly can eat the roots of the plants causing them to wilt, and allium leaf miner will damage the leaves. This can be managed by covering the crop with mesh, or in the case of onion fly, an application of nematodes. If white rot or onion fly occur, then try to avoid growing alliums in that bed for a few years.

WHEN THE CROP IS READY

Spring and summer sowings should be harvestable from late spring to late autumn, when plants are about 15cm (6in) tall. Autumn sowings can stay in the ground over winter for harvest in late winter and spring. As direct sown crops are thinned, the seedlings can be eaten. Carefully twist the plants out of the soil. With multi-sown clumps, harvest the largest spring onions first, trying to disturb the roots as little as possible so that the rest can carry on growing.

STORING AND COOKING TIPS

This crop is best eaten fresh, although they will store in the fridge for a week or so. Try chopping raw into salads or incorporating into a range of dishes from omelettes to stir-fries and soups.

Above: When ready, twist the plants out of the soil, harvesting only as needed.

AT A GLANCE:

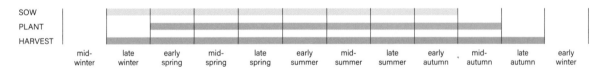

SOW	
PLANT	
HARVEST	

mid-winter · late winter · early spring · mid-spring · late spring · early summer · mid-summer · late summer · early autumn · mid-autumn · late autumn · early winter

Planting Overview: Suitable for pots; start in modules or outside; a good crop to fill the 'hungry gap'.

Varieties to Try: 'White Lisbon' (good over winter, will form small onions if left in the ground), 'North Holland Blood Red' (deep red bases to the plants, mild flavour), 'Eiffel' (long white stems, base does not form bulbs).

'White Lisbon'

'North Holland Blood Red'

Onions and shallots

It's very satisfying to watch onions plump as they reach harvestable size, and some varieties are great for growing through winter. If stored correctly, they can be eaten for much of the year. Shallots are small, sweet onions grown in the same way as other types.

WHAT YOU NEED

Grow in full sun in fertile, well-drained soil with a neutral or alkaline pH.

SOWING AND PLANTING

Beginners are often encouraged to sow 'sets', which are immature onions that start to grow again once planted. They are quicker and less fiddly than

seeds, but more expensive. Seeds take longer but the range of varieties is greater, and seed-grown plants are less prone to bolting. Both can be started inside in late winter, and inside or outside in early autumn, late winter or early to mid spring.

Sets can be planted into pots inside and planted out once they have sprouted, or put straight outside. When planting, leave the tip visible and aim for a 10cm (4in) spacing. Cover new sets with fleece until they have rooted.

Onion seeds are suitable for multi-sowing. Sow into modules, aiming for 3–4 seedlings per module. Plant out after 5–6 weeks at 15–20cm (6–8in) spacing. Alternatively, sow into drills 1cm (½in) deep and 15cm (6in) apart, thinly sowing the seed along the base and then covering. Thin to 10cm (4in) as seedlings emerge.

HOW TO GROW THE CROP

Water so that the onions do not dry out, but note that overwatering reduces the intensity of flavour. Onions in pots need watering more regularly and occasionally feeding. Remove any flowers that appear. Some varieties are more reliable over winter, and they all do best if well established before winter.

Leek rust can affect onions, as can downy mildew: remove affected leaves. If onion white rot or onion fly occurs, causing the plants to wilt and die, then remove affected plants and avoid

Left: Once you've traced your line of onion sets at 10cm (4in) spacing, push them into the soil with just the tip showing.

growing alliums in affected areas for a few years. Areas affected by onion fly can be treated with nematodes. Allium leaf miner will damage the leaves; protect crops with mesh.

WHEN THE CROP IS READY

The bulbs begin to swell during early summer, when they do most of their growing. Harvest any time once the foliage begins to yellow and dry. Different varieties mature at different rates, so the harvest can be staggered. Shallots and overwintering onions mature early, freeing up the ground while there is still plenty of time to get a summer crop established.

STORING AND COOKING TIPS

In sunny weather, leave the onions to dry outside or else place on a slatted surface inside so air can circulate. Once the leaves are papery, store in sacks or use the leaves to create a plait for hanging. Store in a light, cool, dry, frost-free location. Only store undamaged bulbs otherwise rot can set in.

Right: Unless they are being stored, onions can be harvested at any time.

AT A GLANCE:

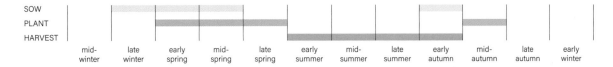

	mid-winter	late winter	early spring	mid-spring	late spring	early summer	mid-summer	late summer	early autumn	mid-autumn	late autumn	early winter
SOW												
PLANT												
HARVEST												

Planting Overview: Grow from sets or seeds; good for overwintering; suitable for multi-sowing.

Varieties to Try: 'Red Baron' AGM (red onion, strong flavour, stores well), 'Senshyu Yellow' (Japanese winter type, reliable over winter, good yields), 'Autumn Champion' (syn. 'Shakespeare') (good for autumn planting, good-sized bulbs), 'Griselle' (shallot, great flavour, long bulb type).

'Red Baron' AGM

'Senshyu Yellow'

Garlic

As easy to grow at home as a pack of spring bulbs, garlic matures as summer passes its midway point. The bulbs provide a distinctive flavour and can be stored for use through much of the year. Hardneck garlic produces larger cloves with a stronger flavour compared to softneck types.

WHAT YOU NEED
Grow in full sun and in fertile, well-drained soil with a neutral pH. Wet soils are more prone to diseases and are best avoided.

SOWING AND PLANTING
Garlic is grown from cloves, the individual sections of a garlic bulb. Buying from a reputable seller ensures the cloves are suitable for the climate, and free from disease. The cloves are best planted in late autumn or early winter as the winter cold triggers the plant to form a good bulb. Discard the smallest cloves, which can be used in the kitchen. Early spring plantings are also possible.

If the soil in your garden sits wet over winter, start garlic in pots in cold frames to help reduce disease issues, then plant out in the spring. Garlic is more usually started in situ, however – plant the cloves 10–15cm (4–6in) apart with the tips 3cm (1in) below the soil surface.

HOW TO GROW THE CROP
Garlic is low maintenance and needs no protection over winter. It needs little watering except in long dry spells. Remove brown leaves as they appear, as well as any flower stalks: these are more common on hardneck varieties.

Rust can often occur on the leaves – increased spacing of plants will improve air flow to reduce this. Allium leaf miner and leek moth can both affect garlic and can be kept off with insect-proof mesh. If white rot occurs, alliums should not be grown in any affected beds for a few years.

WHEN THE CROP IS READY
Autumn-planted garlic can be ready as soon as early summer, and spring-planted garlic in mid- to late summer. The leaves will turn yellow, indicating that the bulb has stopped growing. Carefully lift using a hand fork, being careful not to damage the basal plate. If the bulb is split at harvesting, this indicates it has been left too long.

Left: Plant individual garlic cloves from the end of autumn about 3cm (1in) deep.

WHY ARE VAMPIRES AFRAID OF GARLIC?

It is unclear where myths about vampires came from, but one theory is the disease porphyria. Sufferers of this disease exhibit traditional vampire characteristics, such as an intolerance to sunlight. They are also intolerant of sulphur-rich food, such as garlic.

STORING AND COOKING TIPS

Leave garlic bulbs to dry on the surface of the soil, or bring inside and place on a slatted surface to allow for air circulation. Drying usually takes 2–4 weeks. Once dry, cut off most of the leaves and store in a sack in a cool and dry location. Hardneck types will keep for 4–5 months and softneck varieties for a couple of months longer. Use in a wide range of dishes from soups to stews and stir-fries. The flower buds are also edible, as are the young leaves.

Above: 'Wet garlic' is garlic that is harvested a little bit early, before it has a chance to form a proper clove, and has a mild flavour.

AT A GLANCE:

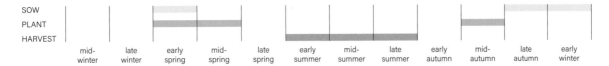

SOW											
PLANT											
HARVEST											
mid-winter	late winter	early spring	mid-spring	late spring	early summer	mid-summer	late summer	early autumn	mid-autumn	late autumn	early winter

Planting Overview: Best sown before winter; a low-maintenance crop; softneck varieties store longer than hardneck.

Varieties to Try: 'Solent Wight' AGM (softneck, well adapted to cooler climates), 'Provence Wight' (softneck, large bulbs with fat cloves), 'Lautrec Wight' (hardneck, purple-tinged cloves).

'Lautrec Wight'

'Solent Wight' AGM

Leeks

Leeks are a classic winter crop, but they can be grown for earlier harvesting in late summer and autumn. Leeks sown for winter harvest will stand through the winter into spring, making them a crop you will rely on during the 'hungry gap'. They are low maintenance and provide a mild onion flavour.

WHAT YOU NEED
Grow in full sun, and in well-drained, fertile soil with a neutral pH.

SOWING AND PLANTING
Leeks remain in the ground for many months so starting inside, or starting in a seedbed, allows for a catch crop before the plants go in the ground, making more efficient use of the space. Sow from late winter through the spring.

Inside, sow into modules, aiming for between 3 and 4 seedlings per module if multi-sowing. They should germinate within a fortnight and be ready to plant after 6–8 weeks. Plant at 10cm (4in) spacing for baby leeks, 15–20cm (6–8in) for individual plants, or 25cm (10in) for multi-sown clumps. Plant deeper than the modules to increase the length of the white shank.

Outside, wait until spring and then sow seeds 1cm (1/2in) deep into a seedbed. Transplant to their final growing position after 6–8 weeks.

Alternatively, sow straight into the final location in drills 20cm (8in) apart, thinning to 15cm (6in) spacing. Cover early sowings with fleece as excess cold can trigger bolting.

HOW TO GROW THE CROP
Water regularly while establishing, and then only in dry spells. Leeks in pots will need watering and feeding throughout the growing season. Remove any yellowing leaves, as well as any flower spikes. There is no need to earth up the stems unless a long white shank is particularly desired.

Leeks are generally hardy and need no winter protection. They also tend to be trouble-free, although there are a few notable problems:

Below left: For a long, white and tender shank, plant leek seedlings deeply.

Below: To make thick, kitchen-worthy leeks, keep the ground around the crop free from weeds.

onion white rot, which is most prevalent in damp soil, and onion fly, which can damage the crop's roots and cause wilting. Onion fly can be treated with nematodes – try to avoid growing alliums in affected beds for several years afterwards. In order to avoid leek rust, increase the spacing between plants to improve air circulation, and grow resistant varieties.

Leek moth will damage the leaves and shank of the plant. Its mating can be disrupted with pheromones, but the only reliable way to prevent damage is to cover the plants with insect-proof mesh from planting until mid autumn, when the second generation of larvae pupates. It is possible to tackle Allium leaf miner and onion fly in the same way.

WHEN THE CROP IS READY

Baby leeks are slightly sweeter, but leeks are usually harvested when more mature. Those sown early can be ready by late summer or early autumn. Leeks sown later will stand through the winter into spring. Carefully harvest leeks with a hand fork. For multi-sown clumps, harvest the largest leek first, leaving the rest to keep growing.

STORING AND COOKING TIPS

This crop is best harvested as needed, although leeks will store in the fridge for around a week. Try steaming, adding to stews, or making into soup. All the leaves are edible, as are the flower buds, although leeks are best harvested well before they get the opportunity to flower.

Above: Carefully harvest leeks using a fork, as and when needed, and leave the rest to keep growing.

AT A GLANCE:

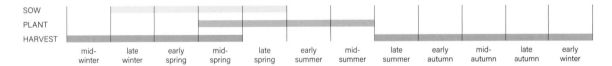

SOW											
PLANT											
HARVEST											
mid-winter	late winter	early spring	mid-spring	late spring	early summer	mid-summer	late summer	early autumn	mid-autumn	late autumn	early winter

Planting Overview: Start seed inside or out; water well until established; may need protecting from leek moth.

Varieties to Try: 'Musselburgh' (very hardy, heavy cropper), 'Oarsman' AGM (vigorous, uniform stems), 'Below Zero' (good rust resistance, stands well through winter).

'Below Zero'

'Musselburgh'

Chives

This easy-to-grow perennial will provide a harvest of mild onion- or garlic-flavoured leaves for many years, used mainly as a culinary herb. The beneficial insects in your garden will also love this plant.

The common chive, *Allium schoenoprasum*, reaches about 30cm (12in), but there are other species, such as garlic/Chinese chives (*A. tuberosum*), fat-leaf chives (*A. cepa*), and Siberian/blue chives (*A. nutans*), all of which are grown in the same way. Garlic chives will reach 50cm (20in) and have flat rather than cylindrical leaves, fat-leaf chives can reach 80cm (2½ft) and have flat leaves with a sweet onion flavour, while Siberian chives can reach 60cm (24in).

WHAT YOU NEED
Grows in fertile, well-drained soil. Does best in full sun but will tolerate light shade.

SOWING AND PLANTING
Sow seed in spring. If starting inside, sow into modules, aiming for 3–4 seedlings in a cluster. Once decent roots are established, plant at 20cm (8in) spacing, or 30cm (12in) for species other than the common chive. Chives can also be sown directly in drills 20–30cm (8–12in) apart and then thinned into clusters. Mature clumps can be lifted and divided in spring or autumn every few years. Young plants can also be bought in the spring and summer.

HOW TO GROW THE CROP
Water well when establishing or after dividing, and then again during dry spells. This plant is

Left: The common chive is a useful perennial herb, a salad ingredient and a very pretty ornamental.

Below: Divide mature clumps in spring or autumn to increase your stock.

good in containers, where it will need more regular watering and occasional feeds. Provide those in the ground with an annual mulch of well-rotted organic matter.

The plants will produce attractive flowers in the summer. Common chives have lilac flowers, garlic chives white and Siberian chives mauve-blue. The flowers are great for attracting beneficial insects but do reduce leaf growth so can be removed before they open if desired. Otherwise, simply remove spent flowerheads and yellowing leaves as they appear. The plants will die back to the ground over winter; they are winter hardy.

WHEN THE CROP IS READY

The leaves and flowers of this crop are edible and can be picked as needed from mid spring to mid autumn using a cut-and-come-again method. Pinch off what is needed and leave the rest to keep growing. Regular harvesting will keep new growth coming. If pots of chives are brought inside over winter, then it is possible to keep harvesting small amounts all year.

Above: Snip off leaves as and when they are needed – they are best fresh.

STORING AND COOKING TIPS

This plant is best eaten fresh but can be stored in the fridge for a few days. They should be eaten raw and add a mild onion flavour to any dishes they are added to, including salads, omelettes and soups. To store longer, freeze into ice cubes and then defrost as needed, although they will have less flavour afterwards.

AT A GLANCE:

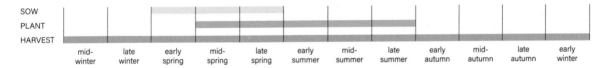

SOW											
PLANT											
HARVEST											
mid-winter	late winter	early spring	mid-spring	late spring	early summer	mid-summer	late summer	early autumn	mid-autumn	late autumn	early winter

Planting Overview: The several species of chive are all grown in the same way; water well; pick regularly to encourage more fresh leaves.

Varieties to Try: As well as the species listed above, try *A. schoenoprasum* 'Cha Cha' (unusual flower heads containing mini cylindrical green leaves) and *A. cepa* 'Quattro' (larger leaves and attractive lilac flowers).

'Cha Cha'

'Quattro'

Elephant garlic

As the name suggests, this long-lived perennial plant produces bulbs twice the size of regular garlic, yet it has a milder taste. This giant of the garlics is, in fact, a closer relative of leeks. The plant is also ornamental, with large purple flowerheads on tall stalks.

WHAT YOU NEED
Elephant garlic grows well in full sun, in any free-draining soil rich in organic matter. Thrives in moist soil but will not tolerate waterlogging.

SOWING AND PLANTING
Plant cloves 10–15cm (4–6in) deep, 20cm (8in) apart, in early to late autumn.

Below: Elephant garlic is easy to grow in containers, but these must be at least 30cm (12in) deep.

HOW TO GROW THE CROP
In the first year, the plants might produce only monobulbs; in the following years, the bulbs will split and produce cloves. It is said that removing the flowers from these plants will help to produce large bulbs. After harvesting, save some cloves for replanting in the autumn.

WHEN THE CROP IS READY
Lift the bulbs after flowering, when the foliage starts dying down. Let them dry in the sun or in a warm dry place indoors. Larger plants are more likely to have split into cloves – harvest these first and leave the smaller plants in the ground for the following year.

STORING AND COOKING TIPS
Elephant garlic is delicious roasted, in soups, or used in all ways that normal garlic would be. The scapes (stalks with flower bud) have the flavour of mild garlicky asparagus and can be stir-fried or sautéed with butter. Store the same way as garlic.

AT A GLANCE:

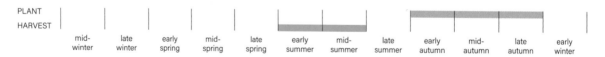

	mid-winter	late winter	early spring	mid-spring	late spring	early summer	mid-summer	late summer	early autumn	mid-autumn	late autumn	early winter
PLANT									▬	▬	▬	
HARVEST						▬	▬					

Planting Overview: Thrives in full sun and moist soil rich in organic matter but will not tolerate waterlogging; remove flowers to produce larger bulbs.

Wild garlic

Wild garlic is a hardy perennial woodland plant, native to Britain. It is one of the most popular crops to forage but can also be successfully grown at home. All parts of the plant are edible. The tender leaves are used to add a garlic flavour to a variety of dishes.

WHAT YOU NEED

Grow in shade or partial shade in moist, free-draining soil rich in organic matter. It prefers slightly acidic soil.

SOWING AND PLANTING

Wild garlic is propagated by seeds or bulbs. Sow seeds in the autumn or early spring direct. Cover lightly; they will germinate in spring when the soil warms up. Alternatively, plant the bulbs in early autumn.

HOW TO GROW THE CROP

The crop grows best with a good amount of moisture. With the right conditions, the plant will spread fast and become a nuisance. To prevent this, grow the bulbs in pots.

WHEN THE CROP IS READY

The leaves are ready to harvest from early spring, the flowers a little later, and the bulbs after the leaves have died down, in early autumn.

Above: Wild garlic, with its edible and ornamental qualities, is ideal for a container garden in shaded areas.

STORING AND COOKING TIPS

The leaves are best used fresh but will last for a few days in the fridge. Leaves can also be frozen for a few months. Dry leaves and crush them with salt to make garlic salt and store in an airtight container. Leaves are added to salads, omelettes and other dishes or can be made into a garlicky pesto. The flower buds and bulbs can be pickled.

AT A GLANCE:

	SOW	PLANT	HARVEST

mid-winter · late winter · early spring · mid-spring · late spring · early summer · mid-summer · late summer · early autumn · mid-autumn · late autumn · early winter

Planting Overview: Easy to cultivate; can spread fast (so be warned); suitable for container growing.

Society garlic

This attractive perennial, also known by the scientific name *Tulbaghia violacea*, is native to South Africa and is often seen in ornamental gardens. As an edible crop, it is grown for its leaves, stems and flowers which smell and taste of garlic.

Above: Similarly to garlic, both the leaves and flowers of society garlic are edible.

The name 'society garlic' was given to the plant because the garlic flavour can be enjoyed without the antisocial bad breath afterwards.

WHAT YOU NEED

Society garlic is best grown in sun or partial shade in well-drained soil.

SOWING AND PLANTING

Sow seeds direct in spring, thinning the seedlings to 25cm (10in) apart. Alternatively, divide mature clumps in late autumn after flowering finishes. Plant the divisions at the same depth as the original plant.

HOW TO GROW THE CROP

Water in dry spells. It has a long flowering season and is suitable to grow in containers, where it will need regular watering and an occasional feed. For areas with harsh winters (–5°C/23°F and lower), cover the clumps over winter with a good layer of mulch; if grown in containers, move indoors.

WHEN THE CROP IS READY

Harvest leaves and flowers regularly from spring to autumn to encourage further production.

STORING AND COOKING TIPS

Leaves and flowers are best eaten fresh. Leaves can be made into pesto and stored in the fridge for a week or in the freezer for a few months.

AT A GLANCE:

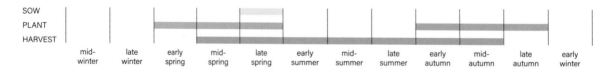

	mid-winter	late winter	early spring	mid-spring	late spring	early summer	mid-summer	late summer	early autumn	mid-autumn	late autumn	early winter
SOW												
PLANT												
HARVEST												

Planting Overview: Easy-to-grow attractive plant suitable for container growing; if temperatures over winter fall below –5°C (23°F) protect clumps with mulch.

Varieties to Try: 'Silver Lace' (striped green and white leaves, pink/lilac flowers), 'Kilimanjaro' (grass-green leaves and pale purple flowers), 'Pearl' (grey-green leaves and white flowers).

Egyptian walking onion

As the name suggests, Egyptian walking onions (*Allium × proliferum*) have a long history. They are hardy perennials which produce plantlets, or small bulbs, on the tops of the flower stalks. This is the plant's way of propagating itself.

The stems bend to the ground when the bulblets become heavy, and as they touch the ground, they root. This is how the plant 'walks' around the vegetable garden.

WHAT YOU NEED

These onions will thrive when planted in a sunny position in rich, well-drained soil. They will not tolerate waterlogging.

SOWING AND PLANTING

Plant the plantlets in the spring or autumn, 25cm (10in) apart and 5cm (2in) deep.

HOW TO GROW THE CROP

Egyptian walking onions are hardy evergreen plants that are easy to propagate by using the plantlets. Collect these for eating and to reduce the spread of the plant. Rejuvenate older plants by thinning or splitting the clump after a couple of seasons.

WHEN THE CROP IS READY

The basal stems are picked like spring onions through the season. The plantlets are ready to harvest by midsummer. Harvest basal bulbs in the autumn and winter.

STORING AND COOKING TIPS

The stems and the small aerial bulbs are used in salads like spring onions. The bulbs can be pickled. Use the basal bulbs in the same way as shallots.

Stems can be stored for a few days in the fridge, the plantlets and bulbs will store for a number of months in a cool, dry place.

Below: Harvest the small aerial bulbs of Egyptian onions for eating (an alternative to spring onions) or planting.

AT A GLANCE:

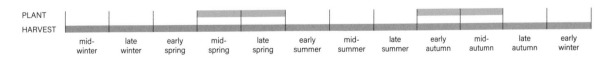

	mid-winter	late winter	early spring	mid-spring	late spring	early summer	mid-summer	late summer	early autumn	mid-autumn	late autumn	early winter
PLANT												
HARVEST												

Planting Overview: Easy to grow and propagate; will not tolerate waterlogging; to rejuvenate the plants, split or thin the clump after a few seasons of growth.

CHAPTER 5

FRUITING VEG

Growing fruiting veg sustainably

Fruiting vegetables may sound like a contradiction in terms, but botanically speaking, anything that develops from the flower part of a plant is classed as a fruit. This means that fruiting vegetables are a broad and diverse category, ranging from sweetcorn to sweet peppers and summer squash.

Some of these crops, including chillies, aubergines and melons, will grow well with a little bit of extra warmth. To grow them sustainably (without any artificial heat), a greenhouse or polytunnel can come in handy. Without cover they are still well worth trying outdoors, especially in milder areas and in sheltered sites. Some traditional greenhouse crops, predominantly tomatoes and cucumbers, will grow perfectly well outside in lots of areas as long as attention is paid to the choice of variety grown.

To contribute to your sustainable, year-round supply of fresh produce, fruiting vegetables provide plenty of options for long-term storage, even if they do not offer winter harvests. Chillies can be dried, tomatoes frozen as sauce, and winter squashes stored for months. You can even process some of your summer glut of courgettes into tasty chutneys for use over the following year.

Try adding even more variety to your diet with unusual crops including chayote, cucamelon and gherkins. Eating lots of fruiting veg really helps ensure that your body is receiving a broad range of nutrients. There are so many good reasons to grow these plants at home, so which is going to be your new favourite?

Some fruiting vegetables, notably tomatoes and aubergines but also melons, are available as grafted plants. While more expensive, grafted plants confer resilience to most soil-borne diseases and can be more productive. These two qualities mean grafted tomatoes in particular are increasingly used in commercial horticulture.

Left: The tomato: is it a fruit, a vegetable or both? Easy to grow in a greenhouse; choose your varieties and planting position carefully if growing outdoors.

Right: Fruiting veg generally requires a bit of warmth, lots of light, plenty of food and water and, in some cases, something to climb on.

Sweetcorn

The most satisfying thing about this summer crop, apart from feasting on its juicy cobs, is watching it explode into growth from just a handful of dried seeds or corn kernels. At home, you can grow full-size or baby sweetcorn, or multicoloured popcorn varieties.

WHAT YOU NEED

Grow in a sheltered location, in full sun and in fertile, moisture-retentive soil.

SOWING AND PLANTING

Sweetcorn is best started indoors in mid to late spring to give it a long enough season. Sow two seeds 1.5cm (5/8in) deep in a 9cm (3³/₄in) pot and thin to one after germination, usually within a fortnight. Plant out at around 10cm (4in) tall once all risk of frost is passed.

In milder areas, sweetcorn can be sown directly outside in early summer, but naturally enough the seeds are very attractive to mice. Station sow two or three seeds per desired location and thin to one after germination.

As sweetcorn is wind pollinated, plant it in a block with 35–40cm (14–16in) spacing for most varieties, although baby sweetcorn should be planted in a row to prevent pollination. If you are growing a 'supersweet' variety, plant it away from other varieties as cross-pollination can result in poor flavour.

HOW TO GROW THE CROP

Sweetcorn needs plenty of water when establishing, and then again when the cobs are forming. If more than one shoot appears from the base, they can all be left on the plants, sometimes providing an extra, small cob for harvest. Plants in really exposed locations may need staking.

Sometimes badgers and birds can try to take the crop so netting can help deter them. Sparsely

Above: Start sweetcorn indoors to give it a head start and also to protect the seeds from mice.

Left: Once the risk of frost has passed, plant out in blocks of at least eight plants to ensure pollination.

filled cobs at harvest are due to poor pollination, often due to wet weather damping down pollen and limiting its spread.

Consider growing sweetcorn with winter squashes underneath them to cover the ground. Alternatively, sow a quick-growing crop such as radish in between the sweetcorn plants when they are first planted.

Above: Pierce a kernel with your thumbnail to see if the cobs are ready to harvest.

WHEN THE CROP IS READY

Sweetcorn is generally ready in late summer to mid autumn when the tassels on the cobs turn brown. To check, peel back the top part of the cob and pierce a kernel. If the liquid is creamy then it is ready; if it has turned paste-like then the cob is overripe. However, popcorn is harvested when it has started to dry out on the plant, and baby corn is harvested when immature so the whole cob can be eaten. To harvest, carefully twist and pull the cob downwards to snap it off the plant.

STORING AND COOKING TIPS

Sweetcorn is best eaten straight after harvesting, either raw or lightly steamed. It can also be frozen and will store for several months. Baby sweetcorn makes a great addition to salads and stir-fries. Popcorn kernels need to be dried on the cob before they are stored. Once fully dried they will store in an airtight jar for months before being popped in a lidded saucepan with a little oil.

AT A GLANCE:

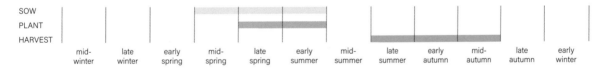

	SOW	PLANT	HARVEST

mid-winter   late winter   early spring   mid-spring   late spring   early summer   mid-summer   late summer   early autumn   mid-autumn   late autumn   early winter

Planting Overview: Most reliable when started indoors; plant most varieties in blocks for wind pollination; harvest when tassels turn brown.

Varieties to Try: 'Swift' AGM (extra-sweet variety, fast growing, reliable), 'Double Red' (red leaves and cobs, rich flavour), 'Fiesta' (attractive multicoloured popcorn variety), 'Minipop' (baby sweetcorn, sweet and crunchy).

'Double Red'

'Swift' AGM

Courgettes, marrows and summer squashes

Courgettes are a staple of the summer plot, producing a large volume of fruits; marrows are simply courgettes left to grow larger. Both are types of summer squash, and there are many other varieties too. They are distinguished from winter squashes by being harvested younger and not developing hard outer skins. All types of summer squash are grown in the same way.

WHAT YOU NEED

Grow in a sunny location with rich, moisture-retentive soil.

SOWING AND PLANTING

Best started indoors to ensure a longer season of growth. Sow two seeds per 9cm (3¾in) pot in mid to late spring and thin to one after germination. Plant out once large enough to handle and all risk of frost is passed. Spacing varies from 90cm (3ft) up to 1.5m (5ft) for trailing types. In milder areas, sow seed direct in early summer, sowing two or three seeds per station, at about 2cm (¾in) depth, and thinning to one.

HOW TO GROW THE CROP

Courgettes and other summer squashes need plenty of water, particularly as they are establishing and once they start setting fruit. When watering, try to direct water to the roots to reduce wastage. As a space-saving measure, trailing types can be trained vertically. Smaller varieties can grow up sturdy stakes, whereas larger ones will cover an obelisk. Compact forms can be grown in containers, although these need plenty of water and weekly feeds to crop well.

Powdery mildew commonly occurs on members of this plant family. To reduce this, grow resistant varieties and space the plants out

Left: Start the seedlings early so that they are a reasonable size once summer is underway and it is warm enough to plant them out. A heated propagator will help to germinate the seed.

to increase air flow. Remove infected leaves when they appear. If the plants are not setting fruit this can be due to them being immature or stressed, or it may be due to low temperatures inhibiting the production of female flowers. Cool weather can also cause fruits to rot off, but this usually resolves itself when the weather improves.

WHEN THE CROP IS READY

Regular harvesting ensures more fruits are produced. Unless aiming to grow marrows, courgettes are harvestable from 10cm (4in) in length, usually from midsummer to mid autumn. Check the plants every couple of days to prevent them getting too large. To harvest, carefully cut the fruit from the plant. Summer squashes are harvested in the same way, with the harvestable size depending on the variety, although they should never get too large as this impairs the texture and flavour.

Right: Harvest courgettes before they get too big, otherwise they become marrows.

STORING AND COOKING TIPS

All of these crops are best eaten fresh, although they will store in the fridge for a few days. Young courgettes can be eaten raw but larger fruits are better lightly steamed, roasted, stuffed or made into chutney. The flowers are also edible.

AT A GLANCE:

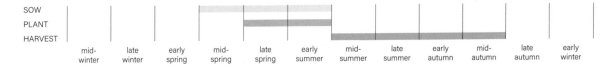

SOW											
PLANT											
HARVEST											
mid-winter	late winter	early spring	mid-spring	late spring	early summer	mid-summer	late summer	early autumn	mid-autumn	late autumn	early winter

Planting Overview: Best started indoors; provide plenty of water; harvest regularly to prevent fruits getting too large.

Varieties to Try: 'Defender' AGM (high-yielding courgette, classic green fruits), 'Orelia' AGM (yellow-fruited courgette, good mildew resistance), 'Sunburst' AGM (summer squash, flattened yellow fruits), 'Astia' AGM (dark green courgettes, compact growth habit).

'Defender' AGM

'Sunburst' AGM

Winter squashes

Winter squashes are among the easiest and most rewarding crops to grow. They come in a wide range of colours and sizes that far surpasses anything from the supermarket. Winter squashes are distinct from summer squashes in that they develop a hard skin. This allows many of the varieties to be stored after harvest to be enjoyed through the 'hungry gap' and beyond. Squashes either have a bush-forming or trailing habit. Botanically, squashes and pumpkins are the same – the heaviest example ever grown reached 1,226kg (2,702lb).

WHAT YOU NEED

Grow in full sun in moisture-retentive, but not waterlogged, soil. Squashes are hungry plants so a rich, fertile soil is needed for them to perform at their best.

Below and right: Plant out only after the risk of frost has passed and once the young plants have developed a few true leaves. Dig a hole large enough for the root ball, planting at the same depth as the plant was in its container, and water in well.

SOWING AND PLANTING

All varieties are frost tender. To ensure a crop, especially in cooler climates, the squashes should be started off indoors so that they have a headstart once the weather warms up and a longer growing season overall. In milder areas it may be possible to sow direct outdoors.

If direct sowing, squashes can be station sown. This means sowing two or three seeds in each location where a squash plant is to grow, about 2cm (3/4in) deep, and then thinning to one.

The spacing for these will vary from 90cm (3ft) for the smaller bush varieties to over 1.5m (5ft) for some trailing varieties. Sow the seeds in late spring or early summer once all risk of frost has passed.

For sowing indoors, sow two seeds per 9cm (3¾in) pot in mid spring, about 1.5cm (¾in) deep. Keep the seedlings warm and they should germinate within a fortnight. Thin to one seedling and plant out once the seedlings have developed a few true leaves and the temperatures have warmed up and there is no more risk of frost.

HOW TO GROW THE CROP

Winter squashes are relatively easy once established. They cover the ground, therefore helping to suppress weeds, and the main maintenance is in controlling their growth, especially with the trailing varieties. Trailing squashes will produce more than one shoot, and the shoots can themselves produce sideshoots. These can be left to run but, if space is limited, they will need pruning and training into position. One way to control their spread is to build a sturdy structure to train them up. This allows the plants to be planted closer together, fitting more crops into the space. This vertical technique is most suitable for plants with smaller fruits but can be attempted with larger varieties.

Squash leaves may also need removing if they develop powdery mildew. This fungal disease is evident when a white powdery substance can be seen on the leaves, and these should be removed to limit the spread of the disease. Some varieties are more susceptible than others, and the disease spreads most easily when the plants themselves are stressed by environmental factors such as a lack of water. Spacing the plants out can help improve air flow and, therefore, reduce the spread of the disease.

Squashes need plenty of water due to their large leaves, but should not require feeding if the soil is adequately rich. When watering, try to direct the water at the roots not the leaves to reduce wastage.

Above: Trailing varieties can be trained up sturdy supports, to save space, and to keep their developing fruits off the ground, where they might rot.

If you see that some fruits are rotting and dropping off the plants, this can be a natural way for the plants to focus their energies on other fruits. If you are aiming to grow the largest squash possible, remove all fruits but one from the plant. If no fruits are setting, it can be due to overly low temperatures inhibiting the production of female flowers, overly hot weather inhibiting the production of male flowers, or immature or stressed plants.

WHEN THE CROP IS READY

Winter squashes are ready to harvest in mid autumn, and should all be harvested before any frosts. As the leaves of the plant die back, cut away those around the fruits to aid the ripening process.

To harvest, use a sharp knife or pair of secateurs to cut them from the plant. Leave the stalk intact, ideally with a little bit of the stem of the plant still attached in a T-shape, to reduce the chance of any rot seeping down into the fruit.

STORING AND COOKING TIPS

Before storing winter squash, they need to be cured. This is a process whereby the skins of the squashes harden to extend their life and increase resistance to rot. This is done by exposing the harvested fruit to sun, either in a greenhouse or outside. If left outside, they are best raised on bricks or wooden pallets so that the fruits are off the damp soil. After a couple of weeks, check the fruits are undamaged and then store in a cool, frost-free location. The length of storage depends on the variety, ranging from a few months up to nine or ten months.

Winter squashes can be cooked in a range of ways. For example, smaller ones can be stuffed whereas larger varieties need to be cut up and steamed or roasted.

Left: 'Crown Prince' winter squashes are well known for their pale blue skins and tasty orange flesh. They also store very well.

AT A GLANCE:

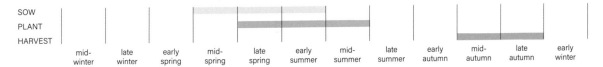

	mid-winter	late winter	early spring	mid-spring	late spring	early summer	mid-summer	late summer	early autumn	mid-autumn	late autumn	early winter
SOW												
PLANT												
HARVEST												

Planting Overview: Best started indoors; both bush and trailing varieties are available; provide plenty of water; try training up over structures to save space.

Varieties to Try: 'Crown Prince' AGM (large fruits, trailing, light blue skin, sweet orange flesh, amazing flavour, stores well), 'Baby Boo' (small fruits, trailing, white skin, pale flesh, nutty flavour), 'Bonbon' (medium fruits, trailing, dark green skin, great flavour), 'Uchiki Kuri' (medium fruits, trailing, dark orange skin, orange flesh, stores well), 'Hunter' AGM (medium fruits, trailing, butternut type), 'Gold Nugget' (medium fruits, bush type, golden orange skin, buttery taste), 'Honey Bear' AGM (small fruits, bush type, dark green skin, orange flesh), 'Tromboncino' (trailing with bizarre fruits, usually harvested young as a summer squash but can be left to grow as a winter squash with a relatively short storage life).

'Bonbon'

'Gold Nugget'

'Uchiki Kuri'

'Baby Boo'

Cucumbers

Fresh homegrown cucumbers offer a taste not found in shop-bought produce. The fruits come in a range of shapes and colours and are an easy crop to grow. Gherkins are cucumber varieties with tiny fruits used for pickling. They are grown in the same way, with the fruits harvested when small.

WHAT YOU NEED
Grow in a sunny, sheltered location, in fertile soil.

SOWING AND PLANTING
Cucumbers started inside tend to germinate more reliably. Sow two seeds per 9cm (3¾in) pot in early to mid spring, or slightly later for outdoor crops, and thin to one after germination, which should take a couple of weeks. Plant out once large enough, ensuring the frost risk is passed if planting outside. Space at 30–40cm (12–16in) if training the plants vertically. Outside, sow seeds in early summer once the soil has warmed up and the risk of frost has passed. Sow three seeds per station, thinning to one after germination.

HOW TO GROW THE CROP
Cucumbers are usually grown inside, but can be grown outdoors in milder regions. Smooth-skinned varieties are generally better indoors, with ridge types grown outdoors. This crop can trail on the ground but is best trained vertically. This saves space and raises the fruits away from slugs. Tie the plant into a post or trellis as it grows, or twine around a vertical string secured at ground level. Indoor cucumbers will reach a greenhouse roof, while outdoor ones can reach over 2m (6½ft). As the vines grow, remove sideshoots one leaf beyond a female flower to improve air flow. Stop non-fruiting sideshoots at two leaves.

Cucumbers need plenty of water. If they are in good soil they should not need feeding. In containers, which should be at least 30cm (12in) in diameter, the plants will require more water, as well as feeding every fortnight. Make use of vents and shading to prevent greenhouses overheating.

Remove leaves that get powdery mildew, or those that die off. If plants develop mottling and distorted growth, this may be cucumber mosaic virus and the plants should be removed. For cucumbers grown inside, damping the floor with water when it is hot keeps humidity high and deters red spider mite and powdery mildew.

Left: Cucumber seeds germinate much more readily indoors, particularly if they have the encouragement of a heated propagator.

Cleaning the greenhouse or polytunnel in winter removes overwintering red spider mite and greenhouse whitefly.

WHEN THE CROP IS READY

Cucumbers are harvestable from midsummer indoors, or late summer outdoors, through to mid autumn. The fruit size will depend on the variety, and smaller varieties start to crop a little quicker. Look for the tip of the fruit rounding off. If the outer skin starts to crack, this indicates the fruit is overly mature. Cut the cucumbers from the plant with a sharp knife.

STORING AND COOKING TIPS

This crop should be eaten as fresh as possible but will keep in the fridge for a couple of weeks. Cut raw into salads or sandwiches. Gherkins should be pickled for storing.

Right: Whether trailing or climbing plants, cucumbers will benefit from a support where they will display their fruit for easy picking.

AT A GLANCE:

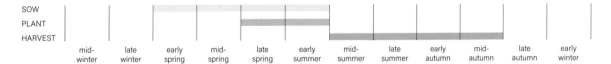

SOW												
PLANT												
HARVEST												
	mid-winter	late winter	early spring	mid-spring	late spring	early summer	mid-summer	late summer	early autumn	mid-autumn	late autumn	early winter

Planting Overview: Can be grown inside or out; provide plenty of water; train vertically to save space and protect the fruits.

Varieties to Try: 'Marketmore' AGM (tasty, reliable outdoors), 'Socrates' AGM (best inside, excellent taste), 'Mini Munch' AGM (bite-sized fruits), 'Crystal Lemon' (round yellow fruits, vigorous), 'White Wonder' (syn. 'Bianco Lungo') (white, mild fruits), 'Diamant' (good gherkin variety for pickling).

'Crystal Lemon'

'Mini Munch' AGM

Chilli peppers

Gardener cooks really get a lot out of growing chillies. They don't take up much space – they are easily grown in a pot on a windowsill, for example – and they make a very colourful and rewarding harvest. Chillies store for months, either dried or pickled.

There is a great variety of chillies available, and to grow them well it is good to know which type you have. Cayenne and jalapeño chillies belong to *Capsicum annum* species, and they fruit earlier than chillies from other species, such as habaneros (*Capsicum chinense*). Habanero chillies are some of the hottest in the world and are best grown indoors in cooler climates.

WHAT YOU NEED
Choose a sunny site with a lot of warmth to grow chillies outdoors. Alternatively, grow indoors on a sunny windowsill or in a greenhouse or polytunnel. They grow alongside tomatoes or cucumbers very nicely. Plant in fertile, free-draining soil or use a peat-free multipurpose compost if growing in a container.

SOWING AND PLANTING
Seed offers the best choice of varieties, but many specialist mail order nurseries offer a good range of baby plants. It is simplest to germinate seed in a heated propagator, as they require a temperature of about 20°C (68°F), which is hard to sustain in the early part of the year, even on a windowsill. The plants will benefit from an early start and begin to flower from early summer onwards. Germination is usually swift but be prepared to wait up to 30 days.

When the plants have grown their second set of leaves, they can be transferred to larger pots, then when they are about 10–20cm (4–8in) tall they can be planted into their final growing positions. Be aware that they are sensitive to cold, so only move them outside once the risk of frost has passed. Planting distance depends on the eventual size of the plant, from 30cm (12in) to 1m (3ft). Pinch out the growing tips at this stage so they become bushier.

HOW TO GROW THE CROP
Chilli plants come in different sizes, from small bushy plants to tall shrubby types. The taller plants will need supports as they become laden with fruit. They can be supported with canes and string.

Left: Support the taller chilli varieties with stakes to prevent plants breaking under the weight of the fruit.

If grown in pots, water regularly and feed weekly with a general-purpose organic fertiliser until flowers form, then continue with organic tomato feed throughout the summer.

WHEN THE CROP IS READY

Harvest is usually 12–16 weeks after sowing. The fruit can be picked at any time, when immature, fully ripened or any time in between. Fully ripe fruit develops more flavour; the heat will not change much with ripening. At the end of the season, bring the plants undercover to help the fruit ripen, so they can be dried and stored.

STORING AND COOKING TIPS

Chillies can be used fresh, both raw or cooked, but be aware that some pack immense heat and need to be handled with care. They are also a very versatile store cupboard crop. Either dry the fruit by stringing them up for later use, or pickle them in oil to make a spicy condiment.

Right: Chillies are ideal for containers. To get good crops from pot-grown plants, water and feed regularly.

AT A GLANCE:

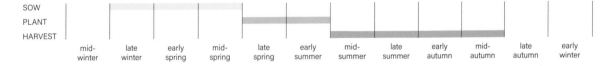

	SOW	PLANT	HARVEST

mid-winter · late winter · early spring · mid-spring · late spring · early summer · mid-summer · late summer · early autumn · mid-autumn · late autumn · early winter

Planting Overview: Grow in full sun in a warm sheltered spot or inside; choose a variety to suit the location; support tall plants as they fruit; water and feed well if growing in containers.

Varieties to Try: 'Padron' (mild when green, prolific), 'Apache' AGM (red, reliable), 'Cherry Bomb' (mild, fleshy, small red fruit), 'Hungarian Hot Wax' AGM (large, mild, ripening from yellow to red), 'Lemon Drop' (very hot with citrusy flavour, yellow fruit).

'Cherry Bomb'

'Lemon Drop'

Sweet peppers

Sweet peppers come in a range of colours and sizes, from long and pointed to round bell peppers. They make a superb crop if you have enough room in your greenhouse, fruiting with generosity if they are happy.

WHAT YOU NEED

This crop needs heat to grow and fruit well, so best results are achieved in a polytunnel or greenhouse. In mild areas it can be grown outside; choose a sheltered location with full sun and fertile, free-draining soil.

SOWING AND PLANTING

Start seed indoors in late winter or early spring. Sow into modules and keep warm before potting seedlings into 9cm (3¾in) pots. The final pots

should be at least 30cm (12in) across. Outside, wait until night temperatures are reliably above 12°C (54°F) then plant at 30–45cm (12–18in) spacing. Varieties with larger fruits take longer to ripen so dwarf varieties are more suitable outside.

HOW TO GROW THE CROP

Water regularly to prevent plants drying out. Pots will need most water and a fortnightly feed. In greenhouses, use ventilation to keep temperatures below 30°C (86°F), and damp down to increase

Left: Sow the tiny seeds indoors from late winter, ideally with the heat of a propagator.

Above: Peppers can be harvested green or allowed to change colour and sweeten.

humidity. This promotes plant growth and reduces issues such as fungal disease, red spider mite and greenhouse whitefly. Pinch out the plant tips once they reach 30cm (12in) to encourage branching. Tall types may need staking.

WHEN THE CROP IS READY

Fruits are ready from midsummer into autumn. They can be harvested green, but will gradually change colour and sweeten. The size and colour will depend on the variety grown. Carefully cut from the plant using secateurs.

STORING AND COOKING TIPS

After removing the seeds, the fruits can be eaten in salads or stir-fries, roasted and eaten as a side dish or as a soup ingredient, or they can be stuffed and baked. If you have a glut, consider preserving or pickling – after all, homegrown sweet peppers are a real treat and must not be wasted!

Right: Sweet peppers are a very rewarding crop to grow – not just for their amazing colours, but also their stunning flavours.

AT A GLANCE:

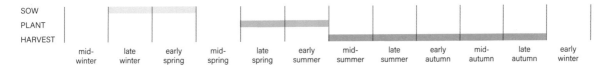

SOW											
PLANT											
HARVEST											
mid-winter	late winter	early spring	mid-spring	late spring	early summer	mid-summer	late summer	early autumn	mid-autumn	late autumn	early winter

Planting Overview: Start seeds indoors; grow plants in a warm location; best crops are produced in greenhouses.

Varieties to Try: 'Bianca' AGM (pale yellow bell peppers, large fruits), 'Corno di Toro Rosso' AGM (pointed red fruit, good flavour), 'New Ace' (dark green bell peppers, turning red as they age), 'Topgirl' (red fruit, dwarf variety).

'New Ace'

'Topgirl'

Aubergines

From the same family as the tomato, aubergines are tender, heat-loving plants. They produce edible fruits which are used in many cuisines. Aubergine does not have much taste on its own, but the spongy flesh absorbs flavour well.

WHAT YOU NEED

Best grown in full sun, in free-draining soil rich in organic matter. In temperate climates it is best in a greenhouse or polytunnel.

SOWING AND PLANTING

Sow seeds indoors in 9cm (3³/₄in) pots from late winter to mid spring and keep at room temperature. Plant outdoors when the danger of frost passes. Baby plants are often seen for sale in nurseries and garden centres. Grafted plants are also available, which are stronger and cope better with cooler weather.

HOW TO GROW THE CROP

Aubergines are grown much like tomatoes (see pp166–9), but they must have plenty of warmth, a sheltered position and a good supply of water. They are suitable to grow in large pots but will need regular watering and feeding. Stake to prevent the heavy fruit breaking the plant.

Below left: Instead of using stakes, train aubergines on hanging strings to support the plants from above.

Below: Under the right conditions, aubergine plants can be very prolific. Harvest fruit when the skin is shiny.

Red spider mite, whitefly and aphids can be a problem, particularly if grown under glass. Ventilate the greenhouse or polytunnel to improve airflow and damp down in the morning to increase humidity and deter red spider mite.

WHEN THE CROP IS READY
The fruit is ripe when it reaches full size and has a shiny skin. If the skin becomes dull and matt, the fruit has passed its prime.

STORING AND COOKING TIPS
Aubergines store for a few days in the fridge. They can be partially cooked and frozen, or preserved in olive oil with garlic and herbs. This versatile vegetable is great in curries, grilled, stewed, baked or stuffed with meat or rice. It is a main ingredient of some iconic dishes, such as Italian parmigiana melanzane, Greek moussaka and Lebanese baba ghanoush.

Above: Aubergine fruit comes in various shapes and colours. This is the white variety 'Clara'.

AT A GLANCE:

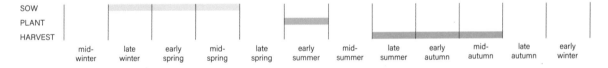

SOW												
PLANT												
HARVEST												
mid-winter	late winter	early spring	mid-spring	late spring	early summer	mid-summer	late summer	early autumn	mid-autumn	late autumn	early winter	

Planting Overview: Plant after last frost under cover, or in a sunny sheltered place; aubergine needs plenty of water, warmth and nutrients; stake before the plant becomes heavy with fruit; monitor plants for pests.

Varieties to Try: 'Bonica' F1 AGM (large black fruit, reliable), 'Galine' F1 AGM (small egg-shaped black fruit, reliable), 'Patio Baby' (small black fruit, compact), 'White Knight' (slim white fruit, reliable), 'Green Knight' (slim green fruit, reliable), 'Clara' AGM (large white fruit, reliable), 'Pinstripe' (small purple striped fruit, compact).

'Bonica' AGM

'Pinstripe'

Okra

Okra is an attractive tender annual plant from the mallow family. It produces green-ribbed edible seedpods, which are popular in many world cuisines.

WHAT YOU NEED
Since okra is a heat-loving vegetable from the tropics, it needs a sheltered position in full sun and plenty of moisture. It will grow well in free-draining soil rich in organic matter.

SOWING AND PLANTING
Sow in spring, two seeds per module or pot. For faster germination, keep above 20°C (68°F) and soak the seeds in warm water overnight before sowing. When the seedlings emerge, thin to the strongest one. After germination, the young okra plants need light to avoid becoming leggy. Plant out after the danger of frost has passed.

HOW TO GROW THE CROP
In temperate climates, it is most productive if grown in a greenhouse or polytunnel.

Avoid planting out early, as cold will slow down growth. Water regularly and stake the plants as they can become top-heavy with fruit, and break.

WHEN THE CROP IS READY
The pods are harvested immature, when they are between 5–12cm (2–5in) long. Mature pods are too tough to eat.

STORING AND COOKING TIPS
Okra is used in curries, stews and can be fried. The fruit is mucilaginous and when cut it becomes slimy, making it a useful thickener in various dishes. To avoid the 'sliminess', do not cut the pods, just fry them whole. Okra will keep well for a few days in the fridge; it can be blanched and stored in the freezer, or pickled.

AT A GLANCE:

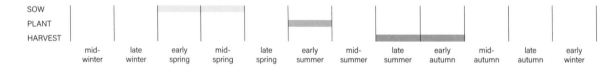

	SOW	PLANT	HARVEST

mid-winter · late winter · early spring · mid-spring · late spring · early summer · mid-summer · late summer · early autumn · mid-autumn · late autumn · early winter

Planting Overview: Heat and moisture are required for good pod production; best grown under cover; stake for support.

Varieties to Try: 'Clemson Spineless' (reliable, cropping within 60 days, good for temperate climates), 'Red Burgundy' (attractive flowers with red pods), 'Baby Bubba' (compact, reliable cropper in cooler climates).

'Clemson Spineless'

'Red Burgundy'

Chayote

All parts of this perennial plant from the cucumber family – also known by the scientific name *Sechium edule* – are edible. It is mainly cultivated for its green fruit that taste of cucumber and courgette with a hint of apple.

WHAT YOU NEED
Chayote is best grown in a sheltered place, in full sun or partial shade outdoors, or in a greenhouse or polytunnel. The plants prefer a well-drained soil rich in organic matter.

SOWING AND PLANTING
Plant the whole fruit in spring indoors in a pot, with the wider end in the soil and tilted to the side, and the top end exposed. Water in, then again when the first shoots start growing. Overwatering at this stage can cause rotting of the planted fruit. Plant outdoors after the danger of frost passes, or indoors when the fruit has sprouted and the plant has a good root system.

HOW TO GROW THE CROP
Chayote will flower and fruit when the days start getting shorter. It needs a sturdy structure to climb and requires a regular supply of water.

WHEN THE CROP IS READY
Harvest in the autumn, when the fruit is about the size of a fist and shiny. Keep some of the fruits

Above: Chayote is a vigorous, heat-loving climber grown as an annual in temperate climates.

over winter in a dry, frost-free place, for growing the following season.

STORING AND COOKING TIPS
The crisp fruit is used raw in salads and smoothies. It can be cooked in stir-fries and a variety of sweet or savoury dishes. It will store in the fridge for a month, or can be frozen, pickled or fermented in brine.

AT A GLANCE:

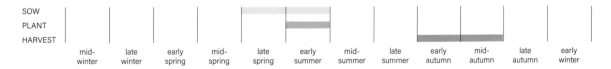

SOW												
PLANT												
HARVEST	mid-winter	late winter	early spring	mid-spring	late spring	early summer	mid-summer	late summer	early autumn	mid-autumn	late autumn	early winter

Planting Overview: Plant in a warm, sheltered place; provide support for the plant to climb; water regularly after the first shoots appear; save a few fruit over winter for growing the following year.

Tomatoes

Tomatoes come in a huge range of flavours, colours, shapes and sizes. Cordon tomatoes are tallest, with some varieties reaching nearly 2m (6½ft) in height. Bush tomatoes are more compact, and are good for pots and hanging baskets.

WHAT YOU NEED

Grow in full sun and in a sheltered location. Outdoor growing is possible in milder areas, but the crop is generally more reliable undercover, in a greenhouse or polytunnel. Choose a site with moisture-retentive, fertile soil which has been enriched with organic matter. This crop can also be grown in large pots or growbags.

SOWING AND PLANTING

Tomatoes can be bought as young plants, but growing from seed provides a wider choice. Sow seed indoors in late winter or early spring for crops that are to be grown undercover – they germinate quickly in a heated propagator. Wait until mid spring for those going outside. As tomatoes cannot be planted out until after the last frost, usually in late spring or early summer, sowing any earlier can result in elongated, overly large plants.

Sow thinly into 9cm (3¾in) pots, lightly cover with compost and keep warm. Germination should occur within a week. Gradually thin the seedlings until eventually only one is left in the pot. Ensure the young plants get plenty of light to stop them becoming leggy. When the plant is about 20cm (8in) tall and has developed good roots, it can be planted. Bury the plant up to the first leaves as any stem below ground level will produce more roots. Spacing varies depending on the variety, but is usually 50–60cm (20–24in) for cordons, and closer for bushes. Beefsteak cordons should be spaced a bit wider.

Left: Grafted tomatoes are grown in the same way as seed raised. They are expensive but more resistant to soil-borne diseases and can produce higher yields.

HOW TO GROW THE CROP

Cordon tomatoes need support, such as a bamboo cane. Alternatively, tie a piece of string to a peg in the soil near the base of the tomato and attach the top to the greenhouse roof or an overhead support. As the tomato grows, wind the string around the stem. To train cordons, the sideshoots need to be removed regularly. These are vegetative shoots produced in the leaf axils, in between the leaf and the main stem of the plant. If caught young these can be pinched out using fingers, but secateurs may be needed for larger ones. Removing sideshoots helps improve air flow, and ensures the plant's energy is focused on the main stem and the fruit it produces. Put small side shoots in water and they will form roots and a new plant. With cordon beefsteak tomatoes, the individual trusses may need support as the fruits get quite heavy. Bush tomatoes do not need training or support unless they are carrying particularly large fruit.

Tomatoes need regular watering, particularly those in pots or growbags. Those growing in the ground should not need feeding but a regular balanced feed will help those in containers. Keeping plants well watered helps to prevent blossom end rot. This disorder, characterised by black discolouration at the base of the fruits, is caused by calcium deficiency, often triggered because the plants cannot take up calcium from dry soil even if it is there.

Tomato blight is indicated by back lesions on the stem of the plants and fruits turning brown. This fungal disease spreads best in humid, warm weather. Growing plants under cover will largely protect them; outside it is safer to grow blight-resistant varieties. They can still get blight and carry on to produce a harvest. Remove any badly infected plants; they can be composted if the heap gets hot enough. Crop rotation is not essential (see p26), but it is a sensible precaution to take after a bad episode of blight.

Remove any yellowing or diseased leaves. Also, as the fruits start to mature, remove the lower leaves to expose the tomatoes to sunlight,

Top: Not all tomatoes are red, so it is useful to know what colour a particular variety is, so you know when it is ripe.

Above: Pinch out sideshoots from the leaf axils to encourage the plant and fruits to maximum production.

ensuring a reasonable number of leaves are left. This will help the fruits to ripen quicker.

WHEN THE CROP IS READY

Tomatoes are harvestable from midsummer through to mid autumn. The larger beefsteak tomatoes will take longer to ripen than cherry tomatoes. Ensure the expected colour of the variety is known to help judge when it is ready.

If a fruit is ripe, it can be detached from the plant with a twist. If the fruit resists, then it is not quite ready. Overripe tomatoes will start to split. At the end of the season, put any unripe tomatoes on a sunny windowsill to ripen. Placing a ripe banana nearby speeds up ripening as it gives off the plant hormone ethylene.

STORING AND COOKING TIPS

Tomatoes were once considered poisonous. The botanical name comes from the Latin for 'wolf peach', and the plants were originally brought to Europe as ornamental curiosities. In reality, it was the high lead content of the plates they were served on, which was partly dissolved by the acidic tomato juice, that was causing the poisoning, not the fruits.

This crop is wonderful when eaten fresh from the plant; the fruits have a relatively short shelf life. Putting them in the fridge will extend their life, but damages the flavour. Gluts are quite common. These can be made into a range of sauces and preserves for storage.

Right: Individually, ripe fruit can be detached with a gentle twist; alternatively and if required, remove whole trusses with secateurs.

AT A GLANCE:

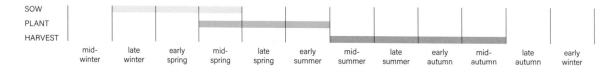

SOW											
PLANT											
HARVEST											
mid-winter	late winter	early spring	mid-spring	late spring	early summer	mid-summer	late summer	early autumn	mid-autumn	late autumn	early winter

Planting Overview: Start seed inside; cordon tomatoes will need training up a support; larger tomatoes take longer to ripen; outside, grow blight-resistant varieties to avoid disease.

Varieties to Try: 'Crimson Cherry' (cordon, blight resistant, attractive trusses of cherry tomatoes), 'Gardener's Delight' (cordon, great flavour, not blight resistant), 'Mountain Magic' (cordon, blight resistant, medium fruits), 'Sungold' AGM (cordon, golden fruits, not blight resistant), 'Costoluto Fiorentino' AGM (cordon, beefsteak, ribbed fruits), 'Black Cherry' (cordon, deep red-purple fruits, very prolific), 'Tumbling Tom Red' or 'Tumbling Tom Yellow' (bush, red or yellow fruits depending on variety, not blight resistant), 'Red Alert' (vigorous bush, highly productive, blight resistant), 'Tumbling Tigress' (bush, red and green striped fruits).

'Black Cherry'

'Crimson Cherry'

'Costoluto Fiorentino' AGM

'Gardener's Delight'

Melons

Closely related to cucumbers and squashes, melons are frost-tender trailing annual plants. There are many different types, such as cantaloupe, honeydew, the classic watermelon and even cucamelons. Melons are cultivated for their large, sweet and juicy fruit that is best eaten fresh on its own or in salads.

Each fruit contains around 95 per cent water and is a sought-after refreshment in hot weather. Melons need plenty of attention during the growing season, but the work is worthwhile for the delicious fruit they provide. There is nothing better than the sweet smell and taste of ripe homegrown melon.

WHAT YOU NEED

Melons are heat- and moisture-loving plants. In temperate climates, they grow best in a greenhouse or, alternatively, in a sheltered place outdoors in full sun or partial shade, in rich free-draining soil. Mulching with well-rotted horse manure or other organic matter will benefit the plant during the growing season.

SOWING AND PLANTING

Sow in mid spring, with one or two seeds per 9cm (3¾in) pot. Thin to just one seedling. Plant under glass from late spring; for outdoor crops wait until early summer, after the last frost. Cover newly planted seedlings with fleece if temperatures drop below 15°C (59°F).

HOW TO GROW THE CROP

Water regularly. If grown in large containers, feed weekly with high-potassium fertiliser. Melons can be trained vertically on supports or left trailing

Above: Mulch newly planted melon seedlings with organic matter to keep the soil around the plant moist.

Left: Watermelons make large fruits that need plenty of warmth and moisture, and a rich soil to form.

on the ground. They can be left to grow without intervention, or pruned and trained to speed fruiting and keep the plant neater. There are different ways to train melons. For example, cut off the tip of the main shoot so that five leaves remain – this will stimulate the growth of side shoots. When these develop, choose four and either position them in different directions on the ground, or train them vertically on supports. To produce good-quality fruit, allow a maximum of six fruit per plant and stop the fruiting shoots two or three leaves after the developing fruit.

To ensure fruit production, pollinate the flowers manually by transferring pollen with a paintbrush. If growing plants vertically, support the ripening melons with little hammocks as the fruit gets heavier.

Above: If the plants are trained vertically, support the heavy fruit with slings made from netting or hessian.

WHEN THE CROP IS READY

The sweet smell and cracking around the stem are signs that cantaloupe and honeydew melons are ready. Watermelon is a bit trickier to establish its ripeness. Perhaps the best way is to knock on the fruit – if it sounds hollow, the fruit is ready.

STORING AND COOKING TIPS

It is best to eat melons fresh on their own, or as part of a fruit or savoury salad. Melons will store for a few days in the fridge. The fruit can also be juiced, grilled, or used in drinks and sorbets.

AT A GLANCE:

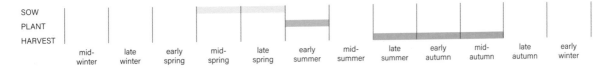

SOW											
PLANT											
HARVEST											
mid-winter	late winter	early spring	mid-spring	late spring	early summer	mid-summer	late summer	early autumn	mid-autumn	late autumn	early winter

Planting Overview: Best to grow under cover, water regularly; if in containers feed weekly with high potash fertiliser; melons can be trained to grow vertically on supports or left trailing on the ground; ensure adequate pollination.

Varieties to Try: Cantaloupe melons 'Emir' AGM, 'Alvaro' AGM and 'Ogen' AGM (suitable for outdoor growing), 'Lottie' (resistant to downy mildew), 'Sugar Baby' (slow-maturing watermelon), 'Early Moonbeam' (fast-maturing watermelon).

'Lottie'

'Sugar Baby'

Gourds and luffa

These frost-tender plants from the cucumber family are cultivated in a similar way to their relatives. They produce edible or non-edible fruit that varies greatly in colour and shape.

Edible gourds, such as bitter gourd, bottle gourd and fig-leaf gourd, are used in cuisines across the world, in savoury or sweet dishes. Gourds can also be used for non-culinary purposes, such as musical instruments, storage jars or water carriers (bottle gourds), and as cleaning sponges (luffas).

WHAT YOU NEED
In temperate climates, most gourds will do better if grown in a greenhouse or polytunnel. Fig-leaf and bottle gourds can be grown outdoors in a

warm, sheltered spot. Gourds do best in well-drained soil rich in organic matter.

SOWING AND PLANTING
Sow one or two seeds in pots indoors in mid spring, thin to one seedling and plant indoors in late spring, or outdoors when the danger of frost has passed. Water well and provide support if grown vertically.

HOW TO GROW THE CROP
Gourds are vigorous vines and need lots of space. If grown in a greenhouse, train the plants vertically to save space. Water regularly as they need moisture and humidity to grow well.

Help to pollinate plants manually to ensure fruit production, by transferring pollen between flowers with a paint brush. Gourds can be grown in large containers but will need lots of water and a weekly feed.

WHEN THE CROP IS READY
For edible uses, many gourds are harvested immature. The mature fruit is harvested when the fruit stalk turns brown and dries out; this is a sign that the fruit is not fed by the plant any more and is ready to harvest.

Left: Gourds are unusual plants, most typically grown as curiosities or for a bit of fun, yet some have practical uses and others are edible.

STORING AND COOKING TIPS

Immature fruit from edible gourds store well in the fridge for a few days and are used in a similar way to courgettes, in stews, curries, stir-fries or pickles. They can also be cooked for a couple of minutes, cooled and stored in the freezer. Mature fruit of the fig-leaf gourd is made into a traditional dessert in France called angel hair. This gourd can be stored for years in a dry, frost-free place.

Mature bottle gourds are dried, hardened and then made into birdhouses, water carriers or musical instruments. Mature luffas are dried, the rind is peeled, and the fibrous skeleton is used as a sponge. As the name suggests, fruit of bitter gourd is bitter. To remove some of the bitterness, add salt to the gourd pieces and leave for 10–20 minutes, wash the gourd, dry and then cook. Bitter gourd is said to have many health benefits.

Above: Bottle gourds including varieties 'Birdhouse' and 'Swan Neck'. The leaves, stems and seeds are all edible.

AT A GLANCE:

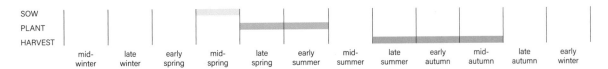

	SOW	PLANT	HARVEST

mid-winter · late winter · early spring · mid-spring · late spring · early summer · mid-summer · late summer · early autumn · mid-autumn · late autumn · early winter

Planting Overview: Grow the more tropical gourds in a greenhouse or polytunnel; train vertically to save space; mulch around plants and water regularly; ensure good pollination by pollinating manually.

Varieties to Try: Fig-leaf gourd (*Cucurbita ficifolia*) (vigorous, prolific, stem and seeds are also edible), bottle gourd (*Lagenaria siceraria*) 'Birdhouse', 'Swan Neck', 'Serpente di Sicilia' (Italian variety, long, snake-like fruit, good for cooking when immature), snake gourd (*Trichosanthes cucumerina*) (best grown indoors, young shoots and leaves are also edible), wax gourd (*Benincasa hispida*) (good for culinary purposes, best grown indoors, leaves, stems,

Cucurbita ficifolia

Luffa acutangula

flowers and seeds are also edible), luffa (*Luffa aegyptiaca* or *L. acutangula*) (immature fruit is good for cooking, dried mature fruit is made into cleaning sponges, best grown indoors, leaves, stems, flowers and seeds are also edible).

CHAPTER 6

BRASSICAS

Growing brassicas sustainably

The term brassicas refers to all crops in the cabbage family. This ranges from relatively quick growers such as pak choi to long-term crops including Brussels sprouts, and even a few perennials like perennial kale. The variety of choice means that everybody can find space for a brassica plant in their garden.

When growing brassicas sustainably, it is important to consider how to best grow the crops alongside the animals that like to feed on them, such as pigeons and cabbage caterpillars, or diseases including clubroot. There is no need to attempt to eliminate these from the garden by the use of chemicals; instead, some simple steps – including promoting soil health, netting and variety selection – can make all the difference. With careful planting, and an acceptance that we share our gardens with a biodiverse range of animals, it may even be possible to grow some brassicas without a net!

This group of plants is also good for providing a fresh and sustainable food source throughout the winter. Crops including kale and Savoy cabbage are winter staples, while sprouting broccoli can be grown to come to fruition in the 'hungry gap' of early spring.

You could also attempt to grow a range of perennial crops like perennial broccoli and sea kale. These crops are lower maintenance than annuals because they do not need sowing and planting every year, and have the added sustainability benefit of ensuring that your soil is always covered with a crop. Forced sea kale is a wonderful spring treat for you to enjoy.

Brassicas are seen in most vegetable gardens for a good reason: they are often quite tasty and will provide fresh harvests long after the heat of summer. They really are essential year-round vegetables.

Left: Fine netting or mesh is a prerequisite to growing brassicas successfully as it excludes most major predators, such as cabbage white butterlflies, without having to resort to chemicals.

Right: Cabbages are a good crop for the year-round vegetable grower as there are varieties for cropping during every season.

Cauliflower

The heads or 'curds' of cauliflowers are probably among the most unusual vegetable crops, particularly the lime green fractal patterns of the Romanesco varieties. They are free from fat and cholesterol, low in sodium and high in vitamins C, K and folates, which are essential during pregnancy. Above all, they are tasty and can be grown for harvest from summer to early spring.

WHAT YOU NEED

Grow in full sun or light shade in a sheltered location in fertile soil. A neutral to alkaline pH is preferable if possible.

SOWING AND PLANTING

Cauliflower can be sown directly from late spring in drills 2cm (3/4in) deep and 45–60cm (18–24in) apart. It is best started, however, indoors from late winter to early summer. Certain varieties are suitable for sowing at specific times and will produce different-sized heads. Sow about 1cm (1/2in) deep in module trays; it should germinate

in 10–14 days. Transplant into 9cm (3³/4in) pots once large enough to handle and grow on.

Once the plants have several true leaves they can be planted out at 45–60cm (18–24in) spacing, depending on the variety. Mini cauliflowers can be planted closer. Firm the plants in well because root rock can limit their growth. After planting, place a disc of cardboard around the base of the stem to stop the cabbage root fly laying its eggs.

HOW TO GROW THE CROP

Keep well watered throughout the growing period. Cauliflowers will need protection from cabbage caterpillars. The easiest method is to cover them with butterfly-proof netting from planting time until harvest, checking the plants before planting to ensure there are no eggs present already.

Brassicas such as cauliflower can also be susceptible to clubroot disease. If this does occur, avoid planting brassicas in the same location for a few years. Crop rotation is not always essential unless issues have occurred, especially if other crops are grown in between plantings of brassicas.

If the cauliflowers are not forming heads, it is usually because their growth has been checked at some point, often by excess cold at planting time, root disturbance or a lack of water. Winter-cropping varieties may need to have their heads protected with horticultural fleece if really hard frosts are forecast.

Left: Once pot-grown seedlings have several true leaves they are ready to plant out.

WHEN THE CROP IS READY

The plants get quite large before harvest, up to 60cm (24in) tall. The heads of mini varieties will only reach around the size of a tennis ball, while other varieties can reach 30cm (12in) across. Late winter sowings should be ready in summer, spring sowings in autumn, and midsummer sowings from winter to early spring. Harvest before any flower buds start to open. To harvest, use a sharp knife to cut below the head.

STORING AND COOKING TIPS

Cauliflowers are best eaten fresh, although they will store in the fridge for a few days. Try cooking up a grilled cauliflower steak or making some cauliflower cheese. They are great for low-calorie diets, but maybe not if covered with cheese.

Above: Winter-cropping cauliflowers may need their heads protecting with fleece if the curds are not to be damaged.

AT A GLANCE:

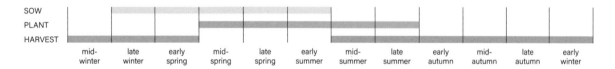

	SOW	PLANT	HARVEST
mid-winter	late winter	early spring	mid-spring	late spring	early summer	mid-summer	late summer	early autumn	mid-autumn	late autumn	early winter

Planting Overview: Best started inside; harvests through much of the year; firm in plants and water well; protect from pigeons and butterflies.

Varieties to Try: 'Triomphant' AGM (stands through winter, white heads), 'All the Year Round' (harvest spring to winter), 'Sunset' (autumn harvests, bright yellow heads), 'Veronica' AGM (Romanesco type, summer to autumn harvests), 'Graffiti' AGM (autumn harvests, purple heads).

'Graffiti' AGM

'Veronica' AGM

Calabrese broccoli

As distinct from their close cousins sprouting broccoli, Calabrese broccoli produce the classic large green heads one would usually associate with broccoli. They look impressive in the veg patch and have a mild flavour. Like all brassicas, they are a good source of vitamins and antioxidants.

WHAT YOU NEED
Grow in full sun or partial shade in a sheltered location. Fertile, well-drained soil with a neutral to alkaline pH is ideal if possible.

SOWING AND PLANTING
Sow direct from late spring to early summer, or sow indoors from late winter to early summer. Outside, sow seeds at a depth of around 1.5cm (5/8in), with a final spacing between plants of 40cm (16in). There are compact varieties that can be grown closer together. Cover direct sowings with horticultural fleece to aid germination.

Broccoli is easiest started indoors where the seeds should be sown into modules, with germination occurring within two weeks. Thin to one seedling per module and transplant to 9cm (3¾in) pots once the seedlings are large enough to handle. Once the plants have several true leaves they can be planted outside, ideally during a spell of cooler weather. Position the plants deeper than in the pots and firm in well to prevent root rock. A cardboard disc around the base of each plant helps to prevent problems with cabbage root fly.

HOW TO GROW THE CROP
As a brassica, broccoli is susceptible to cabbage caterpillars. The simplest way to protect the plants from these is to cover them with butterfly-proof netting from planting time up until harvest. Larger varieties reach about 60cm (24in) tall and may benefit from staking. Water well, especially when plants are establishing and the heads are starting to form. Without adequate water, plants can start to bolt in hot, dry conditions. If issues such as club root arise, then crop rotation can be useful in future years, but it is not essential if no problems have occurred.

Left: Plant out pot-grown seedlings, slightly deeper than they were in the pots, in late spring, ideally during a spell of cool weather.

WHEN THE CROP IS READY

The unopened flowerheads are harvested when 10–15cm (4–6in) in diameter. This is usually from late summer through to autumn, depending on sowing time and the variety being grown. In milder areas, later sowings may stand through the winter, but broccoli is less reliable in this respect when compared to other brassicas. To harvest, use a sharp knife to cut the whole head just above some leaves. If the plant is left in place, it can reshoot and produce some mini broccoli heads for harvest later.

STORING AND COOKING TIPS

This crop is best eaten fresh, but will store in the fridge for around a week. It is hard to beat the taste of lightly steamed broccoli, but it can also be eaten raw, pickled or stir-fried. Bear in mind that the stem and leaves, especially the young ones, are also edible, not just the head.

Above: Broccoli heads are ready when they look like this, just before the flowers open.

AT A GLANCE:

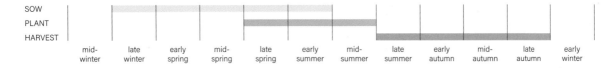

SOW											
PLANT											
HARVEST											
mid-winter	late winter	early spring	mid-spring	late spring	early summer	mid-summer	late summer	early autumn	mid-autumn	late autumn	early winter

Planting Overview: Easiest started inside; firm in plants well; protect from cabbage caterpillars.

Varieties to Try: 'Green Magic' AGM (reliable, fast maturing), 'Kabuki' AGM (compact variety, best for autumn harvests), 'Marathon' AGM (reliable for late summer harvests).

'Green Magic' AGM

'Marathon' AGM

Sprouting broccoli

The diminutive but extra tasty form of Calabrese broccoli, sprouting broccoli comes in purple or white. Apart from the lovely flavour, it is a valuable crop because the plants stand in the ground for several months, with most varieties coming ready in the 'hungry gap' in late winter and early spring.

WHAT YOU NEED
Grow in full sun or light shade in a sheltered location. Fertile, well-drained soil with near neutral pH is ideal.

SOWING AND PLANTING
Sow from late spring to midsummer, although fast-growing varieties can be sown in mid spring to enable a harvest the same year. Most varieties of sprouting broccoli will stand in the ground for many months so it is best started indoors, allowing another crop to make use of the outdoor space in the meantime. Alternatively, it can be sown outdoors, ideally covered with horticultural fleece to aid germination.

Inside, sow into modules and transplant individual seedlings into 9cm (3¾in) pots once large enough to handle. Germination should occur within two weeks. Plant out once they have several true leaves. Firm in well, positioning the plants slightly deeper than they were in the pots. Placing a disc of cardboard around the base will help to deter cabbage root fly. These plants can reach up to 1m (3ft) in height so space widely at 60–70cm (24–28in). Some varieties are more compact.

HOW TO GROW THE CROP
Sprouting broccoli is best covered with butterfly-proof netting from planting time until harvest to keep off pigeons and cabbage caterpillars. Water well when establishing and then during dry spells. If planted in exposed locations, the plants may benefit from staking. Besides that, the plants are fairly low maintenance, they just need the lower leaves removed as they turn yellow and die away. If issues, including clubroot, occur then crop rotation may be helpful in future years but it is not essential otherwise. Plants started indoors are more able to cope with clubroot anyway as they are larger when getting established.

Left: Cardboard root collars help protect young plants from root fly, as does fine mesh netting.

WHEN THE CROP IS READY

It is the unopened flower buds that are harvested; they look like miniature heads of broccoli. Fast-growing varieties may be ready by midsummer, but most varieties will be ready to harvest from late winter to mid spring and are harvested by using a sharp knife. Cut just above where the shoot branches and more flowering shoots of a smaller size will be produced. The stems and leaves of this plant are also edible, particularly the young leaves.

STORING AND COOKING TIPS

This crop can be frozen but as there is often little fresh produce available when this crop is being harvested it is usually eaten fresh. Try lightly steaming, grilling or adding to a stir-fry. White varieties have a slightly milder flavour than purple ones.

Right: Harvest the unopened flowerheads with a sharp knife, then enjoy them fresh, lightly steamed.

AT A GLANCE:

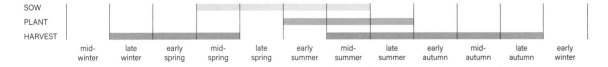

	mid-winter	late winter	early spring	mid-spring	late spring	early summer	mid-summer	late summer	early autumn	mid-autumn	late autumn	early winter
SOW												
PLANT												
HARVEST												

Planting Overview: Best started indoors; protect from cabbage caterpillars; provides a harvest in the 'hungry gap'; firm in well at planting.

Varieties to Try: 'Claret' AGM (purple, vigorous, heavy cropping, ideal for overwintering), 'Burbank' (white, great taste, fast growing), 'Cardinal' AGM (purple, good flavour, more compact than some other varieties).

'Burbank'

'Cardinal' AGM

Pak choi

This small leafy plant, also called bok choi, comes in green, white and red, and it is fairly easy to grow. Incredibly, it contains over 70 antioxidants, as well as minerals and vitamins. Pak choi is fast growing and forms upright rosettes if left to mature, but the leaves are edible at any stage.

WHAT YOU NEED

Grow this crop in full sun or light shade, especially in the summer, on moisture-retentive, slightly alkaline soil.

SOWING AND PLANTING

While pak choi can be sown all year, it grows best in the cooler conditions of spring and autumn. Sow in early to mid spring or late summer to early autumn. In between these times, sowings are best done for baby leaves not full heads.

Pak choi can be sown outside from mid spring once the soil has warmed up. Sow in drills 1.5cm (5/8in) deep and 25cm (10in) apart, thinning the seedlings to 20–25cm (8–10in) if growing for mature plants, or 10cm (4in) for baby leaves.

Inside, sow into modules, thinning to one seedling after germination. Plant out once the plants have a few true leaves. Early and late sowings benefit from protection with fleece.

HOW TO GROW THE CROP

Water well until established, then do not let the plants dry out as pak choi likes damp conditions. In warmer weather, pak choi can run to seed before maturing so focus on growing in cooler conditions and provide plenty of water. Pak choi will survive light frosts, but should be harvested before severe weather occurs. In containers, it grows well so long as it has sufficient water. Remove any yellowing leaves as they appear.

As a relatively fast-growing crop, pak choi is less susceptible to cabbage caterpillars than other brassicas, although cabbage root fly can cause issues. Covering young plants with horticultural fleece helps them get off to a good start, and surrounding the plants with other, taller crops helps disguise them from pigeons. Covering with fleece from spring through to early autumn keeps off flea beetles, although they will grow without this protection. Crop rotation is not essential if the plants are growing well, as pak choi is a fairly short-term planting and the bed is likely to get a variety of crops throughout the year.

Left: Pak choi is best sown and grown during the cooler months of spring and autumn, when it is less likely to bolt.

TATSOI

Tatsoi is an Asian green closely related to pak choi and can be grown and treated in essentially the same way. A light frost in autumn can slightly improve the flavour. Try 'Yukina Savoy', which has a slightly stronger mustard flavour than other varieties. Red tatsoi is also available.

WHEN THE CROP IS READY

Pak choi can be harvested as baby leaves in about six weeks, harvesting in the cut-and-come-again style for repeat harvests until flowering. The flowers are also edible. Once a plant has flowered it can be replaced. Full hearts are ready around two months after sowing, and can be cut at ground level to harvest.

STORING AND COOKING TIPS

This crop is best eaten fresh but will store in the fridge for a few days. Baby leaves can be eaten raw but it is best lightly cooked, such as in a stir-fry.

Above: Full pak choi hearts are quite distinctive and are cut at ground level.

AT A GLANCE:

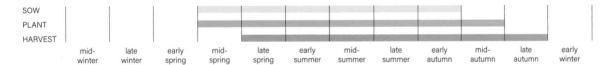

SOW												
PLANT												
HARVEST												
	mid-winter	late winter	early spring	mid-spring	late spring	early summer	mid-summer	late summer	early autumn	mid-autumn	late autumn	early winter

Planting Overview: Prefers the cooler, damp conditions of spring and autumn; harvest either as baby leaves or mature heads.

Varieties to Try: 'Yuushou' (green with white stems, less prone to flowering, good yield), 'Red Choi' AGM (red-leaved variety, good flavour), 'Choko' F1 AGM (slightly better in summer than some varieties), 'Ivory' AGM (dark green leaves, crispy white stems).

'Red Choi' AGM

'Yuushou'

Kale

Annual kales range from cavolo nero types to frilly purple and variegated varieties. The leaves are high in nutrients and they have great ornamental value. Asparagus kale has grey-green leaves; it can be harvested for these, but it also produces sprouts in the spring, which can be harvested like a green version of sprouting broccoli.

WHAT YOU NEED

Grow in full sun or light shade in a sheltered location. Ideally the soil will be rich, well drained and of a neutral pH.

SOWING AND PLANTING

Sow from mid spring to midsummer. Kale can be sown outdoors, ideally under horticultural fleece to aid germination, but it is best started indoors. This allows a catch crop to make use of the space before the kale, which will be in the ground for many months. Sow seeds individually into modules and transplant into 9cm (3¾in) pots. Once they have several true leaves, the plants can be planted outside at 45cm (18in) spacing, or 30cm (12in) for compact varieties. Bury the lower part of the stem, up to the first leaves, in the soil and firm in well. A cardboard disc around the base at planting time helps to control cabbage root fly.

HOW TO GROW THE CROP

Kale is best protected with butterfly netting from the moment of planting. Red and purple varieties seem to suffer slightly less from pigeons and cabbage caterpillars so can be tried without this. Taller varieties, which grow up to 90cm (3ft), benefit from staking, especially if being grown in more exposed locations.

As crops started indoors are larger at planting time, they are more resilient to clubroot than those that are direct sown, but crop rotation may still be useful if this issue occurs. It is not essential

Left: Sow seeds in modules so that the plants are ready to go in the ground as soon as the preceding catch crop has been harvested.

Below: Curly kale varieties benefit from extra protection from flying insects as their leaves are harder to clean.

otherwise, especially if other crops are grown between crops of brassicas. Most kale varieties are reliably hardy, but some cavolo nero types can be destroyed in really hard winters. Water regularly during establishment and then only during dry weather. Plants should not need feeding.

WHEN THE CROP IS READY

Kale sown early should be ready to crop as baby leaves by early summer, but it is more usually cropped from late summer through to early spring. Simply snap off the lower leaves carefully when they have reached the desired size. If this is done regularly enough it should prevent yellow leaves from appearing, but if they do these can be removed to the compost heap. Baby kale leaves can be harvested using the cut-and-come-again method once the plants have reached a height of around 10cm (4in).

STORING AND COOKING TIPS

Kale provides a rare fresh harvest through the winter so is best eaten fresh. It will store in the fridge for a couple of weeks and can be stir-fried, steamed, or made into kale crisps in the oven.

Above: 'Nero di Toscana', also known as black kale, is considered a gourmet crop.

AT A GLANCE:

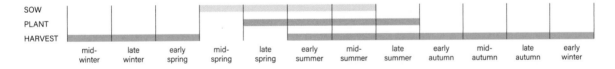

	SOW	PLANT	HARVEST

mid-winter | late winter | early spring | mid-spring | late spring | early summer | mid-summer | late summer | early autumn | mid-autumn | late autumn | early winter

Planting Overview: Best started indoors; plant deep and firm in well; protect most varieties from pigeons and cabbage caterpillars.

Varieties to Try: 'Emerald Ice' (variegated leaves), 'Scarlet' (vibrant purple, curly leaves), 'Nero di Toscana' (cavolo nero type, long, dark green leaves), 'Kapitan' AGM (green leaves, very hardy, also good as baby leaves), 'Starbor' AGM (green leaves, compact variety).

'Scarlet'

'Starbor' AGM

Brussels sprouts

Brussels sprouts, known by the scientific name *Brassica oleracea* var. *gemmifera*, are a winter staple, particularly at the Christmas table, offering fresh harvests in the coldest months. The flavour, especially with recent breeding, is tasty and mild. The health benefits of these 'mini cabbages' are numerous.

WHAT YOU NEED

Grow in a sheltered location with full sun or partial shade. Ideally the soil will be slightly alkaline, and reasonably water retentive.

SOWING AND PLANTING

For autumn harvests, sow seeds of an early variety in early to mid spring. For winter and early spring harvests, choose a later variety and sow in mid to late spring. Plants can be successively cropped so not many are needed.

Sow seeds outside, at 2cm (3/4in) deep, from mid spring. Either start them in a separate location at 10cm (4in) spacing and transplant, or sow into the final location at 60cm (24in) spacing, preferably with an intercrop.

Inside, sow two seeds per module, cover with compost, then thin to one on germination. Once true leaves have developed, transplant into 9cm (3¾in) pots and plant out 6–8 weeks after sowing. Plant at 60cm (24in) spacing, burying the bottoms of the stems and firming in well. Placing a cabbage collar around the base deters cabbage root flies.

HOW TO GROW THE CROP

Sprouts need plenty of water until established, and then only in really dry weather. As they grow, up to 1m (3ft) for non-compact varieties, staking helps keep them upright. The crop is fully hardy, and tastes slightly sweeter after a frost. Regularly remove lower leaves as they turn yellow.

Sprouts benefit from covering with butterfly netting to keep off cabbage caterpillars and pigeons. Crop rotation is not essential in healthy soil, especially if other crops are grown in between plantings of brassicas. If club root occurs, starting crops inside helps to mitigate any issues as the plants are often strong enough to grow through. There are also resistant varieties.

If sprouts either do not form or 'blow' (fail to stay tight and round), this can be due to a lack of water, poor soil lacking nutrition, choice of variety, or excess wind rock because the plant was not properly firmed in.

Left: Mid- to late-spring planting is best for a Christmas crop of Brussels sprouts.

WHEN THE CROP IS READY

Early plants can be ready from mid autumn, and others through winter into early spring. When a sprout is a tight, walnut-sized ball it can be snapped off. The lower sprouts mature first, allowing for successional harvests. Alternatively, remove the whole plant by cutting around the base to sever fibrous roots and then twisting. The stem will contain sprouts of varying sizes, although some varieties are more uniform. The young leaves at the top are also edible.

Above: Brussels sprouts form on a long stem and they can either be harvested individually or the whole stem cut down.

KALETTES

Kalettes, also known as flower sprouts, are a cross between kale and Brussels sprouts. They look like fluffy sprouts and can be grown in the same way. They are most commonly green with purple ribbing. Grow the straight species or try 'Autumn Star' for a slightly earlier harvest and 'Christmas Rose' for a fresh harvest through the festive period.

STORING AND COOKING TIPS

To avoid overcooking, try steaming, roasting or stir-frying. Sprouts are best eaten fresh and harvested as needed, although a full stem can be stored, hanging, in a frost-free shed for a few weeks. They can also be preserved in the freezer for several months.

AT A GLANCE:

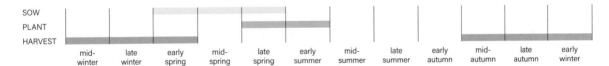

SOW											
PLANT											
HARVEST											
mid-winter	late winter	early spring	mid-spring	late spring	early summer	mid-summer	late summer	early autumn	mid-autumn	late autumn	early winter

Planting Overview: Grow for autumn or winter harvests; protect from cabbage caterpillars; firm in well to prevent wind rock.

Varieties to Try: 'Igor' AGM (classic green, stands really well over winter), 'Brodie' AGM (mild, almost sweet flavour, good yield), 'Red Rubine' (attractive purple variety), 'Crispus' AGM (club root-resistant, good for autumn harvests), 'Long Island Improved' (more compact variety).

'Crispus' AGM

'Brodie' AGM

Cabbages

Cabbages are a diverse crop, varying in seasonality and coming in a range of sizes and colours from red to white. They can provide a harvest through many months of the year, from early harvests in summer and autumn to overwintering and harvesting in winter and spring. Savoy cabbages are deeply veined with purple tinges. Check the seed packets for the specifics of each variety.

WHAT YOU NEED

This crop grows best in full sun, although partial shade also works. Ideally grow in rich, moisture-retentive soil that is of a neutral or alkaline pH.

SOWING AND PLANTING

Cabbage seeds can be sown outside but are easiest started inside. This gives the young seedlings protection as they start growing so should ensure they are stronger at planting time and more able to cope with any issues. This also allows for a catch crop in the bed before planting.

If starting outside, sow early cabbages in spring, and overwintering cabbages in summer. They can be started in a seedbed, an area away from their final location, and then transplanted once an earlier crop has finished. Alternatively,

sow direct into their end location. With the latter option, a quick intercrop such as radish can help make more efficient use of the bed space. Sow 2cm (¾in) deep and gradually thin to the desired spacing. This will vary depending on the variety, but generally ranges from 30–45cm (12–18in), with winter cabbages usually being the furthest apart. Covering with horticultural fleece will protect the young seedlings and aid germination.

If starting the seed inside, sow from late winter to mid spring for early cabbages and in

Below left: Cabbages are best started indoors in modules for later planting.

Below: Young cabbage plants will need plenty of water to help them establish.

Above: You will get the best results if you grow your cabbages under protective mesh netting, as it excludes most predators.

Right: Cardboard root collars are a simple way to prevent the cabbage root fly from laying its eggs.

the summer for overwintering types. Sow into modules and germination should occur within a fortnight. Thin to one seedling per module and then transplant into 9cm (3¾in) pots. Plant out once they have several true leaves. Position the plant slightly deeper than the original depth and firm in well to prevent root rock. A cardboard disc around the base of the stem at planting time should ensure there are no issues with cabbage root fly.

Above: Cabbages form different heads, some less tight than others, like this spring cabbage.

HOW TO GROW THE CROP

Cabbages grow best if protected from cabbage caterpillars. These are the young of large and small white butterflies and the cabbage moth. Cover the plants with butterfly-proof netting from planting time until harvest, keeping the netting on over winter as pigeon protection.

Like all brassicas, cabbages are also vulnerable to the fungal disease club root. This causes a distortion of the roots and means the plants struggle to grow because they cannot access the water and nutrients they need. This is less likely to occur in soils with a neutral or alkaline pH. Club root-resistant varieties are available. If it does occur then crop rotation – avoiding growing

brassicas in that area for a few years – can be considered. If no issues have arisen then crop rotation is not essential, especially if another crop or two has been grown in the soil between crops of brassicas.

Provide plenty of water to the plants as they are establishing, and then during hot and dry spells. If the cabbage heads split before harvest, this can be a sign that they were lacking water while growing. The plants should not need feeding if the beds have been prepared with mulch during the previous winter.

WHEN THE CROP IS READY

All cabbages are ready to harvest once a tight head has formed in the centre of the plant. Depending on the variety, this can take 4–6 months. Check regularly as the heads will start to deteriorate if left too long. If a cabbage fails to form a proper head, this can be due to damage to the growing point while the plants were young, or because the plant is growing in unsuitable conditions, such as those lacking moisture or experiencing severe temperature fluctuations.

Depending on sowing time, early cabbages can be harvested from late summer through to late autumn. Overwintering types can be harvested as needed through the winter and spring.

To harvest, use a sharp knife to cut off the cabbage at ground level. The rest of the plant can then be twisted out of the soil, leaving most of the fibrous roots behind to rot down in situ. Alternatively, cabbages harvested in the spring or summer can be encouraged to produce a second, smaller crop. To do this, score a cross 1cm (½in) deep into the stump.

STORING AND COOKING TIPS

Summer and autumn cabbages can be frozen for use later in the year, but overwintering types are best left in the ground until they are needed. Cabbage can also be preserved through pickling or fermenting to make sauerkraut. Red cabbages are great braised with a little apple, sugar and vinegar, while all cabbages can be added to dishes such as stir-fries. When preparing cabbages in the kitchen, be aware that a friendly slug may have made the journey as well, so check the centre of the plants carefully. They are still perfectly edible, just carefully cut out any damaged parts and send the slug to the compost heap.

Right: Harvest cabbages with a sharp knife once they have formed a tight head.

AT A GLANCE:

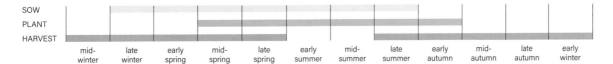

| | mid-winter | late winter | early spring | mid-spring | late spring | early summer | mid-summer | late summer | early autumn | mid-autumn | late autumn | early winter |

Planting Overview: Sowing times depend on type of cabbage; protect from cabbage caterpillars; water well during establishment.

Varieties to Try: 'Rookie' AGM (red, early, great colour), 'Greyhound' (white, early, very fast growing), 'January King' (Savoy, overwintering, large heads), 'Spring Hero' (white, overwintering, crisp, sweet flavour), 'Lodero' (red cabbage, club root- resistant).

'Spring Hero'

'Rookie' AGM

'Greyhound'

'January King'

Perennial kale

Most of the kales we grow as annuals are, in fact, biennial. Both types are descendants of the perennial wild cabbage, as are many other well-known brassicas such as broccoli, cauliflower and Brussels sprouts.

Perennial kales are hardy to –10°C (14°F) and have a lifespan of between 5 and 15 years. They are easily propagated by softwood cuttings (see opposite) from late spring to mid autumn. The great advantage of growing a perennial kale is the continuous harvest of nutritious leaves with minimal effort.

WHAT YOU NEED

Grows best in a rich soil in full sun, but will tolerate most soil types and grows happily in heavy shade. On acidic soil, there is more chance of club root infection so neutral or alkaline soil is most suitable.

SOWING AND PLANTING

Since most types of perennial kale do not set viable seed, taking cuttings is the most reliable way to propagate new plants. The cuttings are best taken in spring or autumn and should be 15–20cm (6–8in) long. Rooted cuttings can be purchased online and at specialist nurseries.

Below: Perennial kale provides a supply of nutritious leaves throughout the year. It is a short-lived perennial that will keep cropping for 5–10 years.

Ideally space 1–1.5m (3–5ft) apart, as plants have a tendency to spread laterally.

HOW TO GROW THE CROP

Water well on planting and in dry periods, until established. It can be grown alongside other brassicas, and as the plants suffer the same problems as biennial kales, a fine mesh or netting will protect from cabbage butterflies and pigeons. Being perennial, however, the plants usually recover quickly from any damage if left uncovered. Remove any yellow lower leaves regularly.

WHEN THE CROP IS READY

Perennial kale can be harvested all year round, but the cooler months give leaves the best flavour. They are especially tender and sweet in spring and if harvested at this time they can be eaten raw if sliced thinly and added to a mixed salad.

STORING AND COOKING TIPS

After harvest, wash and rehydrate the leaves by submerging in fresh cold water for an hour. Drain well, slice into thin ribbons and store in the fridge in a polythene bag. This way, the leaves will last for two weeks. Alternatively, blanch for two minutes, then dry and freeze. Cook in much the same way as other types of kale: steam, boil, sauté, or make kale crisps.

TAKING CUTTINGS

Softwood cuttings from perennial kale are straightforward. The plants are very responsive and cuttings seem to produce roots readily. To insure against losses, make a good number of cuttings from sideshoots with ridged stems, and trim these to 15–20cm (6–8in) long, removing the larger leaves and leaving the growing tips untouched. Place in a pot of moist compost with the lower two-thirds of the cutting buried, and leave the pots in a shady place. Within 14 days, roots should start to form. Alternatively, cuttings can be placed straight into the ground.

AT A GLANCE:

	mid-winter	late winter	early spring	mid-spring	late spring	early summer	mid-summer	late summer	early autumn	mid-autumn	late autumn	early winter
PLANT												
HARVEST												

Planting Overview: Hardy perennial; water well until established; covering plants to protect from bird and insect damage can be advantageous, but is not usually necessary.

Varieties to Try: 'Daubenton's' (the main green type; plain large leaves with a paler midrib), 'D'Aubenton Panaché' (attractive variegated type with white leaf margins), 'Taunton Deane' (prolific and tasty with purple mid ribs).

'Daubenton's'

'D'Aubenton Panaché'

Perennial broccoli

This sprouting broccoli is called 'nine star' because of its many heads or 'stars'. Similar in appearance to cauliflower, the plants can live for three to five years.

WHAT YOU NEED

Best grown in full sun and will do well in free-draining soil rich in organic matter, that is ideally of a neutral or alkaline pH.

SOWING AND PLANTING

Sow seed from early to late spring in modules. Transplant seedlings when two sets of true leaves have developed, spacing plants 1m (3ft) apart.

HOW TO GROW THE CROP

Cover the plants when young to protect from pigeons and caterpillars. Slugs can be an issue for seedlings. Water well until established and stake if plants become top heavy.

Above: As the appearance suggests, perennial broccoli tastes like a cross between cauliflower and broccoli.

CIMA DI RAPA/BROCCOLI RAAB

Another type of sprouting brassica is cima di rapa, a fast-maturing vegetable with sprouting flower buds that can be eaten raw or cooked. Best sown directly in early spring, plants can begin cropping in late spring if kept well watered. Snap off the central flower stalk when around 10–15cm (4–6in) long.

WHEN THE CROP IS READY

In late winter the following year, a central flower bud will emerge. Cut the flower bud when the stalk is 15–20cm (6–8in) long to stimulate the production of side shoots for further harvest.

STORING AND COOKING TIPS

Store in a bag in the refrigerator for a week or more. Can be eaten raw in a salad, but the flavour is better when lightly steamed or boiled and dressed with olive oil and lemon juice.

AT A GLANCE:

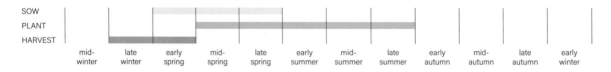

	SOW	PLANT	HARVEST
mid-winter			
late winter			
early spring			
mid-spring			
late spring			
early summer			
mid-summer			
late summer			
early autumn			
mid-autumn			
late autumn			
early winter			

Planting Overview: Hardy short-lived perennial (3–5 years); water well until established; cover plants when young to protect from pigeons; slugs can be an issue for young plants.

Sea kale

Native to coastal Britain, sea kale is a hardy perennial plant that was popular in Victorian kitchens. As an edible crop, it is mainly cultivated for the tasty and healthy blanched tender young shoots, although all parts of the plant are edible.

WHAT YOU NEED
Sea kale grows best in well-drained, neutral or slightly alkaline soil, in sun or partial shade.

SOWING AND PLANTING
Propagate by seeds or root cuttings. Sow seeds in early spring in modules. To aid the erratic germination, remove the seeds from the watertight casings that protect them. Take root cuttings in early spring, place vertically in a pot or directly in the ground, leaving the top of the cutting just above soil level. Final spacing is 60cm (24in) apart.

HOW TO GROW THE CROP
Sea kale is a drought-tolerant plant, but young plants benefit from extra water after planting and in dry spells. Avoid planting in ground where brassica club root is a problem. The tender blanched shoots are produced by covering the crowns in early spring. Refrain from blanching plants in their first year to allow them to establish.

WHEN THE CROP IS READY
In early to mid spring, harvest young blanched or unblanched shoots. The mature leaves can

Above: Sea kale is hard to come by in the shops, which is all the more reason to grow your own.

be harvested throughout the season, while the flowers and young seedpods can be harvested in the summer.

STORING AND COOKING TIPS
Use the shoots fresh as they do not store well. Blanched young shoots are used like asparagus. Cook older, more bitter leaves in the same way as kale. The flowers and young seedpods are also a great addition to salads.

AT A GLANCE:

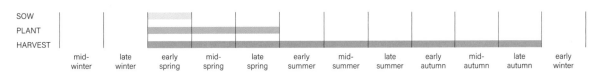

SOW												
PLANT												
HARVEST												
	mid-winter	late winter	early spring	mid-spring	late spring	early summer	mid-summer	late summer	early autumn	mid-autumn	late autumn	early winter

Planting Overview: Established plants are drought-tolerant; water young plants in dry spells; can suffer the same problems as other brassicas; do not blanch plants in their first year.

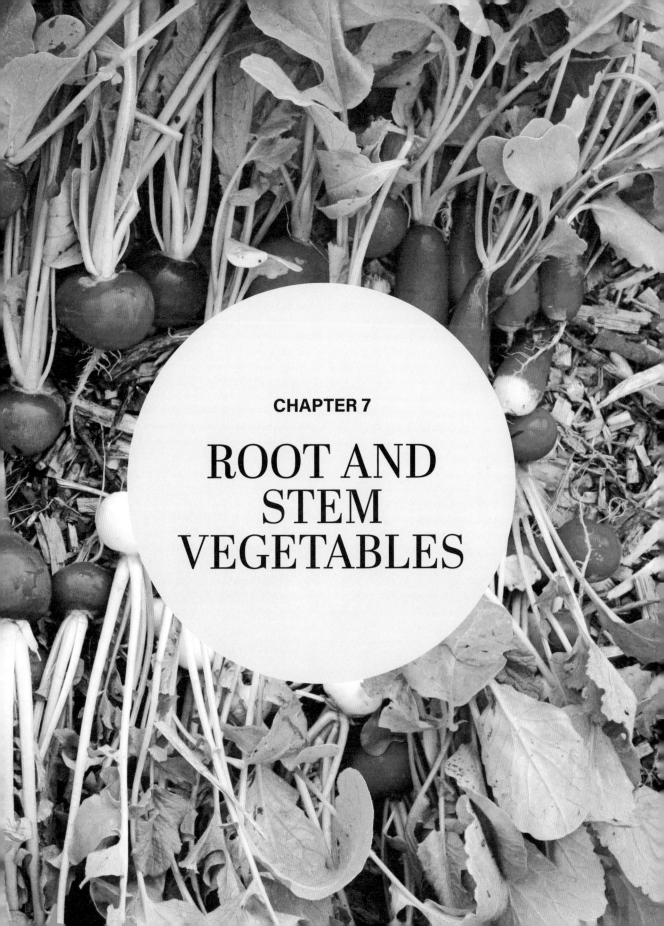

CHAPTER 7

ROOT AND STEM VEGETABLES

Growing root and stem vegetables sustainably

This broad category of edible crops incorporates everything from crisp-textured fresh radishes, the elongated tap roots of carrots and the swollen stem bases of beetroot, to the emerging stems of springtime asparagus. There are many unusual crops in the group, including oca and agretti. This chapter also covers some salad vegetables, such as celery, to heartier winter crops like swede and celeriac, meaning there is something here for every day of the year.

With the right growing conditions, many of these crops are largely trouble-free and can provide relatively easy access to a sustainable, year-round supply of homegrown produce. Parsnips are a winter staple, while asparagus is perfect for the hungry gap, and crops such as potatoes can store for many months. It is always worth remembering how important a range of crops like these is in your diet, and that the fresher the produce, the more nutritious it will be.

In recent years, people have been experimenting more and more with new crops to add even greater variety to their diet, helping them to 'eat the rainbow'. Sweet potatoes come in a range of colours beyond the supermarket orange, while kohlrabi can add flashes of purple. Yacon is a wonderful crop from South America, and skirret is long overdue a comeback into our diets. But remember to source plants with caution if you are intending to grow anything that could be new or exotic to your country (including from seed), as they can carry new pests or diseases, sometimes without showing symptoms, or may prove to be invasive. Oca, for example, can be very hard to get rid of once established and may be best in a container.

If you are seeking a diverse range of crops with sustainable, year-round potential, then you really must add some of these wonderful roots and stems to your plot in the coming year.

Left: Potatoes are perhaps the most versatile root crop there is, but their ubiquity may give you a reason to experiment with more unusual varieties that are not commonly found in the shops.

Right: Colourful carrots and beetroots give meaning to 'eat the rainbow'.

Beetroot

This easy-to-grow crop makes a colourful and useful addition to your vegetable garden. Whether harvested as baby beets, or allowed to grow large, beetroot is a tasty plant that comes in a range of bright colours and stores well after harvest.

WHAT YOU NEED

Beetroot grows best in full sun or partial shade. It likes a fertile and reasonably well-drained soil that has been enriched with plenty of organic matter so that it does not dry out too quickly.

SOWING AND PLANTING

The cooler spring and autumn months are most suitable for beetroot, but it can also be grown in summer. Sow directly outside or start inside, with germination taking up to 14 days. Inside, they can be sown from late winter to early spring in modules. This works well for multi-sowing – aim for four or five plants per module, bearing in mind that some seeds are multi-germ, meaning there may be more than one seedling per seed. Plant out once the first true leaves are showing.

Outdoor sowing can be done from mid spring in drills around 2.5cm (1in) deep. Either sow in multi-sown clusters or individually, and plan to thin the resulting seedlings to 10–20cm (4–8in) apart in all directions. Use the wider spacing for multi-sown clumps. Two or three sowings can provide beetroot for much of the year.

HOW TO GROW THE CROP

Beetroot is generally trouble-free. Water regularly until the seeds have germinated or seedlings established. After that, ensure they do not dry out and become woody, although excess water favours leaf growth over beets. Pots will need more regular watering. Plants in reasonable soil will not need feeding, but those in pots may benefit from a balanced feed fortnightly. If the plants are only

Left: Begin by sowing beetroot seed either directly or in modules for later transplanting.

producing small beets, this is generally due to a lack of water or poor soil, so try mulching with organic matter before planting again. Beetroot can bolt, especially if sown in cold weather or hot dry spells. Regular watering and bolt-resistant varieties will help prevent this.

WHEN THE CROP IS READY

Harvest the young roots as highly tender baby beets, although larger ones will not turn woody if the soil is good. With multi-sown beetroot, twist out the largest individual, leaving the rest to keep growing. This allows for a successional harvest from one sowing. Otherwise, simply twist the plant out when ready.

STORING AND COOKING TIPS

To store beetroot, twist off the leaves and store the roots in a cool, dark, dry place. They can keep for several months. Remember the leaves are also edible and can be used in salads. If there is no risk of hard frosts, the roots can be stored in the ground. Try using baby beets in salads and roasting or steaming the larger ones.

Top: Gradually thin the rows so that the remaining plants are well spaced.

Above: In good soil, beetroot can be harvested from small up to a weight of 2kg (4lb 8oz) and not go woody.

AT A GLANCE:

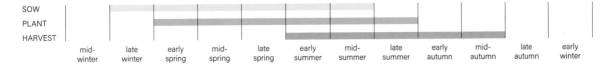

	mid-winter	late winter	early spring	mid-spring	late spring	early summer	mid-summer	late summer	early autumn	mid-autumn	late autumn	early winter
SOW												
PLANT												
HARVEST												

Planting Overview: Needs rich soil; start inside or out; good for multi-sowing; water well until established; harvest as baby or larger beets.

Varieties to Try: 'Burpees Golden' (slightly sweeter, yellow), 'Boltardy' AGM (classic red, bolt-resistant), 'Chioggia' (mild taste, attractive pink and white circles in the flesh), 'Red Ace' AGM (great taste, deep red).

'Chioggia'

'Burpees Golden'

Carrots

Carrots are a classic crop to grow in the vegetable garden, and they come in a wider range of shapes and colours than might be expected. Homegrown carrots are sweeter than those from the supermarket, a real delicacy when harvested young. The foliage can be made into pesto.

WHAT YOU NEED

Carrots grow best in relatively light soil that is fairly free of stones, which can cause the roots to fork. Grow in full sun, although light shade also works, and in fertile, fairly well-drained soil.

SOWING AND PLANTING

This crop is best sown directly outside as the root disturbance of transplanting can encourage forking. Shorter-rooted varieties and baby carrots can be grown in pots. In milder areas, sow from late winter under fleece, otherwise wait until the soil has warmed up in early spring. They can be sown until midsummer; regular sowing provides a successional harvest. Create drills about 1cm (1/2in) deep and 20cm (8in) apart, thinly sprinkle in the seeds, then water well until germination, which can take a couple of weeks.

Unless the variety is resistant to carrot root fly, they are best covered with fleece or insect-proof mesh from the moment of sowing until harvest. If the seedlings do not appear, slugs, snails or root fly are probably the reason.

HOW TO GROW THE CROP

Seedlings need to be thinned to 5–10cm (2–4in) apart, depending on the variety and desired size. They should not need feeding and, while they should not dry out completely, they are fairly drought-tolerant. Excess water can cause leaf growth at the expense of the root. Carrots in pots will need more water and fortnightly feeding.

Left: Carrots are best sown directly in drills, then thinned as they start to grow.

WHEN THE CROP IS READY

If growing full-sized carrots, earlier sowings will need about four months until harvest, but later sowings may be ready after three months. Sometimes, the shoulders of the carrots poking above the ground is a good indication they are ready. It is a good idea to start harvesting some of them early as baby carrots to avoid a glut later on. To harvest, grasp the base of the leaves and gently pull. If they are resistant, which often occurs in drier soils, then a hand fork can help to ease them out gently.

STORING AND COOKING TIPS

Carrots will store in the fridge – or in a cool, dark, frost-free place – for a few months. However, they are best stored in the ground until needed, but should be lifted before heavy frosts. Gluts can be made into soups and frozen, and the leaves used for pesto. Baby carrots are a delicacy best enjoyed in salads, while mature ones can be steamed, roasted or added to soups or stews.

Above: In containers, short or round varieties that will not be confined by the depth of the pot are a good choice.

AT A GLANCE:

SOW											
HARVEST											
mid-winter	late winter	early spring	mid-spring	late spring	early summer	mid-summer	late summer	early autumn	mid-autumn	late autumn	early winter

Planting Overview: Sow in a light soil; direct sow outside; protect from root fly unless they are resistant; harvest as baby carrots or mature roots.

Varieties to Try: 'Tozresis' AGM and 'Flyaway' AGM (root fly-resistant, good flavour), 'Rondo' (round variety good for pots), 'Autumn King' (classic, good for growing a little later in the season), 'Rainbow' (for colours from yellow to deep purple).

'Autumn King'

'Rondo'

Celery

Traditionally, celery was quite a labour-intensive crop to grow as it required earthing up the stems to keep them white and tender. Modern self-blanching varieties take the pain away.

WHAT YOU NEED
Grow in full sun and rich, moisture-retentive soil.

SOWING AND PLANTING
Start seeds indoors in mid spring, sowing into modules and covering lightly with soil. Keep at around 15°C (59°F) until germination, about three weeks. Thin to one seedling per module. Plant out from early summer 20–25cm (8–10in) apart.

Below: The flavour of homegrown celery is something to savour, and it's probably the best-known stem veg.

HOW TO GROW THE CROP
Water regularly in hot, dry weather; feeding should not be necessary. Growing celery in pots is best avoided as they dry out too quickly. Sometimes the plants will produce side shoots; removing these is not necessary. If you are allergic to celery, take care when handling the plants. Blanching is often recommended when growing celery, but this should not be necessary with most modern varieties.

WHEN THE CROP IS READY
Spring-sown crops should be ready by autumn. The individual stalks are unlikely to get as large as those in the shops, but they will be much tastier. Either harvest successionally by snapping off the outside stalks, or use a sharp knife to cut below ground level and harvest the whole plant.

STORING AND COOKING TIPS
Celery is best eaten fresh but can keep in the fridge for a couple of weeks; try placing limp stems in a glass of water to revive them. Eat raw in salads, stir-fry, use in stocks or to enrich stews and soups.

AT A GLANCE:

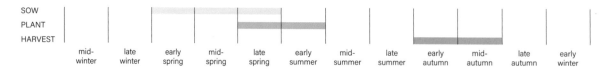

	mid-winter	late winter	early spring	mid-spring	late spring	early summer	mid-summer	late summer	early autumn	mid-autumn	late autumn	early winter
SOW												
PLANT												
HARVEST												

Planting Overview: Start seed indoors; water well; choose modern, self-blanching varieties; plants can bolt if it is too cold.

Varieties to Try: 'Hadrian' AGM (reliable, succulent stems), 'Octavius' (slow to bolt, good flavour), 'Giant Pink' AGM (attractive colour).

Celeriac

Celeriac is great for winter harvests. It is a root vegetable with a similar taste to celery but is much easier to grow. Although it has quite an odd appearance, don't let that put you off growing it as it is quite versatile in the kitchen.

WHAT YOU NEED
Grow in moisture-retentive soil, in full sun or partial shade.

SOWING AND PLANTING
Sow seeds indoors in mid spring and cover lightly with soil. Keep at around 15°C (59°F) until germination, about three weeks. Thin the seedlings to one per module. Cold weather can trigger bolting so plant outside 30cm (12in) apart from early summer, once the plants have true leaves.

HOW TO GROW THE CROP
Celeriac needs plenty of water so it is best grown in the ground, not in pots. While the soil should remain moist, they should not need feeding. Remove leaves if they are damaged or yellowing.

WHEN THE CROP IS READY
Harvest from mid autumn. Look at the swollen stem to judge the desired size, then carefully loosen the soil and twist the plants out. The longer celeriac is left before harvest, the stronger the flavour will be.

STORING AND COOKING TIPS
Celeriac can be stored in the ground over winter and harvested as needed. However, plants can rot in the winter wet, particularly in heavy soils. Instead, they can be lifted and stored in early winter. Twist off the leaves and brush off excess soil before storing in a cool, dark, frost-free place. They can keep for several months. Remove the knobbly outer skin before use. Try adding celeriac to mash, roasting it, or grating into salads.

AT A GLANCE:

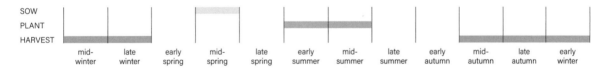

	SOW	PLANT	HARVEST

mid-winter · late winter · early spring · mid-spring · late spring · early summer · mid-summer · late summer · early autumn · mid-autumn · late autumn · early winter

Planting Overview: Start seeds indoors; provide plenty of water; good for storing over winter.

Varieties to Try: 'Monarch' AGM (smoother skin, good flavour), 'Prinz' AGM (large roots, resistant to leaf diseases), 'Ibis' AGM (fast growing).

'Monarch' AGM

'Prinz' AGM

Florence fennel

Florence fennel is an attractive plant for the vegetable garden with feathery foliage. The swollen base of the stems is the main part that is eaten, providing an aniseed-like flavour, but the whole plant is edible. It is very closely related to herb fennel (see p248), except herb fennel does not form a swollen base.

WHAT YOU NEED

Grow this crop in full sun in a sheltered location. Moisture-retentive rich soil is ideal; avoid heavy or waterlogged ground.

SOWING AND PLANTING

Florence fennel seed can be sown from early to midsummer, either indoors or outside, when temperatures are warm enough to help avoid the plants prematurely bolting or running to seed. Sowings from late spring are possible if done indoors and with bolt-resistant varieties. Inside, sow in module trays to help avoid root disturbance. Thin to one seedling per module and plant out once they are large enough to handle. Transplanting outdoors should be done in cool and damp weather to help the plants establish and reduce the risk of bolting.

To sow outside, create drills about 1.5cm (5/8in) deep and 35cm (14in) apart. Sow the seed thinly along the base and cover lightly with soil. Keep the seeds well watered; germination should occur in a couple of weeks. Thin the resulting seedlings to about 20–25cm (8–10in) apart. You can use closer spacings if you are planning to harvest the crop as baby heads.

HOW TO GROW THE CROP

This crop is best grown in the ground because it needs plenty of water to grow well. The plants will need regular watering in hot and dry weather. If the plants do start to flower, the base will turn woody, but they are still useful as a way of attracting beneficial insects and pollinators into the garden, and the leaves, stems and flowers can still be harvested. There should be no need to feed crops grown in the ground.

Left: Plant Florence fennel outside in the summer, as plants may bolt in cold weather.

WHEN THE CROP IS READY

Florence fennel is ready to harvest when the swollen base has reached an appropriate size. This can be at any time from baby bulbs up to a full-sized crop. Larger crops are usually ready after three to four months. To harvest, either twist out, or use a sharp knife to cut just below ground level and remove the plant. The root may reshoot, and the leaves can be put into salads.

STORING AND COOKING TIPS

This crop is best eaten soon after harvesting but will store in the fridge, or in a cool and dry location, for a few weeks. The swollen bases can be roasted or grilled and go well with fish. Every part of the plant can also be chopped raw into salads.

Above: The base of Florence fennel will swell as it grows and can be harvested at any time.

AT A GLANCE:

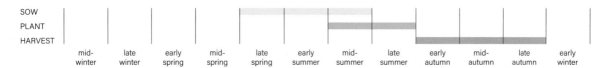

	mid-winter	late winter	early spring	mid-spring	late spring	early summer	mid-summer	late summer	early autumn	mid-autumn	late autumn	early winter
SOW												
PLANT												
HARVEST												

Planting Overview: Sow seed in early to midsummer, or late spring under cover; keep well watered; grow bolt-resistant varieties.

Varieties to Try: 'Dragon' AGM (excellent bolt resistance), 'Rondo' AGM (quicker-growing variety), 'Chiarino' (intense aniseed flavour), 'Romanesco' (large base, highly bolt-resistant).

'Romanesco'

'Rondo' AGM

Parsnips

Once germinated, parsnips are one of the simplest crops to grow and reward you with a tasty harvest through the cold winter months. The slightly sweet, earthy taste of a freshly harvested parsnip with your Christmas dinner is hard to beat.

WHAT YOU NEED

Parsnips are best in full sun. They prefer light, well-drained, fertile soils. Removing any large stones helps to prevent the roots from forking.

SOWING AND PLANTING

The trickiest part of growing parsnips is getting them to germinate. Where possible, use fresh seed, although seeds bought a year or two ago can still germinate well if they have been kept in a fridge. Parsnip seeds can be sown from mid to late spring; mid spring is ideal as it gives you time to resow if the seeds do not germinate.

To avoid root disturbance, sow the seeds directly outside in drills about 1cm (½in) deep and 30cm (12in) apart. Sow the seed along the base of the drill, cover with soil and water well. The seeds should germinate in about three weeks, but can take a little longer. Sowing a row-marker crop such as radish, which germinates quickly and will be harvested before the parsnips get too large, makes good use of the bed space and can help in identifying the parsnip seedlings from any other seedlings that appear. Thin the parsnip seedlings to 10–15cm (4–6in) spacing.

HOW TO GROW THE CROP

Parsnips will occupy the ground for many months, but they are low maintenance. Beyond removing the yellow leaves and watering, they need little care as they grow. Young plants need most water, but all should be watered in hot and dry weather otherwise the roots can become more susceptible to parsnip canker. Canker-resistant varieties are

Below left: Thin the parsnip seedlings, as they appear, to 10–15cm (4–6in) spacings.

Below: As they occupy the ground for a long time, grow an intercrop alongside to maximise the space.

available. Adequate water also helps to prevent the roots from splitting. There will be few, if any, leaves left over the winter months.

WHEN THE CROP IS READY

Parsnips are usually ready to harvest in the autumn but they are best left until after a hard frost as this will lead to them developing a slightly sweeter flavour. It is best to make sure they are all harvested before early spring as they turn woody if they put on too much new growth.

STORING AND COOKING TIPS

It is easiest to leave parsnips in the ground and harvest them as needed. Very hard frosts make harvesting almost impossible; if such conditions are expected, the roots can be lifted and stored in a cool and dry location for a few months. Parsnips can be steamed or roasted; honey-glazed parsnips are particularly good.

Right: Dig parsnips as they are needed, ideally before they get too woody but after a hard frost.

AT A GLANCE:

SOW											
HARVEST											
mid-winter	late winter	early spring	mid-spring	late spring	early summer	mid-summer	late summer	early autumn	mid-autumn	late autumn	early winter

Planting Overview: Sow direct outside; germination may take a while; water well in dry spells; harvest as needed through the winter.

Varieties to Try: 'Albion' AGM (canker-resistant, sweet flavour), 'Countess' (reliable, good crops), 'Gladiator' AGM (large, well-flavoured roots).

'Albion' AGM

'Gladiator' AGM

Sweet potatoes

This tender perennial crop is grown in temperate zones as an annual. These are trailing plants that belong to the morning-glory family and are decorative as well as productive. They are cultivated for their edible storage roots, although the young shoots and leaves are also edible. This is a staple food in many countries and comes in varied flesh and skin colours, from yellow to orange and purple.

WHAT YOU NEED

Sweet potatoes grow best in rich, free-draining soil in full sun. In temperate climates, bigger yields are achieved under cover. They are sensitive to cold soil. When planting, the soil should be 15°C (59°F) or above. To help warm the soil, cover with reusable black fabric two weeks before planting.

SOWING AND PLANTING

Sweet potato plants are grown from 'slips'; these are long shoots that have been removed from sprouted sweet potato tubers. Slips can be bought, but also propagated at home by placing a tuber horizontally in a container and half-covering it with moist, free-draining soil. Keep the container in a warm spot indoors or in a propagator at 18°C (64°F). This should be done 6–8 weeks before you wish to plant them.

When the shoots/slips are about 10cm (4in) long, break them off and pot up to allow root development. Rooted slips should then be planted 30–40cm (12–16in) apart in rows 90cm (3ft) apart, after the danger of frost has passed and the soil has warmed up. They can be planted through black fabric, to keep the plant roots warm.

HOW TO GROW THE CROP

Sweet potatoes need a temperature of 20–25°C (68–77°F) to produce good crops. To crop reliably in unpredictable summers, they are best grown in polytunnels or cold frames. Watering is especially important in hot spells, when plant growth can be rapid. If planted outdoors, grow in a sheltered warm position.

As a space-saving option, sweet potatoes can be grown in large containers, or the trailing vines can be trained to grow up a trellis or arch. In containers, the plants will need regular feeding throughout the growing season.

WHEN THE CROP IS READY

In temperate climates, sweet potatoes reach maturity in 90–120 days. The storage roots, or tubers as they are more commonly called, are ready to harvest in autumn, after the first frost catches the foliage. Severe cold will spoil the roots if they are left in the ground any longer.

Left: To grow sweet potatoes in containers, choose large ones and plant just one plant per pot.

Right: Harvest sweet potatoes in autumn. Use a border fork to lift the crown in the same way as you would do with normal potatoes.

Take care when harvesting, as the tubers will not store well if damaged. After harvesting, the tubers need a period of curing in a hot sunny spot indoors. This encourages them to stay dormant, hardens the skin for better storage and improves flavour.

STORING AND COOKING TIPS

After 1–2 weeks of curing, store the tubers in a dark, cool and frost-free place; they should last until spring. They are delicious roasted, made into chips or boiled and mashed. The young shoots and leaves can be used like spinach.

AT A GLANCE:

PLANT											
HARVEST											
mid-winter	late winter	early spring	mid-spring	late spring	early summer	mid-summer	late summer	early autumn	mid-autumn	late autumn	early winter

Planting Overview: Grow from slips in spring; plant rooted slips out when the soil has warmed, preferably under cover; keep well watered.

Varieties to Try: 'Beauregard' (reliable, red skin with orange flesh, bushy), 'Erato Violet' (purple skin and flesh, rich in antioxidants), 'Kaukura' (reliable, ornamental purple foliage), 'Evangeline' (bushy growth).

'Beauregard'

'Kaukura'

Potatoes

With careful planting and storage, it is possible to eat homegrown potatoes all year round. This makes them indispensable for the year-round veg grower, and this is no bad thing since potatoes are a kitchen staple. Varieties are either first or second early, or maincrop. First early or 'new' potatoes are usually smaller and slightly sweeter than maincrop varieties.

WHAT YOU NEED

Potatoes grow best in full sun and rich, moist but well-drained soil.

SOWING AND PLANTING

Potatoes are grown from seed potatoes, which are available to buy from late winter. It is advisable to buy new from a certified supplier each year to ensure they are disease-free. Before planting, seed potatoes can be chitted for four to six weeks. This involves leaving them somewhere light but out of direct sun so they start to sprout; this means they will start growing more quickly once planted. This is most useful with early potatoes, but it is not essential, and there is no need to worry if sprouts are not produced.

Potatoes can be planted through the spring with first earlies generally planted a couple of weeks before second earlies, and maincrops a couple of weeks later again. However, they can all be planted from mid spring. There is no need to remove any sprouts, and be careful not to damage any that are there. When planting, dig a hole, place the potato in the hole with shoots facing upwards, then cover with soil. If the potatoes are going to be earthed up, plant them about 15cm (6in) deep, otherwise a depth of 25cm (10in) is ideal. Space first and second earlies about 30cm (12in) apart and main crops 40cm (16in) apart. Shoots should appear after a couple of weeks.

Potatoes, ideally the smaller early varieties, can also be grown in sacks. Part-fill the sacks with soil,

Left: Use old egg boxes to sprout (or chit) your seed potatoes, which gives them a bit of a start ahead of planting.

position the potatoes, then cover with more soil. Place one tuber in a 30cm (12in) diameter sack and three in a 60cm (24in) diameter sack. Placed in a greenhouse, sacks can facilitate an early harvest in the spring. Alternatively, sacks planted in mid- to late summer will be ready through the early winter up until Christmas, so long as they are brought inside when the weather gets colder.

Above left: A bulb planter will help you plant potatoes with minimal soil disturbance.

Above: Emerging foliage can be 'earthed up' to prevent light reaching the tubers.

Below: Growing potatoes in sacks offers versatility with growing options.

HOW TO GROW THE CROP

Potato foliage is frost-tender, so plant late enough to avoid frosts, cover emerging foliage with fleece when frost is forecast, or earth up. This involves covering the emerging shoots with the surrounding soil or extra materials such as compost and straw once they are about 20cm (8in) high, leaving the tops visible. This is repeated a few times through the season. As well as frost protection, earthing up prevents light reaching the potato tubers, turning them green and poisonous. However, earthing up is not essential. Seed potatoes planted a little deeper have enough space below ground for tubers to develop. If any do turn green, cut off the green part and the rest of the tuber remains edible. Potatoes in sacks need earthing up until the soil surface is just below the top of the sack.

Potatoes do not need feeding or regular watering, but they will need water in dry spells. If potatoes lack water, a disorder called hollow

heart can occur, meaning the potatoes develop a hollow centre and become inedible. Potatoes in sacks benefit from regular watering and a fortnightly feed.

When growing potatoes, keep an eye out for blight, particularly in damp, humid weather in late summer. Infected foliage goes black and should be removed; the tubers will eventually turn putrid and very smelly. Harvesting the crop early ensures it is not infected, although first and second early potatoes are usually harvested before blight strikes anyway. There are blight-resistant maincrop varieties available.

If blight has been a problem, then crop rotation ensures any infected tubers left in the soil cannot reinfect future crops. If a crop has been particularly badly eaten by insects, such as eelworms, then crop rotation is also useful. However, crop rotation is not essential and potatoes can be grown in the same soil each year, particularly if there have been intermediary crops until early spring.

WHEN THE CROP IS READY

First early potatoes are ready around 12 weeks after planting, second earlies 14 weeks, and main crops 16–20 weeks. Maincrops will continue growing until mid autumn, although slug damage can increase. Flowering, or the leaves turning yellow, can indicate the crop is ready, but the best indicator is to use your hand to feel under the soil. In healthy no-dig soil, potatoes can be harvested without digging – gather together all the foliage and pull the plant; it should come up with the potatoes attached. You can then use your hand, or a trowel, to find any remaining tubers.

Below: Flowering is an indication that it is time to investigate if the tubers are large enough to harvest.

STORING AND COOKING TIPS

Potatoes store well in a cool, dry, frost-free and dark location. After harvesting, excess soil should be brushed off and the tubers left to dry for a few hours before storing. Those in storage should be checked occasionally for rot. Potatoes can be stored until late winter or early spring, and even if they turn a little soft or start to sprout, they are fine once cooked. Peel off any signs of scab before cooking. In general, first and second early potatoes are better eaten as salad potatoes, while maincrops make excellent mash, chips or roasties.

Above: A crop of first early potatoes, planted at the beginning of spring, will be ready in early summer.

AT A GLANCE:

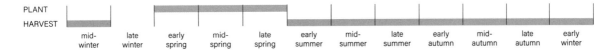

PLANT											
HARVEST											
mid-winter	late winter	early spring	mid-spring	late spring	early summer	mid-summer	late summer	early autumn	mid-autumn	late autumn	early winter

Planting Overview: There are lots of options with regards to chitting, planting depth and earthing up; try growing in sacks for early or late harvests.

Varieties to Try: 'Rocket' (first early, heavy cropper), 'Charlotte' AGM (classic second early, waxy texture), 'Sarpo Mira' AGM (maincrop, blight resistant), 'Desiree' AGM (maincrop, great for mash), 'Swift' (first early, waxy texture), 'Kestrel' (second early, produces consistently sized tubers), 'Vivaldi' AGM (first early but can be left to grow larger and harvested later), 'Jazzy' AGM (second early, small tubers with a strong flavour), 'Pink Fir Apple' AGM (maincrop, waxy, wonderful taste, smaller than many maincrops), 'Cara' (maincrop, good blight and drought resistance).

'Charlotte' AGM

'Desiree' AGM

'Rocket'

'Sarpo Mira' AGM

Radishes

Radishes add a crisp, peppery taste to salads. Most are fast growing and they come in a range of colours – there are even varieties suitable for winter harvest. In Oaxaca, Mexico, the Night of the Radishes festival celebrates this crop with incredible sculptures made from oversized radishes.

WHAT YOU NEED

Grow radishes in fertile, moisture-retentive soil in full sun or light shade.

SOWING AND PLANTING

Salad radishes can be sown from late winter or early spring until late summer, although the heat of midsummer is best avoided. Winter radishes can be sown in late summer or early autumn. The earlier and later sowings are best covered with fleece to aid germination. Radishes can be started indoors, but the speed of growth generally makes it easier to start outside. Germination occurs in just over a week. Inside, use module trays to enable multi-sowing, aiming for five seedlings per cell, or three for winter radish.

Plant out clumps at around 10cm (4in) spacing, or 20cm (8in) for winter radish. Outside, create drills 1cm (1/2in) deep and 10cm (4in) apart, or 15cm (6in) for winter radish. Thinly sow the seed along the base of the drill and cover with soil. Thin to 2–3cm (¾–1in) spacing, or 15cm (6in) for winter radish. Radishes can also be sown directly into pots, and regular sowings will ensure a successional harvest.

RAT'S TAIL RADISH

Also known as edible-podded radishes, these are grown for their seed pods, which have a slight spicy taste. The pods are picked immature during the summer months. They are often more successful than salad radishes in hot summers, and there are green- or red-podded varieties available.

HOW TO GROW THE CROP

Radishes are fairly low maintenance. Once germinated, they benefit from being kept moist otherwise they may flower prematurely. Pots and summer sowings are most prone to this. During the spring and summer they need protecting with horticultural fleece or insect-proof mesh as flea beetles can eat the leaves and roots of radishes, while cabbage root flies eat the roots. Winter radishes can reach around 40cm (16in) tall, and can be left without protection in milder areas, but may benefit from being covered by horticultural fleece elsewhere.

Left: Radish thinnings should be enjoyed raw.

WHEN THE CROP IS READY

Salad radishes can be ready to harvest in as little as 4–6 weeks during the summer months. If left too long they become tough. Winter radishes are larger and take longer to mature, but can be ready by early winter, and then provide a crop during the following months. Simply twist the radish out of the ground when it is ready.

Above: Simply twist salad radishes out of the ground when they are ready.

MOOLI

Also known as daikon or Oriental radish, this is a type of winter radish, although some varieties are suitable for earlier sowing. It forms a long white tap root and is slow growing, taking 3–4 months to be ready for harvest. Cook like winter radishes, or serve thinly sliced or grated in salads and pickles. Mooli roots can be lifted and stored if necessary. 'Neptune' produces particularly long white roots.

STORING AND COOKING TIPS

Salad radishes are best eaten raw and can be stored in the fridge for up to a week. Winter radishes can be harvested as needed through the winter and early spring, or lifted in early winter and stored in a cool location for a few months. They can be added to stews in a similar way to turnips and have a slightly milder taste than salad radishes.

AT A GLANCE:

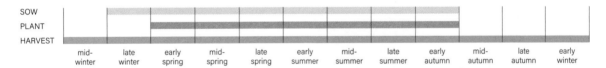

	SOW	PLANT	HARVEST
mid-winter	late winter	early spring	mid-spring
late spring	early summer	mid-summer	late summer
early autumn	mid-autumn	late autumn	early winter

Planting Overview: There are salad and winter types of radish; generally easiest to sow outside; keep moist to encourage the radishes to swell.

Varieties to Try: 'French Breakfast 3' (salad variety, cylindrical red roots with white tips, reliable), 'Bright Lights' (salad variety, multicoloured, quite large roots), 'Black Spanish Round' (winter variety, black skin, sharp-flavoured white flesh), 'Green Luobo' (winter variety, mild flavour, green flesh).

'Black Spanish Round'

'Bright Lights'

Kohlrabi

Kohlrabi is a fast-growing hardy vegetable from the brassica family. It is grown for its above-ground swollen stem that can be green, white or purple, with white flesh inside. The leaves are also edible. It is often compared to turnip, but the flesh is sweeter with a mild cabbage flavour and a firm, crisp texture. It can be eaten raw or cooked.

WHAT YOU NEED

This crop grows well in sun or partial shade. It enjoys cool, wet conditions and fertile, well-drained soil of neutral or alkaline pH, with organic matter to help moisture retention.

SOWING AND PLANTING

Kohlrabi is best sown in late winter to early spring, or mid- to late summer. It is good to start indoors in modules, as this speeds up the germination. Sow up to three seeds per module, thinning to

one. Plant out when the seedlings have at least two true leaves. Plant slightly deeper than the original depth, 30cm (12in) apart. Placing a brassica collar around the base of the plant prevents brassica root fly damage.

HOW TO GROW THE CROP

Kohlrabi is one of the first crops to grow in spring. Protect the seedlings from low temperatures and insect damage with horticultural fleece or fine mesh, then keep the plants well watered during their establishment. Watering prevents them from bolting and the bulb becoming woody. Feeding is not necessary if the soil is mulched with a good layer of well-rotted organic matter.

To get a good crop of kohlrabi, it is best to cover the whole crop with butterfly netting or mesh to provide protection from cabbage white caterpillars and pigeons. If nets in the garden are undesirable, intersperse these unusual and attractive plants among herbs, flowers or other vegetables; this might help to reduce pest damage. Kohlrabi can be grown in pots but will need extra watering and regular feeding. It can also be grown as a catch crop.

Left: Kohlrabi is a good crop to start indoors in modules so that they are ready to plant out as soon as spring is underway.

WHEN THE CROP IS READY

Spring-sown kohlrabi is best harvested young, when the bulbs are tender and about size of cricket balls. The summer sowing can stay in the ground through autumn and winter, to harvest as needed.

STORING AND COOKING TIPS

The bulbs can be eaten raw, grated into salads and coleslaws, or they can be lightly steamed, roasted or used in stir-fries. The leaves are tasty if cooked like cabbage.

Kohlrabi will last in the fridge up to two weeks or longer if the leaves are removed. It can be pickled, or blanched and frozen for later use. Late crops can be left in the ground and picked as needed through the winter, or harvested in the autumn and stored in a cool, frost-free place.

Above: Harvest kohlrabi by twisting the plant out of the soil and removing the lower leaves. These are edible and taste like cabbage leaves.

AT A GLANCE:

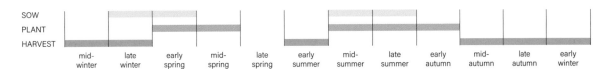

SOW										
PLANT										
HARVEST										
	mid-winter	late winter	early spring	mid-spring	late spring	early summer	mid-summer	late summer	early autumn	mid-autumn	late autumn	early winter

Planting Overview: Start seeds indoors in modules; keep well watered and protect with mesh or net against insect damage and frost.

Varieties to Try: 'Modrava' F1 (purple, compact, reliable, suitable for pots), 'Kolibri' AGM (purple, reliable with uniform bulbs, crisp with good flavour), 'Superschmelz' (heirloom variety with large bulb), 'Kossak' F1 (pale green, reliable with large bulbs, good for winter storage), 'Quickstar' (light green, fast maturing, slow to bolt).

'Kolibri' AGM

'Modrava'

Turnips

Often underused and underappreciated, turnips have a lot to recommend them. They are fast and easy to grow, can be eaten young or mature, and make an important contribution to a healthy diet.

WHAT YOU NEED
Grow in full sun, in rich, moist soil.

SOWING AND PLANTING
Sow from early spring indoors, through to late summer. If multi-sowing, aim for 4–5 seedlings per clump. Inside, start in module trays; outside, create drills 1cm (½in) deep and 25cm (10in) apart. Seeds germinate within 1–2 weeks. Aim for 5–10cm (2–4in) between individual baby turnips and 25–30cm (10–12in) between mature, multi-sown clumps. Successional sowing ensures regular harvests.

HOW TO GROW THE CROP
Water the plants regularly, and cover to protect from insects including flea beetle. In autumn, when the weather is wetter and insects are less prevalent, this crop can be grown in pots.

WHEN THE CROP IS READY
Turnips can be ready in as little as six weeks. All are best harvested before frosts, and before reaching the size of a tennis ball. With multi-sown clumps, minimize root disturbance so other turnips can keep growing. The slightly peppery leaves can also be harvested, although picking too many reduces the growth of the turnip.

STORING AND COOKING TIPS
Baby turnips are best fresh, but larger ones can be stored for a few weeks. Younger turnips are sweeter so are good raw in salads, while larger ones are useful in soups and stews.

AT A GLANCE:

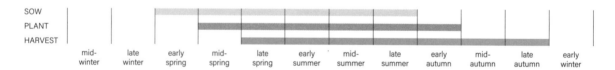

	SOW	PLANT	HARVEST

| mid-winter | late winter | early spring | mid-spring | late spring | early summer | mid-summer | late summer | early autumn | mid-autumn | late autumn | early winter |

Planting Overview: Sow indoors or outside; provide plenty of water; choose appropriate varieties for harvesting small or mature; best in cooler conditions.

Varieties to Try: 'Oasis' AGM (sweet flavour, best harvested small), 'Sweetbell' (salad turnip, crisp texture), 'Purple Top Milan' (harvest from baby roots, up to a larger size).

'Oasis' AGM

'Purple Top Milan'

Swede

Swedes are a hearty root crop, slightly sweeter than turnips. They are also known as Swedish turnips, hence the name 'swede' – this hints at their tough nature, which allows them to be harvested through autumn and winter.

WHAT YOU NEED
Grow in full sun and in rich, relatively moist soil.

SOWING AND PLANTING
Swede can be sown from mid spring to early summer. If starting indoors, sow in modules and thin to one seedling to minimize root disturbance when planting. Outside, create drills 2cm (3/4in) deep and 30cm (12in) apart, and thinly sprinkle the seed. The end spacing should be 20–25cm (8–10in), or 8–10cm (3½–4in) for mini swedes.

Above: Many varieties of swede can be stored in the ground to lift as needed.

HOW TO GROW THE CROP
As they are in the brassica family, swedes are vulnerable to insects, including cabbage caterpillars and gall midge, as well as diseases such as club root. For this reason, it is best to protect the plants with fleece or insect-proof mesh. Provide plenty of water as they grow.

The swollen base should be visible. To harvest, simply twist the plants out of the ground.

STORING AND COOKING TIPS
Store in the ground or lift and store in a cool, dry, frost-free location for several months. Swede is great cooked in stews or added to mash.

WHEN THE CROP IS READY
This crop should be ready after 2–3 months for mini swedes, or 4–6 months for mature plants.

AT A GLANCE:

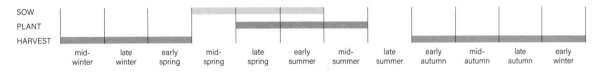

SOW												
PLANT												
HARVEST	mid-winter	late winter	early spring	mid-spring	late spring	early summer	mid-summer	late summer	early autumn	mid-autumn	late autumn	early winter

Planting Overview: Start inside or out; provide plenty of water; protect from insects.

Varieties to Try: 'Gowrie' AGM (purple skin, good for midwinter harvests), 'Helenor' (stores well, can be left in the ground until early spring), 'Marian' (yellow skin, resistant to club root).

Asparagus

This wonderful perennial crop is low maintenance and provides a spring treat every year. The fresh spears are hard to beat and as well as being delicious and tender, they are full of nutrients and antioxidants.

WHAT YOU NEED

Grow in a sheltered site with full sun, in well-drained, fertile soil. Choose your site carefully as asparagus can live for around 20 years and is difficult to move once established.

SOWING AND PLANTING

Asparagus grown from seed should be sown indoors in late winter or early spring and planted in early summer. Outdoor sowings are possible from mid spring but are vulnerable to slugs. However, asparagus is usually grown from crowns. These are one-year-old bareroot plants and can be planted in early to mid spring. Space crowns 35–45cm (14–18in) apart. When planting, dig a hole large enough to spread the roots out. Create a slight rise in the centre and place the middle of the crown on top to aid drainage. Cover with soil, leaving any bud tips just visible.

HOW TO GROW THE CROP

For the first two years after planting, avoid harvesting so the plants can establish. Leave any spears that appear and they will form attractive, feathery fronds up to 1.5m (5ft) high, which can be supported with stakes and string. In subsequent years, allow the foliage to grow once harvesting has finished so the plant can store energy for the following year.

The plant's foliage provides autumn colour before it is cut down at the end of the season to remove overwintering asparagus beetles. These insects damage asparagus foliage. Small populations can be tolerated, but the adults and larvae can also be removed by hand during the growing season and destroyed.

Spread a rich, well-rotted organic mulch in winter to nourish the plants for the coming season. Water well until established, after which the plants will only need watering in really hot, dry spells.

Asparagus is dioecious, meaning the plants are either male or female. Most modern varieties are all male as these produce better spears. Female plants produce berries in autumn, and can be dug out and replaced by male plants. Established plants may be lifted and divided in early spring.

Left: Asparagus spears appear in spring.

Right: Use a sharp knife to cut them just below ground level.

ASPARAGUS ALTERNATIVES

Fiddleheads These are the edible tips of ostrich ferns (*Matteuccia struthiopteris*). The new shoots of this woodland perennial can be harvested from mid to late spring and are best eaten lightly steamed. They taste like a cross between asparagus and broccoli. Be aware that not all ferns are edible.

Solomon's seal The young shoots of this perennial have a taste reminiscent of asparagus. This woodland plant is harvested in spring when the shoots are still tightly coiled. They only need a very light steam before eating.

WHEN THE CROP IS READY

Spears start to appear in mid spring, with some varieties appearing slightly earlier or later, extending the season of harvest. A light harvest may be possible two years after planting, three for plants grown from seed, but a full harvest should wait another year. Cut spears with a sharp knife just below ground level when they are 10–15cm (4–6in) tall. Stop harvesting after around eight weeks.

STORING AND COOKING TIPS

Asparagus spears should be eaten as soon as possible after harvesting. Try lightly steaming or grilling, and serve with butter or a creamy sauce.

AT A GLANCE:

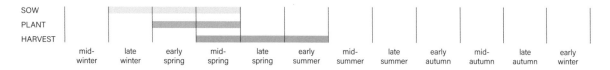

SOW			
PLANT			
HARVEST			

mid-winter | late winter | early spring | mid-spring | late spring | early summer | mid-summer | late summer | early autumn | mid-autumn | late autumn | early winter

Planting Overview: Long-lived perennial; low maintenance; avoid harvesting for the first few years after planting.

Varieties to Try: 'Connover's Colossal' AGM (large, reliable spears), 'Gijnlim' AGM (early season variety, prolific cropper), 'Guelph Millennium' AGM (vigorous, reliable in most soils), 'Backlim' AGM (mid to late season, good flavour).

'Backlim' AGM

'Gijnlim' AGM

Globe artichokes

This perennial provides edible flower buds in summer and attracts insects when left to flower. Cardoons are close relatives, but it is the stem that is eaten.

WHAT YOU NEED
Grow in full sun in a sheltered location with fertile, well-drained soil. Avoid frost pockets or waterlogging over winter, which can be fatal.

SOWING AND PLANTING
Sow seed inside in early to mid spring and pot up seedlings into 9cm (3³/₄in) pots. Alternatively, buy plug plants and grow on before planting out. Average plants reach 1.5m (5ft) high and 1m (3ft) wide. Plant out after the last frost.

HOW TO GROW THE CROP
Provide plenty of water while plants are establishing. Remove yellow leaves and cut down the plants in winter. Divide plants every 4–6 years to encourage vigour. They can also be propagated by basal offsets from established plants.

Choose varieties with appropriate hardiness for your situation, applying a layer of mulch each year as winter protection, and to feed the plants.

WHEN THE CROP IS READY
In the first year, remove the flower stalks to aid establishment. From the second year, harvest the flower buds during the summer, when fully closed and the size of a large orange or grapefruit.

STORING AND COOKING TIPS
Globe artichokes and cardoons are best fresh. Try roasting or frying smaller buds, and steaming larger ones, eating the fleshy bases of the scales with butter or a sauce. With cardoons, trim and peel the fleshy mid rib of young leaves before blanching and adding to a stir-fry.

AT A GLANCE:

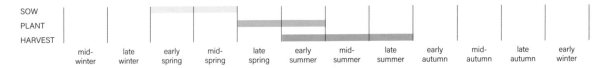

SOW												
PLANT												
HARVEST												
	mid-winter	late winter	early spring	mid-spring	late spring	early summer	mid-summer	late summer	early autumn	mid-autumn	late autumn	early winter

Planting Overview: Large attractive perennial that needs plenty of space; harvest the unopened flower buds; avoid waterlogging; if not harvested as buds, the flowers open in midsummer.

Varieties to Try: 'Purple Globe' (attractive purple flowers), 'Green Globe Improved' (heavy crops, good flavour).

'Green Globe Improved'

'Purple Globe'

Jerusalem artichokes

Jerusalem artichokes are an easy hardy perennial plant from North America, grown for their edible tubers. Some people find them hard to digest.

WHAT YOU NEED
Best in rich, free-draining soil, in sun or semi-shade.

SOWING AND PLANTING
Plant tubers in early spring, about 15cm (6in) deep and 30cm (12in) apart. They can be started in pots indoors and planted out when conditions improve.

HOW TO GROW THE CROP
Moisture is important to form good-sized tubers, so apply a mulch in spring. The plants are vigorous, can grow tall and may need support. The plants are usually trouble-free; however, snails and slugs can cause damage to young shoots.

WHEN THE CROP IS READY
Dig up the tubers from autumn onwards. If any tubers are left in the ground, they will grow the following year.

OCA
This tender annual from the Andes is also cultivated for its edible tubers, which are an alternative to potatoes. They swell late in the season, so for a successful harvest leave them in the ground for as long as possible until the first frost. Keep them confined to a container and source plants carefuly (see p31).

STORING AND COOKING TIPS
Store in the fridge for a few weeks or harvest as needed throughout winter. Start with eating small quantities as the non-digestible sugars in the tubers can cause bloating. Jerusalem artichokes are versatile vegetables that can be roasted, fried or blended into purées or soups.

AT A GLANCE:

PLANT												
HARVEST												
mid-winter	late winter	early spring	mid-spring	late spring	early summer	mid-summer	late summer	early autumn	mid-autumn	late autumn	early winter

Planting Overview: Water well in hot dry spells for good-sized tubers; support plants as they get tall; harvest from autumn onwards.

Varieties to Try: 'Fuseau' (widely available, reliable), 'Gerrard' (red-skinned tubers), 'Dwarf Sunray' (compact 150–180cm/5–6ft tall with regular flower display), 'Dwarf' (truly compact 50–60cm/20–24in tall, red-skinned tubers).

'Fuseau'

'Dwarf Sunray'

Rhubarb

Although often considered a fruit due to its use in desserts, rhubarb is in fact an easy-to-grow hardy perennial vegetable, cultivated for its edible stems. Rhubarb can be harvested from early spring, providing a fruity supplement at a time when most fresh fruit is unavailable.

WHAT YOU NEED

Rhubarb grows well in sunny positions, in free-draining soil rich in organic matter. It is important that the plant is not sitting in waterlogged soil over winter, as the crowns are prone to rot.

SOWING AND PLANTING

Plants can be grown from seed, but the most common way of propagating is by dividing a crown. Young rhubarb plants are also available to buy. The best time to divide rhubarb is when the plant is dormant in late autumn to early winter.

When planting, ensure the tip of the crown is sitting just above the soil; this helps protect the crown from rotting. Space plants 75–90cm (30–36in) apart.

HOW TO GROW THE CROP

In the first year of growth, do not harvest any stems to encourage the development of a strong plant. Mulch around the crown each spring with well-rotted organic matter, but do not cover it as that can cause the crown to rot. When the leaf buds start to swell in early spring, the plant can be covered with a forcing pot in order to produce forced rhubarb, a delicacy with a milder flavour and less fibrous stems. Only force rhubarb over alternating years as consecutive forcing year-on-year can exhaust the plant. Water your rhubarb regularly during the growing season. Removing old spent leaves regularly will help keep the plants healthy. If the plant produces flowers, cut these out to save the plant's energy. Rhubarb can be grown in large containers but will need regular watering and feeding.

WHEN THE CROP IS READY

Rhubarb is ready to harvest when the stems are 30cm (12in) long, usually from early spring to midsummer. However, some late varieties produce well into late summer. When harvesting, pull the stem from the crown in one piece and don't take more than half of the stems from the plant at one

Left: To force the rhubarb stems, cover part of the plant's crown when the leaf buds start to swell.

time. Discard the greenest, leafy parts of the stems as they are poisonous. In other words, just use the red or pink and pale stem bases.

STORING AND COOKING TIPS

Rhubarb stems last up to a week in the fridge and can be frozen or made into jam. Traditionally used in pies and crumbles and for wine making, rhubarb is versatile and can be prepared in many ways – stewed, poached, roasted or made into cordial.

Right: Forced rhubarb stems are tender, sweeter and less fibrous than unforced rhubarb. Uncover the crown after the forced stems are harvested.

AT A GLANCE:

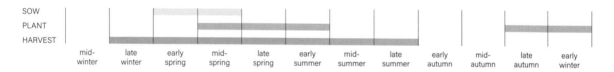

	SOW	PLANT	HARVEST

mid-winter · late winter · early spring · mid-spring · late spring · early summer · mid-summer · late summer · early autumn · mid-autumn · late autumn · early winter

Planting Overview: Plant crowns in late autumn to early winter; ensure the crown sits just above soil level; do not harvest in the first year after planting to help establish a strong plant.

Varieties to Try: 'Victoria' (reliable main season variety), 'Raspberry Red' AGM (deep red stems, early variety), 'Timperley Early' AGM (red stems, very early variety), 'Champagne' (pink stems, early variety), 'Stockbridge Arrow' (red stems with distinctive arrow-shaped leaves, reliable main season variety), 'Livingstone' (late summer variety).

'Raspberry Red' AGM

'Timperley Early' AGM

Yacon and dahlia

Yacon is a tender perennial plant in the sunflower family that originates from the Andes. It produces a large quantity of edible tubers with a crisp texture and tastes like a mixture of pear, apple and celery. More familiar to gardeners are dahlias, but less commonly known is that they also produce edible tubers.

WHAT YOU NEED

Both crops thrive in sunny positions. Yacon needs plenty of space. It can reach over 2m (6½ft) in height and spread over 1m (3ft). Plant in moisture-retentive soil with plenty of organic matter; both plants benefit from a good layer of mulch.

Above: Yacon is a potential source of very damaging pathogens, so ensure tubers are only sourced from established suppliers and have been grown locally rather than imported.

SOWING AND PLANTING

Like dahlias, yacon is usually propagated by tubers. Yacon has two types of tuber – large root tubers that are edible, and knobbly stem tubers concentrated around the main stem, which are used for propagation. In areas with cold winters, the tubers of both crops are best started indoors in mid spring, in pots, with the tuber placed just under soil level. Plant out when the danger of frost has passed. Space at least 90cm (3ft) apart. Water well after planting.

HOW TO GROW THE CROP

In areas with cold winters, yacon and dahlia crowns are best lifted in the autumn and stored indoors. The stem tubers are divided in spring and used for propagation. These tubers can also be purchased from a reliable supplier. The dahlia species traditionally grown as food crops are *Dahlia coccinea* and *D. pinnata*. After planting, water regularly to provide a better yield. Yacon is a large plant and might need staking to avoid the stems breaking in strong winds. Both are easy to grow and generally trouble-free.

WHEN THE CROP IS READY

Both crops need a long season to produce a good harvest. It is best to harvest as late as possible, just when the first frost arrives. Take care when harvesting tubers as they break easily, and damaged tubers do not store well.

STORING AND COOKING TIPS

Tubers will last for 3–4 months in a dry, frost-free place. The flavour improves after a month in storage, becoming sweeter. Tubers are mostly used raw, eaten as a fruit or in salads.

They can also be cooked in curries, stir-fried or used in baking as a crunchy substitute to apple. It is best to peel the skin before eating. The popular way to store yacon in Japan and Korea is by pickling. Tubers can also be processed into a low-calorie syrup, which is used as a sweetener. Yacon contains non-digestible sugars and is good for the gut. It is also said to suppress the appetite. Introduce it into your diet gradually to reduce the bloating effect of the sugars.

Below: A yacon tuber weighs 200–500g (7oz–1lb 2oz); one plant can produce more than 10kg (22lb) of tubers.

AT A GLANCE:

	mid-winter	late winter	early spring	mid-spring	late spring	early summer	mid-summer	late summer	early autumn	mid-autumn	late autumn	early winter
PLANT				▬								
HARVEST										▬	▬	

Planting Overview: After planting, water regularly; stake plants to protect from winds; after autumn harvest, store the small knobbly tubers indoors for planting the following year; purchase tubers or plants from reliable sources to ensure healthy, pathogen-free plants.

Varieties to Try: *Dahlia coccinea* (up to 3m/10ft high), *D. pinnata* (up to 1.2m/4ft high), Yacon 'Inca Red' (produces red tubers).

Dahlia coccinea

Yacon 'Inca Red'

Agretti and samphire

Agretti is a leafy, frost-tender vegetable popular in Italy, and like samphire it is native to coastal areas. The succulent stems and leaves of both are becoming more popular among chefs and deserve to be more widely cultivated.

There are two types of samphire: marsh samphire (*Salicornia europaea*) and rock samphire (*Crithmum maritimum*). They are both wild perennial plants and are traditionally foraged but can also be cultivated from seed. Okahijiki (*Salsola komarovii*) is a Japanese alternative to agretti, and one of Japan's oldest vegetables – now considered a gourmet speciality.

WHAT YOU NEED

Best grown in full sun, on light, free-draining soil rich in organic matter. Agretti is a halophyte, a plant adapted to salty water. However, it is happy in a wide range of conditions and does not need to be by the sea or in salty water to grow successfully.

SOWING AND PLANTING

Sow seeds from late winter to late spring. Seeds are only viable for a short period of time and have a low germination rate. When sowing, use fresh seed and sow more than needed to balance this out. In early spring, start the seeds indoors in modules, three or four seeds per module, and plant out after the danger of frost passes. Plant about 20–30cm (8–12in) apart. Seeds can also be sown direct from late spring. Germination takes up to three weeks.

HOW TO GROW THE CROP

Apart from slightly tricky germination, agretti is an easy crop to grow. Harvest regularly when the stems are succulent and soft, as it promotes further growth. As the plants get older, the stem will get woody, and it will start flowering. You can save your own seeds for next year's crop. Grow in full sun and water regularly for tender leaves. Slugs and snails can be a problem for young plants. For continuous harvest, sow agretti every few weeks. It is suitable to grow in containers.

WHEN THE CROP IS READY

For harvest, cut sections of stem when the young plants are 15–20cm (6–8in) high. Regular harvesting will make the plants bushier, and they will crop for several weeks until the stems become woody.

Left: These young agretti plants are ready to harvest. Cut sections of stems regularly to encourage further growth.

STORING AND COOKING TIPS

Agretti will store for a few days in the fridge but is best used fresh when harvested. It can also be frozen but needs to be blanched first. It can be used in salads, or lightly steamed to accompany fish. The needle-like leaves are salty, crunchy and succulent like samphire. The succulent leaves of samphire can be eaten raw or lightly cooked, traditionally with fish, white meat or pasta.

Right: Harvest samphire regularly to ensure a continuous supply of the tender stems.

AT A GLANCE:

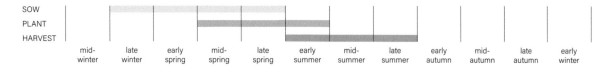

SOW											
PLANT											
HARVEST											
mid-winter	late winter	early spring	mid-spring	late spring	early summer	mid-summer	late summer	early autumn	mid-autumn	late autumn	early winter

Planting Overview: A cut-and-come-again crop which can supply a continuous harvest of succulent leaves for several months; grow in full sun and water regularly for more tender leaves; if grown in containers, use free-draining compost.

Agretti 'Roscano'

Crithmum maritimum

Skirret

This perennial root vegetable used to be part of the European diet for centuries. With the arrival of potatoes to Europe, skirret fell out of favour. Recently it is gaining popularity with chefs and homegrowers for its carrot-parsnip flavour.

WHAT YOU NEED
Skirret thrives in full sun or partial shade in free-draining soil rich in organic matter.

SOWING AND PLANTING
Skirret is propagated by seeds or by crown division. Sow in early to mid spring direct or in modules. The germination is erratic and takes two weeks or more. Final plant spacing is 30cm (12in). Crowns are lifted and divided in early spring. Select crowns with the best-quality roots to propagate. Plant crowns with the shooting tips at soil level.

Below: When harvesting skirret, select the plants with the best-sized roots to propagate for the following year.

HOW TO GROW THE CROP
Skirret is an easy-to-grow hardy perennial crop. It needs plenty of water to grow well. Water regularly and mulch around the plant to keep the soil moist. This will help to stop the core of the root becoming woody. Collect seeds for planting the following year. For more reliable germination, use fresh seeds.

WHEN THE CROP IS READY
The roots are ready to harvest from autumn onwards. Lift the crown and harvest the biggest, smoothest roots. The rest of the crown can be divided and replanted for the following year.

STORING AND COOKING TIPS
Skirret stores well for a few days in the fridge but can be harvested as needed through the winter. Skirret is used raw, parboiled, roasted or fried. It has a sweet carrot-parsnip flavour and a starchy, floury texture.

AT A GLANCE:

	SOW	PLANT	HARVEST
mid-winter			
late winter			
early spring			
mid-spring			
late spring			
early summer			
mid-summer			
late summer			
early autumn			
mid-autumn			
late autumn			
early winter			

Planting Overview: Hardy perennial cultivated for its edible roots; plant crowns or seedlings in spring; water regularly to avoid woody roots; harvest from autumn onwards as needed.

Scorzonera and salsify

Scorzonera is a hardy perennial vegetable grown for its long black edible taproot. Salsify has similar qualities and requirements, but has a white root.

WHAT YOU NEED
Both crops grow best in light, moisture-retentive soil in full sun or partial shade. They will grow well on heavier soils, but the roots may be smaller.

SOWING AND PLANTING
In spring, sow direct 1.5cm (5/8in) deep in rows 30cm (12in) apart. Germination can take up to three weeks and can be erratic. Thin the young plants to a minimum of 15cm (6in) apart.

HOW TO GROW THE CROP
These crops are easy to grow and usually problem-free. For good-quality roots, water regularly. Young shoots, leaves and flowers are also edible.

WHEN THE CROP IS READY
Roots are harvested in the first year from autumn onwards but are best if left in the ground over winter, as the flavour improves with frost.

STORING AND COOKING TIPS
Scorzonera can be stored in the fridge for a few weeks or harvested as needed throughout the

Above: Harvested black roots of scorzonera. Leave small roots on the plant for the following year – they do not deteriorate with age.

winter. This is a useful winter vegetable with a mild asparagus and oyster flavour and is great served with meat, roasted or sautéed in butter. Peeling the roots' inedible skin is best done after cooking for about 10–20 minutes. Ground dried root is used as a coffee substitute. Salsify is delicious in soups, roasted or sautéed and adds interest to the winter diet.

AT A GLANCE:

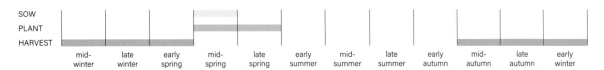

SOW											
PLANT											
HARVEST											
mid-winter	late winter	early spring	mid-spring	late spring	early summer	mid-summer	late summer	early autumn	mid-autumn	late autumn	early winter

Planting Overview: Sow direct, using more seeds than needed to balance the erratic germination; water regularly for good-quality roots; harvest from autumn onwards as needed.

Varieties to Try: Scorzonera 'Duplex' (heavy-yielding heritage variety) and 'Russian Giant' (long, slender black roots with a good flavour).

American groundnut

American groundnut (*Apios americana*), also known as hopniss, is a hardy perennial climber from the legume family native to North America. All parts of this plant are edible, but it is mainly cultivated for its edible tubers, which were a staple food for Native Americans long before colonization. They can be used as a substitute for potatoes.

WHAT YOU NEED

American groundnut is a marsh plant but adapts well to a range of environments. It grows well in rich moisture-retentive soil, in full sun or partial shade. The plants will need a support to climb on.

SOWING AND PLANTING

It is mainly propagated by tubers but can also be propagated by seeds. Plant tubers in mid to late spring 10cm (4in) deep and 30cm (12in) apart. Make sure to provide support for emerging shoots to climb on, in a similar way as for climbing beans, otherwise the shoots will start twining on surrounding plants.

HOW TO GROW THE CROP

It is an easy-to-grow hardy crop that can withstand temperatures of –20°C (–4°F), and lower when dormant. This moisture-loving plant will require regular watering. The tubers reach harvestable size after two or three years. The plant's vigorous shoots can travel over 1m (3ft) in the soil. To keep the plants in an allocated area, and for easier harvesting, plant in large bottomless containers sunk into the ground. It can also be grown in large (50 litre/11 gallon minimum) pots with a base, but the plants will need increased watering and feeding. Fragrant flowers appear in late summer and early autumn and some varieties will start producing pods. The plant is generally problem-free. As a legume, the plant has the ability to fix nitrogen in the soil.

Left: American groundnut is not just a useful edible plant but also a beautiful climber that can be trained on a trellis or arch.

WHEN THE CROP IS READY

Start harvesting in the second or third year during the autumn, after the foliage dies. The tubers are hardy and can be lifted through the winter until spring as needed.

STORING AND COOKING TIPS

The tubers are best kept in the ground through winter until harvested. They can also be stored in cold humid space. They have a flavour like a sweet potato and can be boiled and mashed, roasted or fried. It is also possible to dry and grind them into flour – use it as you would chickpea flour.

The crop is high in protein, calcium and iron, but the tubers also contain non-digestible sugars and may cause bloating. Try only small amounts to introduce them into your diet gradually to avoid an adverse reaction.

Above: The tubers, leaves and flowers of American groundnut are all edible and highly nutritious.

AT A GLANCE:

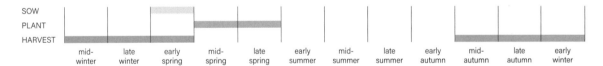

SOW											
PLANT											
HARVEST											
mid-winter	late winter	early spring	mid-spring	late spring	early summer	mid-summer	late summer	early autumn	mid-autumn	late autumn	early winter

Planting Overview: Hardy perennial climber cultivated for its edible tubers; foliage, young pods and beans are also edible; it thrives in moist conditions and will need a support to climb on.

Varieties to Try: 'Nutty' and 'Abundance' are both grown for their high yields.

'Nutty'

CHAPTER 8

HERBS

Growing herbs sustainably

Herbs will enhance the flavour of most, if not all, of the recipes you use when cooking your homegrown vegetables. They are, therefore, an essential addition to the year-round edible palate. A container of herbs near the kitchen is easy to manage and access, allowing for minimal time between plot and plate. It is hard to get fresher and more nutritious than that.

Many herbs are perennials, making them really sustainable to grow. Their roots are always present, supporting and sustaining the soil, and once established, they generally need less water than annuals. Perennial herbs, such as lavender and rosemary, are well known, but there are many others available, including sage, lemon grass and horseradish.

Annual herbs are also important for providing a wide range of flavours throughout the season. Coriander is surprisingly hardy, while others, such as dill and parsley, grow best in the warmer months but can be stored for use at other times of the year. Many of these, and some perennials, will grow well in pots for ease of access.

As well as tasting great, many herbs are beautiful to look at and help to attract beneficial insects and pollinators to your garden. This helps you to garden sustainably, as a thriving ecosystem in your garden helps ensure that natural predator and prey cycles can function, and provides much-needed support to garden wildlife. Chamomile, mint and oregano are just three examples of herbs with this dual purpose, but most herbs will flower well at some point in their life cycle. Chives, another important flowering herb, are discussed alongside the other alliums on pp138–9.

Left: Many herbs, when they are in flower, are magnets for beneficial insects.

Right: Mediterranean herbs are ideal for containers, enjoying the free-draining conditions.

Dill

Dill (*Anethum graveolens*) is an annual herb from the carrot family and is cultivated for its deliciously fragrant, feathery leaves. It is a very versatile plant as the flowers, stems and seeds can all be used.

WHAT YOU NEED
Choose a sheltered position in full sun or partial shade in a freely drained soil rich in organic matter.

SOWING AND PLANTING
Sow directly outdoors from mid spring or indoors in modules or trays from late winter onwards. If sown in trays, prick the plants out when small and plant out when the roots fill the module. Water well after planting. Thin direct-sown seedlings after germination; spacing should be 20–25cm (8–10in) apart. If the temperature falls below freezing, protect seedlings with fleece.

HOW TO GROW THE CROP
Ensure the plants have enough space and are watered well in warm weather to prevent bolting.

For leaf production, choose varieties that are slow to bolt. Sow seeds every four weeks for a continual harvest. Dill is suitable for growing in containers throughout the year; grow in a greenhouse or on a sunny windowsill in cool weather. Slugs can be a problem. This herb self-seeds freely.

WHEN THE CROP IS READY
Harvest the leaves regularly once the plant is about 20cm (8in) tall. Start with the outer leaves.

STORING AND COOKING TIPS
The aniseed-flavoured leaves are best fresh in salads, soups and potato dishes and will add flavour to pickles. They also go well with fish and eggs. The leaves can be frozen and the seeds can be dried and stored in an airtight container.

AT A GLANCE:

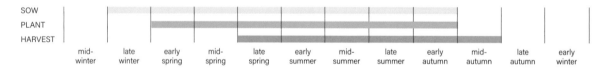

	SOW	PLANT	HARVEST

mid-winter · late winter · early spring · mid-spring · late spring · early summer · mid-summer · late summer · early autumn · mid-autumn · late autumn · early winter

Planting Overview: Protect early sowings; water well; sow every four weeks for continual harvest; grow indoors throughout the season.

Varieties to Try: 'Nano' (compact, good for containers, slow bolting), 'Mammoth' (tall with large flowers), 'Dukat' (reliable, slow bolting, good flavour, lots of leaves), 'Mariska' (also known as florist's dill, quick to flower so good in flower arrangements and for seed production).

'Mammoth'

'Mariska'

Caraway

Caraway (*Carum carvi*) is an easy-to-grow hardy biennial crop in the carrot family. All parts of the plant are edible, but it is mostly cultivated for its pungent seeds. This ancient spice is used in savoury and sweet dishes, commonly in Eastern European cuisines.

WHAT YOU NEED
Caraway will grow in any soil, whether positioned in full sun or partial shade.

SOWING AND PLANTING
Direct sow caraway seeds outdoors in spring or autumn, then thin seedlings to 30–40cm (12–16in) apart. Water well.

HOW TO GROW THE CROP
Water regularly. If grown in containers, make sure they are at least 30cm (12in) deep to accommodate the plants' long tap roots and feed the pots every few weeks. Caraway self-seeds easily.

WHEN THE CROP IS READY
Cut the seedheads off when they turn brown. Hang them upside down in a paper bag in a dry place. When the seeds are dry and fall easily from the flowerheads, they are ready to gather and store. Shake the contents of the bag and clean the seeds from the chaff.

STORING AND COOKING TIPS
Store cleaned seeds in an airtight container. These can be used in baking. Caraway is a traditional addition to rye bread but also goes well with meat or adds flavour to sauerkraut and pickles. The fresh carrot-tasting foliage is great in salads or pesto. The root is used like a parsnip or carrot.

Below: Ready to harvest. Botanically, caraway seeds are not actual seeds but dried fruit of the plant.

AT A GLANCE:

	SOW	HARVEST

mid-winter	late winter	early spring	mid-spring	late spring	early summer	mid-summer	late summer	early autumn	mid-autumn	late autumn	early winter

Planting Overview: Easy-to-grow plant; water regularly; collect and dry seedheads when they turn brown; self-seeds readily.

Tarragon

Tarragon is a perennial herb with aromatic leaves used in many European cuisines. Grow French tarragon (*Artemisia dracunculus* var. *sativa*) rather than its Russian namesake as it is much tastier. The leaves of orange-flowered Mexican tarragon (*Tagetes lucida*) have a similar taste.

WHAT YOU NEED
Best in a sunny position in free-draining soil. It will not tolerate waterlogging.

SOWING AND PLANTING
Available as nursery plants, French tarragon can be planted out in spring after the last frost. Propagate by plant division in spring or by semi-ripe cuttings in summer. Mexican tarragon is easy to grow from seed, treated as an annual in cool climates.

HOW TO GROW THE CROP
Tarragon is an easy-to-grow, drought-tolerant herb. In spring, cut the spent foliage down to the new shoots. Grow frost-tender French tarragon in free-draining compost in pots, moving them indoors in winter. With its orange flowers, Mexican tarragon will enliven both flower and vegetable beds and also attract beneficial insects.

WHEN THE CROP IS READY
Once the plant establishes, pick the young shoot tips from spring to autumn. Regular harvesting will make the plant bushier and ensures a continued supply of leaves.

STORING AND COOKING TIPS
The leaves are best used fresh. Add to dishes at the last minute, as if cooked for too long, they lose their flavour. Leaves can be stored in the fridge for a few days or can be frozen. They can also be dried and stored in an airtight container.

AT A GLANCE:

	SOW	PLANT	HARVEST

mid-winter · late winter · early spring · mid-spring · late spring · early summer · mid-summer · late summer · early autumn · mid-autumn · late autumn · early winter

Planting Overview: French tarragon is a drought-tolerant plant suitable for growing in containers; propagate by semi-ripe cuttings or plant division and move indoors to overwinter.

Mexican tarragon is a tender plant from the marigold family, grown for its fragrant leaves and orange edible flowers. It is similar in taste and use to French tarragon. The flowering tips can be dried and used to make tea.

French tarragon

Mexican tarragon

Coriander

This annual herb is easy to grow for its leaves, flowers and seeds. The foliage is used in many Asian cuisines, while the dried seeds are a classic Indian spice.

WHAT YOU NEED

Grow in full sun, or partial shade in summer. Fertile, free-draining soil is best.

SOWING AND PLANTING

Sow from early spring to early autumn, although summer sowings can flower before a decent leaf harvest. If starting inside, sow into modules, with two or three seedlings per module. Plant out at 20cm (8in) spacing once the plants have true leaves. Outside, create drills 1.5cm (5/8in) deep and 20cm (8in) apart, and thinly sprinkle the seeds.

HOW TO GROW THE CROP

Keep plants moist but not wet to delay flowering. Removing flowers promotes leafy growth, but the flowers and seeds are edible and attractive to wildlife. Later sowings will overwinter in a greenhouse or polytunnel but may need some protection outside in colder areas.

WHEN THE CROP IS READY

The main leaf harvest is early summer to mid autumn, but light harvests can continue with overwintering plants into spring. Pick by taking a few leaves at a time and leaving the rest to keep growing. Flowers can be harvested when they appear, which can be any time from spring to autumn, depending on sowing time. Dry harvested seeds before storing in an airtight container.

STORING AND COOKING TIPS

Eat coriander leaves fresh in Asian-inspired salads, curries and casseroles. Use the lemon-scented seeds to flavour curries and fish dishes.

Below: Coriander foliage resembles parsley but has its own distinctive flavour.

AT A GLANCE:

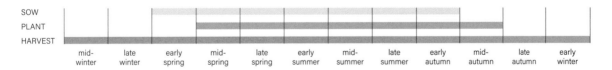

Planting Overview: Provide enough water to delay flowering; harvest leaves individually; the flowers are attractive, especially to wildlife.

Varieties to Try: 'Confetti' AGM (finely divided foliage, good flavour), 'Leisure' (slower to flower so longer leaf harvests), 'Lemon Coriander' (unusual lemony taste).

Turmeric

Turmeric (*Curcuma longa*) is a tender herbaceous perennial plant grown for its edible tuberous roots called rhizomes. Considered a superfood because of its many health-giving properties, it is used as a spice, medicine and food dye.

WHAT YOU NEED
Turmeric thrives in free-draining soil rich in organic matter and needs moisture and temperatures above 18°C (64°F) for successful rhizome production. Best grown under cover.

SOWING AND PLANTING
Turmeric is propagated from rhizomes; these can be purchased from a reliable supplier. Cut the rhizomes into 3–7cm (1–2½in) sections; if they are dry, soak them in warm water for 24 hours before planting. Place the sections flat in pots, with the growth buds facing up, 1–2cm (½–¾in) deep in February. Keep indoors at room temperature. Water after planting and then sporadically until the first shoots appear. After that, water regularly. Plant indoors when the young plants are established, or outdoors when the temperatures are above 15°C (59°F).

Below: Turmeric contains the antioxident curcumin, which has anti-inflammatory properties.

HOW TO GROW THE CROP
Water regularly. Turmeric can be grown in large pots but will need feeding weekly; they must be moved indoors for winter.

WHEN THE CROP IS READY
The tubers are ready for harvesting after the foliage dies down.

STORING AND COOKING TIPS
Turmeric rhizomes are used fresh or dried in curries, stews, soups, as a drink flavouring, in pickles or as a food dye. They can be left in the soil until needed.

AT A GLANCE:

	mid-winter	late winter	early spring	mid-spring	late spring	early summer	mid-summer	late summer	early autumn	mid-autumn	late autumn	early winter
PLANT	▓	▓	▓									
HARVEST										▓	▓	

Planting Overview: Grow indoors or in a sheltered sunny place outdoors when temperatures reach above 15°C (59°F); water regularly; suitable for growing in containers; overwinter indoors in pots with minimal watering.

Lemon grass

Lemon grass (*Cymbopogon citratus*) is a large and attractive tender perennial. The highly aromatic, citrus-flavoured stem bases are used in Asian cooking.

WHAT YOU NEED

Lemon grass is best grown indoors or in a sheltered sunny spot outdoors in summer, and moved indoors for winter. Free-draining soil rich in organic matter is best.

SOWING AND PLANTING

Sow in early to mid spring in trays indoors; the seeds need 20°C (68°F) for successful germination. The growth of seedlings is slow. Wait to transplant them to individual pots when they are a good size. Plant out when danger of frost passes. It can also be propagated in spring by plant division.

Above: Lemon grass grows well in tropical conditions.

HOW TO GROW THE CROP

Lemon grass needs warmth and moisture to produce harvestable stems. It is good to grow in large containers, this way the plant can be moved indoors for overwintering. In containers, regular feeding and watering is needed during the summer. In winter, keep the plants on the dry side and above 5°C (41°F). Remove untidy foliage. If growing indoors, red spider mite, white fly and aphids can be a problem.

WHEN THE CROP IS READY

When the stem bases are as thick as a pencil, cut or pull the thickest stems from the outer parts of the plant base. Alternatively, dig out the plant, harvest as many suitable stems as possible, and plant the remaining part back in the ground or pot.

STORING AND COOKING TIPS

Store for a couple of weeks in the fridge, or freeze. Lemon grass stalks are used to flavour curries and stir-fries or to make citrus-flavoured tea.

AT A GLANCE:

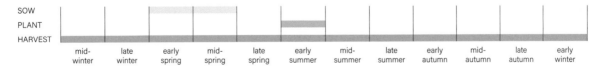

SOW											
PLANT											
HARVEST											
mid-winter	late winter	early spring	mid-spring	late spring	early summer	mid-summer	late summer	early autumn	mid-autumn	late autumn	early winter

Planting Overview: Lemon grass is a tender plant and needs to be overwintered indoors at temperatures above 5°C (41°F); it is good for growing in containers; if grown indoors, watch out for greenhouse pests; water regularly, feed pots weekly.

Herb fennel

Herb fennel (*Foeniculum vulgare*) is grown for its feathery leaves, flowers and seeds. It is a short-lived perennial commonly grown in flower borders as an ornamental herb, especially the highly decorative bronze fennel.

WHAT YOU NEED
Grow in full sun in free-draining soil.

SOWING AND PLANTING
Sow from mid spring to midsummer. Inside sow in modules to minimize root disturbance at planting, and thin to one seedling per module. Outside, direct sow into pots or into the ground. Drills should be 30cm (12in) apart and 1cm (1/2in) deep. Thin to 30cm (12in) spacing.

HOW TO GROW THE CROP
Water well when establishing, after which this plant is fairly drought-tolerant. Those in pots need more water and occasional feeds. Flowers can be removed to encourage more leaves, but they are attractive and good for wildlife. They may need staking as they can reach 1.5m (5ft) tall. Herb fennel dies back before winter and can then be mulched. Dead stems left standing over winter are a wildlife habitat. If seeds are left to ripen, they will self-seed. Young seedlings can be transplanted in spring.

WHEN THE CROP IS READY
The leaves and flowers can be harvested through the season. Regular picking encourages more leaves to grow. The seeds can be harvested by cutting and drying the seedheads in late summer.

STORING AND COOKING TIPS
All parts have an aniseed flavour and go well in fish dishes. The leaves and flowers should be eaten soon after harvesting. The seeds can be dried and stored in an airtight jar for several months.

AT A GLANCE:

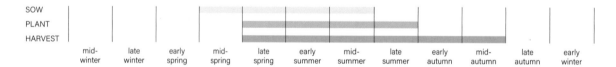

	SOW	PLANT	HARVEST

mid-winter · late winter · early spring · mid-spring · late spring · early summer · mid-summer · late summer · early autumn · mid-autumn · late autumn · early winter

Planting Overview: Try to minimize root disturbance when propagating; flowers are good for wildlife; pick regularly if you wish to encourage more leaves.

Varieties to Try: 'Purpureum' (bronze fennel, slightly hardier than green fennel, deep purple foliage).

Bronze fennel

Green fennel

Angelica

Needing a lot of space to grow, angelica (*Angelica archangelica*) is a beautiful hardy biennial from the carrot family. It makes a large architectural plant with yellow-green flowers and pink stems. All parts are edible.

WHAT YOU NEED
Grow in moist, free-draining soil in full sun or partial shade.

SOWING AND PLANTING
Sow fresh seeds direct in autumn or spring. If sown in spring, germination might be erratic. Leave the seeds uncovered as they need light to germinate. Alternatively, sow in trays in a cold frame and prick out when the first true leaves appear. Plant out 1m (3ft) apart when the seedling roots fill the pot.

HOW TO GROW THE CROP
Water in hot weather, using a surface mulch to keep the soil moist. Angelica will flower in its second year. It is a large plant and is not suitable for pots. It self-seeds easily, but as it looks like some toxic plants, make sure it is identified correctly if using this herb for culinary purposes.

WHEN THE CROP IS READY
Pick the leaves and stalks in spring or early summer when they are tender. Take care when harvesting as the plant can cause a skin irritation.

Above: The yellow-green flowers of angelica are very attractive to pollinating insects.

Collect the seedheads when they turn yellow and put in a paper bag to finish drying.

STORING AND COOKING TIPS
Fresh and sweet, liquorice-flavoured leaves and young stems are used in salads, baking or savoury dishes. The dried leaves are used for tea. Stems are candied and used for cake decorations or can be cooked with other fruit, adding sweetness to jams. The seeds and roots can be used to flavour liqueurs.

AT A GLANCE:

SOW											
PLANT											
HARVEST											
mid-winter	late winter	early spring	mid-spring	late spring	early summer	mid-summer	late summer	early autumn	mid-autumn	late autumn	early winter

Planting Overview: Keep soil around plants moist; sow annually for a continual supply; self-seeds readily; not suitable for pots; identify correctly before consuming.

Chervil

This short-lived herb (*Anthriscus cerefolium*) is best grown as an annual. Its delicate, pretty foliage has a light parsley flavour with a hint of aniseed. This plant is attractive, offering lacy foliage and white flowers in summer and autumn.

WHAT YOU NEED
Grow chervil in light shade in fertile, moisture-retentive soil.

SOWING AND PLANTING
Sow regularly to provide a continual harvest. Sow from early spring to early autumn. Outside, create drills 1cm (½in) deep and 25cm (10in) apart, thinning to 15–20cm (6–8in) after germination. Protect early sowings with fleece. Inside, sow in modules and then thin to one per module, planting out after the last frosts. Try to minimize root disturbance when transplanting.

HOW TO GROW THE CROP
Chervil often runs to seed, after which the leaves turn bitter. Providing plenty of moisture, especially to plants in pots, will delay this. If left to flower, chervil can self-seed prolifically. Autumn sowings can be overwintered in a greenhouse, or under a cloche outside.

WHEN THE CROP IS READY
First harvests can be as soon as two months after sowing, and overwintering plants can provide light harvests into spring. Harvest the youngest leaves using the cut-and-come-again method. The flowers and seeds are also edible.

STORING AND COOKING TIPS
Chervil seeds can be dried and stored but chervil leaves and flowers are best eaten fresh. Use them in soups and stews or as a pretty addition to salads or as a garnish.

AT A GLANCE:

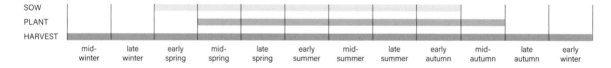

	SOW	PLANT	HARVEST

mid-winter · late winter · early spring · mid-spring · late spring · early summer · mid-summer · late summer · early autumn · mid-autumn · late autumn · early winter

Planting Overview: Repeat sowings provide a continual harvest of this herb; provide protection to overwintering plants; water plants well in order to delay flowering.

Varieties to Try: *Anthriscus var. crispum* (curly-leaved variety), *A. cerefolium* (species form) has flat leaves.

A. cerefolium

A. var. crispum

Lovage

This hardy perennial (*Levisticum officinale*) is a close relative of celery and is easy to grow. It provides a mild celery flavour with a hint of aniseed.

WHAT YOU NEED

Grow in light shade or full sun, in fertile, moisture-retentive soil.

SOWING AND PLANTING

Sow in spring or early summer. Inside, sow individually into modules, planting once decent roots have developed. Outside, sow seeds 1.5cm (5/8in) deep. Young plants can also be bought. Only a couple of plants are needed as this perennial reaches 1m (3ft) wide and 2m (6½ft) high, and lasts several years.

HOW TO GROW THE CROP

Water regularly until established, and then in hot, dry weather. This plant will grow in containers, which need lots of water, but it is more vigorous in the ground. Once flowering starts the leaves turn bitter. The flowers can be removed to encourage leaves or left to attract wildlife. They will self-seed. Cut back in late summer to stimulate young growth. Plants die back over winter, at which point they can be mulched.

WHEN THE CROP IS READY

Seed-sown lovage is harvestable the spring after sowing, but bought plants provide a light harvest in the first year. Pick young leaves regularly throughout the season. The flowers and seeds are also edible in summer and early autumn.

STORING AND COOKING TIPS

Add the leaves and stalks to soups and stews, using flowers and seeds as garnishes.

Below: Lovage is a leafy green herb similar to coriander and parsley.

AT A GLANCE:

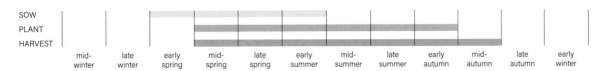

	mid-winter	late winter	early spring	mid-spring	late spring	early summer	mid-summer	late summer	early autumn	mid-autumn	late autumn	early winter
SOW												
PLANT												
HARVEST												

Planting Overview: Most easily established by buying young plants; water well initially; harvest the leaves regularly.

Oregano and marjoram

Oregano (*Origanum vulgare*) and marjoram (*O. majorana*) are from the same genus and grown in the same way. They are compact perennial herbs which add a slightly spicy flavour to dishes. Marjoram is usually milder in flavour.

WHAT YOU NEED
Grow in free-draining soil and full sun, in a sheltered location.

SOWING AND PLANTING
Young plants can be planted from late spring to early autumn. Alternatively, sow seed inside in spring and plant out once good roots have developed. Space at 20–30cm (8–12in). They can also be propagated by layering, dividing in spring or autumn, or softwood cuttings in summer.

Below: Oregano is a low-growing, pretty herb.

HOW TO GROW THE CROP
Once established, both herbs are drought-tolerant. They grow well in pots, which need regular watering, but ensure the plants do not sit in wet soil. Oregano grows in poor soil so should not need mulching, but containers benefit from a balanced feed after flowering. Clip plants in late spring to keep them compact. White or pink flowers are produced in summer, up to 30cm (12in) high. Cut back the stems once the flowers die back. Most varieties are hardy but some benefit from winter protection.

WHEN THE CROP IS READY
Picking leaves regularly through spring and summer will encourage more growth. Flavour is best before flowering. Light harvests are possible throughout the year, especially if plants are protected over winter. Plants grown from seed can take a year to become harvestable.

STORING AND COOKING TIPS
Marjoram leaves are best fresh and oregano dried. Add to pizza, tomato sauces, ragus and meat dishes. Flowers are also edible.

AT A GLANCE:

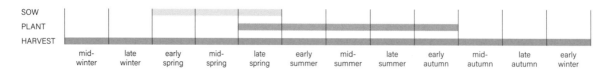

	mid-winter	late winter	early spring	mid-spring	late spring	early summer	mid-summer	late summer	early autumn	mid-autumn	late autumn	early winter
SOW			●	●	●							
PLANT					●	●	●	●	●			
HARVEST	●	●	●	●	●	●	●	●	●	●	●	●

Planting Overview: Both plants are drought-tolerant once established; clip back plants to keep them compact; oregano leaves are best dried before use.

Lemon verbena

This beautiful perennial shrubby herb (*Aloysia citriodora*) is cultivated for its fragrant leaves, which release a strong citrus aroma when touched. The delicate white flowers attract many insects in summer.

WHAT YOU NEED
Lemon verbena is not fully hardy in temperate climates and is best grown in a sheltered sunny spot in well-drained soil.

SOWING AND PLANTING
It is not easy to grow from seed. It can be propagated by softwood cuttings in early spring, but the easiest way is to purchase young plants. Plant out in a sheltered spot or in a container. One plant is usually enough for a sufficient supply of leaves. If more than one plant is grown, space at least 50cm (20in) apart.

HOW TO GROW THE CROP
This plant dislikes waterlogging and might not survive temperatures below –5°C (23°F), so grow it in containers that can be moved indoors for the winter. If it is grown outdoors, mulch the plant thickly before winter, as it will help to protect the roots from cold damage. The top of the plant might die in the winter but, if the roots are protected, it will regrow.

Above: Lemon verbena is a beautifully fragrant plant. The strong citrus scent fills the air when you brush past.

WHEN THE CROP IS READY
Harvest as needed throughout the season.

STORING AND COOKING TIPS
Leaves are used fresh or dried, adding lemon flavour to sweet or savoury dishes. It is also used to flavour oil, vinegar or sugar and is used in ice creams, cocktails and delicious teas.

AT A GLANCE:

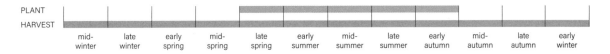

PLANT											
HARVEST											
mid-winter	late winter	early spring	mid-spring	late spring	early summer	mid-summer	late summer	early autumn	mid-autumn	late autumn	early winter

Planting Overview: Best grown from bought plants; protect from cold weather in winter; choose a warm, sheltered spot.

Mint

This perennial herb is easy to grow and comes in a wide range of varieties and flavours useful for sweet and savoury dishes alike. Its roots have a habit of spreading vigorously, so keep plants contained.

WHAT YOU NEED
Grow in full sun or light shade, in fertile, free-draining soil.

SOWING AND PLANTING
Mint can be bought as small plants, which are ideally planted in spring but can be planted through to mid autumn. Propagation is best done by division in spring or autumn because seed can be slow and unreliable. Softwood cuttings can also be taken in spring, and root cuttings in autumn or winter. These plants are vigorous and should be planted in pots to prevent them running through beds. Plant into pots at least 30cm (12in) in diameter. If desired, pots can be

sunk into the soil with the rims above the surface at 30–40cm (12–16in) spacing.

HOW TO GROW THE CROP
Mint will flower in summer. Flowering shoots can be removed to encourage more leafy growth, or left to attract wildlife. Cut back after flowering, or if the leaves are too badly affected by powdery mildew, and a second flush of young growth will appear at the back end of the season. Mint will die back to the ground in winter, at which point it can be mulched, reshooting in spring.

Water plants well, but avoid waterlogging. Those in pots will benefit from a fortnightly balanced feed throughout the growing season. Plants benefit from repotting every couple of years. When repotting, use the 'Pac-Man' method which involves cutting the rootball nearly in two then folding it back on itself so the youngest and most vigorous growth that was on the outside of the container is now in the centre. Alternatively, simply divide the plant in two and repot into two separate containers. A pruning saw can be used to cut through the mint (wear gloves); it is a vigorous plant and should quickly recover. Try to avoid growing different varieties too close together as this can impair their individual flavours.

WHEN THE CROP IS READY
Pick foliage from mid spring to mid autumn. Use secateurs to cut off whole shoots to keep the plant compact and encourage more to be

Left: Mint is best propagated by dividing plants or making softwood cuttings in spring.

produced. If potted mints are brought inside over winter, then light harvests can carry on all year.

STORING AND COOKING TIPS
The youngest growth has the strongest flavour. Fresh mint leaves make a refreshing herbal tea or can be added to a range of desserts and savoury dishes, including sauces, pesto and salads. Leaves can be frozen in ice cubes to add to drinks throughout the year. The flowers are also edible.

Right: Growing mint in pots is a good way to keep it contained.

AT A GLANCE:

PLANT												
HARVEST												
	mid-winter	late winter	early spring	mid-spring	late spring	early summer	mid-summer	late summer	early autumn	mid-autumn	late autumn	early winter

Planting Overview: Best grown in containers to control the spread; pick shoots regularly to encourage more growth; repot every few years to renew vigour.

Varieties to Try: *Mentha* 'Chocolate Peppermint' (dark green leaves tinged red, red stems, mint-chocolate scent), *M.* × *piperita* 'Lime' (citrus scent and flavour, compact to 40cm/16in tall), *M. spicata* (spearmint, classic bright green leaves), *M. spicata* 'Moroccan' (one of the best varieties for mint tea), *M. suaveolens* 'Variegata' (pineapple mint, variegated foliage, fruity flavour).

M. spicata

M. × *piperita* 'Lime'

M. spicata 'Moroccan'

M. suaveolens 'Variegata'

Szechuan pepper

There are two varieties of Szechuan pepper: Chinese (*Zanthoxylum simulans*) and Japanese (*Z. piperitum*). Both are hardy deciduous shrubs or small trees with attractive leaves and thorny branches. The plants are easy to grow and produce seeds covered with red spicy skin, used as a pepper substitute.

WHAT YOU NEED
Grow in rich, well-drained soil in sun, partial or full shade.

SOWING AND PLANTING
Szechuan pepper can be propagated by seed or semi-ripe cuttings. However, it is easiest to buy young plants. Plant out in autumn or spring.

Below: Szechuan pepper shrubs bear attractive red berries and are easy to grow.

HOW TO GROW THE CROP
Water well and mulch around the plant base to keep moisture in the soil. If needed, prune when the plant is dormant. It can be grown in large pots, but regular feed and watering is required. As some species of Szechuan pepper are not self-fertile, grow two or more plants for reliable seed production.

WHEN THE CROP IS READY
Harvest in the autumn when the seeds' pink casings start to open. Dry for a few days indoors, until the casings start peeling off. Discard the seeds and save the aromatic shells.

STORING AND COOKING TIPS
Store the seedcases in an airtight container in a dark place until they are needed. Mix with salt to season meat and other savoury dishes. Szechuan pepper is one of the key ingredients in Chinese five spice. For the best aroma, toast the shells before use. They combine a citrusy flavour with a spicy, peppery numbing effect.

AT A GLANCE:

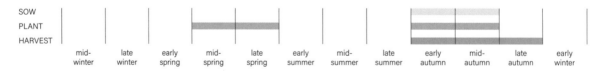

SOW
PLANT
HARVEST

mid-winter | late winter | early spring | mid-spring | late spring | early summer | mid-summer | late summer | early autumn | mid-autumn | late autumn | early winter

Planting Overview: Plant out in spring; feed and mulch during the growing season; keep the roots moist during dry periods; can also be grown in a large container, kept pruned to size.

Cumin

Cumin is a popular spice in Indian cuisine. This tender annual plant from the carrot family has attractive summer flowers that are good for pollinators.

WHAT YOU NEED

In temperate climates, cumin is best grown under cover, but will survive in a sheltered sunny position, or in pots on a warm patio. Cumin prefers free-draining soil and sporadic watering.

SOWING AND PLANTING

To produce ripe seeds, the plant needs a long growing season. To achieve this, sow indoors from early to late spring in modules and plant out after the last frost. Alternatively, sow directly in the ground in a greenhouse or polytunnel. For faster germination, soak the seeds in water overnight before sowing. Cumin dislikes root disturbance, so sowing direct is a better option. Thin to, or plant, 20cm (8in) apart.

HOW TO GROW THE CROP

It is a drought-tolerant plant, so water only when necessary. Ideal for container growing. Seeds can be started directly in pots indoors and moved out when the weather warms up.

WHEN THE CROP IS READY

Collect the seedheads as they turn brown and place them in a paper bag; the seeds will drop from the seedheads when dry.

Above: Cumin is a key ingredient in chilli and curry powders. You can grow your own in a pot on a sunny windowsill.

STORING AND COOKING TIPS

Clean the dried seeds from the chaff and store in an airtight container. Use whole, crushed or ground in curries, chutneys, with meat, or to add an earthy flavour to roasted vegetables, rice or bean dishes. Roast the seeds for a more intense flavour. Edible leaves are used as an aromatic addition to salads.

AT A GLANCE:

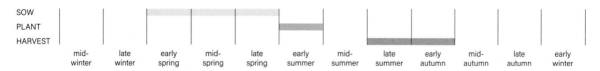

	SOW	PLANT	HARVEST
mid-winter			
late winter			
early spring			
mid-spring			
late spring			
early summer			
mid-summer			
late summer			
early autumn			
mid-autumn			
late autumn			
early winter			

Planting Overview: Best grown under cover and sown directly; ideal for pots; plant out after last frost; needs a long season to produce ripe seeds; water only when needed.

Basil

Basil is a cold-sensitive herb that is treated as an annual in temperate climates. It is cultivated for its green or red aromatic leaves and has a long history of culinary use. The many types of basil have subtle variations in flavour: sweet and Genovese types are used particularly in Italian cuisine, lemon and Thai basil are used in Thai and Vietnamese cooking, while holy basil or tulsi is a sacred plant in the Hindu tradition and used for religious purposes.

WHAT YOU NEED

Basil requires a warm and sunny sheltered spot with freely draining soil. It can be grown indoors or out.

SOWING AND PLANTING

Sow from early spring indoors in modules or trays. Alternatively, sow direct outdoors in late spring to early summer when the temperatures stay above 15°C (59°F). Thin seedlings to 20–30cm (8–12in) apart. If started in trays, transplant seedlings when the first true leaves appear into individual pots. Do not overwater as the seedlings are susceptible to damping off. When young plants establish, and roots fill the modules or pots, plant 20–30cm (8–12in) apart indoors, or outdoors when air temperatures are reliably above 15°C (59°F).

HOW TO GROW THE CROP

Basil is a heat-loving plant and will grow indoors or outdoors in a warm and sheltered sunny spot. It is a compact plant, suitable for growing in containers and will happily grow on windowsills. Water regularly, in the morning if possible, as basil dislikes wet cold roots overnight. Sow every few weeks to assure a continual harvest of fresh leaves. Basil grows well with other plants such as tomatoes, aubergines and peppers.

Below left: Sow the basil seeds in trays or modules in the spring, indoors. They will germinate in a few days.

Below: When the seedlings have a few true leaves, repot into bigger containers, or plant outside when the danger of frost has passed.

WHEN THE CROP IS READY

To harvest basil, cut the tips of the shoots to encourage new growth and further harvest. Keep harvesting foliage throughout the season. Remove any flowering shoots to prolong the leaf harvest. The leaf flavour will begin to deteriorate after plants start blooming.

STORING AND COOKING TIPS

Basil is good fresh in salads, or with mozzarella and tomatoes just tossed in olive oil. It is a traditional herb in Italian cuisine and is an essential ingredient in traditional pesto. It is also used in pasta, pizza, baking and even ice creams. In Thai and Indian cooking, basil is used in curries and dhals. Basil leaves can be stored in the fridge, freezer, or dried and stored in an airtight container. Dried leaves steeped in hot water make delicious tea.

Right: Fresh basil has the best flavour. If you have a glut of basil leaves, dry or freeze them for future use.

AT A GLANCE:

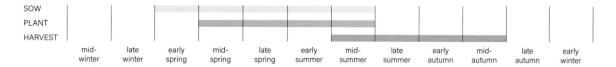

SOW												
PLANT												
HARVEST												
mid-winter	late winter	early spring	mid-spring	late spring	early summer	mid-summer	late summer	early autumn	mid-autumn	late autumn	early winter

Planting Overview: Sow from early spring; plant out only during warm weather; water well; suitable for pots and as an underplanting for tomatoes.

Varieties to Try: *Ocimum* × *africanum* 'Lime' (small, citrus-flavoured leaves), *O. basilicum* 'Lettuce Leaf' (strong growth with large green leaves, good for pesto), *O. b. purpurascens* 'Purple Ruffles' (purple leaves with good flavour), *O. basilicum* 'Thai Sita' (Thai basil, attractive green-purple growth with pungent aniseed flavour), *O. minimum* 'Minette' (Greek type, small leaves, bushy growth with good flavour).

'Lettuce Leaf'

'Purple Ruffles'

Parsley

This nutritious biennial herb (*Petroselinum crispum*) is a classic of European cuisine and produces either curly or flat leaves. Curly-leaved varieties have a milder flavour than those with flat leaves.

WHAT YOU NEED

Grow in full sun or partial shade, in fertile, well-drained soil.

SOWING AND PLANTING

Parsley is biennial but is usually grown as an annual. Sow seed in spring to early summer, or in early autumn. It is slow to germinate. Outside, sow 1cm (½in) deep in drills 15cm (6in) apart and thin to 15cm (6in). Inside, start in modules and plant out once the seedlings have decent roots. Parsley plants can also be bought.

HOW TO GROW THE CROP

Water regularly, especially crops in containers, which will need occasional feeding. Remove any yellowing leaves. Parsley is hardy over winter but the foliage can die down. For winter harvests, bring pots inside or grow in a greenhouse or cold frame. The leaves are not worth harvesting once flowering begins the following spring, but flowers can be left. Parsley is occasionally affected by carrot root fly.

Below: Pot on young parsley plants once they have a decent root system.

Right: Parsley comes in both flat-leaved and curly-leaved forms.

WHEN THE CROP IS READY

Spring sowings provide harvests throughout the summer and autumn. Baby leaves can be harvested earlier; autumn sowings provide a light harvest through winter. Regularly picking individual leaves encourages more growth.

STORING AND COOKING TIPS

The leaves are best used fresh in salads, pasta dishes, omelettes, sauces, stocks and casseroles. Leaves can also be frozen into ice cubes or dried, although these have less flavour. The flowers are also edible.

Right: While curly-leaved parsley has a milder flavour than the flat-leaved variety, it is highly decorative both in pots and as a garnish.

AT A GLANCE:

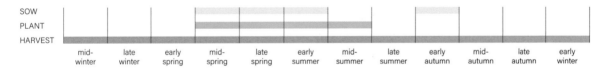

SOW											
PLANT											
HARVEST											
mid-winter	late winter	early spring	mid-spring	late spring	early summer	mid-summer	late summer	early autumn	mid-autumn	late autumn	early winter

Planting Overview: Biennial usually grown as an annual; provide plenty of water; regular harvests will encourage more leaves to be produced.

Varieties to Try: 'Moss Curled' AGM (curly, dark green leaves), 'Bravour' AGM (curly, highly productive), var. *neapolitanum* (also sold as 'Giant of Italy', flat-leaved, great flavour, large leaves), 'French' (flat-leaved, freezes well).

'Moss Curled' AGM

P. var. *neapolitanum*

Rosemary

This evergreen shrub grows well in poor soils. It can reach 1.5m (5ft) in height but is kept smaller with regular trimming or an annual trim after flowering or in early spring. Attractive blue, pink or white flowers appear in early summer.

WHAT YOU NEED
Grow in full sun and in light, free-draining soil.

SOWING AND PLANTING
This plant is generally bought but can be propagated from semi-ripe cuttings in late summer or heel cuttings in spring. Layering is also possible. Seed can be started inside in spring but is slow to germinate and takes several years to be harvestable. Plant in spring through to early autumn, spacing at least 45cm (18in) apart.

Below: Rosemary is an indispensable kitchen herb.

HOW TO GROW THE CROP
Water well initially; rosemary is fairly drought-tolerant so only needs watering in prolonged dry weather once established. Ensure plants do not sit wet. Rosemary grows well in containers, which need regular watering. Repot every few years, and mulch those in the ground over winter, leaving a gap around the base of the stem. Rosemary is generally hardy but may need protection in harsh winters. Trim after flowering, being careful not to cut back into old wood. Even with regular trimming, plants turn woody and can be replaced after several years to keep them fresh and compact. Rosemary beetle may be a problem and should be picked off by hand.

WHEN THE CROP IS READY
Harvest the foliage as needed all year, although new growth has the best flavour.

STORING AND COOKING TIPS
Rosemary sprigs can be used fresh or dried. Add to stews, marinades, pasta dishes, roast meats and as a topping on breads.

AT A GLANCE:

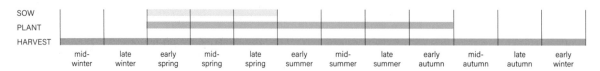

	SOW	PLANT	HARVEST

mid-winter · late winter · early spring · mid-spring · late spring · early summer · mid-summer · late summer · early autumn · mid-autumn · late autumn · early winter

Planting Overview: Propagate from cuttings; water well until established; prune annually to maintain the shape of the plant; young growth has the best flavour.

Bay

This attractive large evergreen shrub has aromatic leaves that are harvestable all year. Bay trees need space, but plants can be kept compact by regular trimming.

WHAT YOU NEED

Grow in full or part sun, in a warm, sheltered location with free-draining soil.

SOWING AND PLANTING

Bay can be bought as a small plant, or as topiary. Plant in spring to early summer: planting later means the plant can struggle over winter. To propagate, take softwood cuttings in early summer or semi-ripe cuttings in late summer. Layering is also possible. Bay seeds are tricky to grow, and bay is dioecious, meaning plants are male or female and one of each is needed for seed production.

HOW TO GROW THE CROP

Water regularly for the first year and then again in dry spells. This plant grows well in large containers, which need frequent watering in summer and occasional feeds. Ensure the plant does not become waterlogged. Regular clipping from late spring through summer will control the size of the plant, otherwise it can reach 7m (23ft) tall. Repot containers every couple of years, and mulch others over winter. This plant is generally hardy but may benefit from fleece over winter. Move containers into a greenhouse if necessary.

Above: Just one or two bay leaves in a soup or stew can really enhance its flavour.

WHEN THE CROP IS READY

Harvest leaves as needed throughout the year.

STORING AND COOKING TIPS

The leaves infuse flavour into soups, sauces and stews as well as sweet dishes. Remove leaves before serving. Fresh leaves are slightly bitter so they are more commonly used dried.

AT A GLANCE:

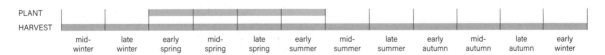

PLANT											
HARVEST											
mid-winter	late winter	early spring	mid-spring	late spring	early summer	mid-summer	late summer	early autumn	mid-autumn	late autumn	early winter

Planting Overview: An evergreen that can be harvested all year; water plants well for their first year; try clipping into shapes for added ornamental value.

Sage

This handsome evergreen shrubby herb (*Salvia officinalis*) is in the same genus as ornamental salvias. As well as silver-green common sage, there are purple-leaved and variegated varieties available.

WHAT YOU NEED

Grow in a sheltered location in full sun with free-draining soil.

SOWING AND PLANTING

Seed is generally only available for common sage. Sow inside in spring and keep warm until germination, planting out after the risk of frost. Young plants can be bought, and sage can be propagated through layering, root and softwood cuttings. Ideally plant in spring, although it can be planted until autumn, avoiding hot, dry spells. Leave around 50–60cm (20–24in) between plants.

HOW TO GROW THE CROP

Water well after planting, but once established this plant is drought-tolerant. Containers should be kept slightly moist. Ensure this plant does not get waterlogged. After summer flowering, cut plants back by a third, and then cut back hard in spring to promote bushy growth, but do not cut into old growth. Plants often get straggly after several years and are best replaced. This plant is winter hardy, but winter protection improves the quality of winter harvests. Mulch in the spring.

WHEN THE CROP IS READY

Pick sprigs of leaves all year; young leaves from late spring through summer have the best flavour.

STORING AND COOKING TIPS

Peppery sage leaves are useful in stuffings, sauces, pasta dishes and marinades. They are best fresh but can be dried or frozen in ice cubes.

AT A GLANCE:

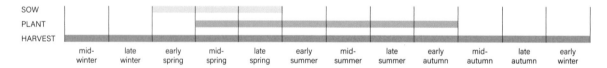

| | SOW | PLANT | HARVEST |

| mid-winter | late winter | early spring | mid-spring | late spring | early summer | mid-summer | late summer | early autumn | mid-autumn | late autumn | early winter |

Planting Overview: Drought-tolerant once established; prune hard in spring to keep plants compact; young leaves produced in the growing season have the best flavour.

Varieties to Try: 'Purpurascens' (purple young foliage), 'Purpurascens Variegata' (purple-flushed cream-edged foliage).

'Purpurascens'

'Purpurascens Variegata'

Thyme

This woody evergreen shrub is compact with varieties offering a range of colours and flavours. White, pink or purple flowers appear in late spring and early summer and attract beneficial insects.

WHAT YOU NEED
Grow in full sun in free-draining soil.

SOWING AND PLANTING
Young plants can be bought to plant from late spring to early autumn. Seeds are sown inside in spring and planted out once well-rooted. Space at 30cm (12in) intervals. Cuttings can be taken in late spring or early summer, or low-growing stems can be layered.

HOW TO GROW THE CROP
Water well until established, after which this crop is mostly drought-tolerant. Thyme grows well in containers, although it will need more water. Ensure plants do not become waterlogged. Trim back after flowering, but do not cut into old wood. This prevents plants becoming too straggly, although they still need replacing every few years to keep them at their best. The ultimate height ranges from groundcover up to 30cm (12in). Most varieties are winter hardy although a few benefit from winter protection.

WHEN THE CROP IS READY
Pick as needed throughout the year; new growth has the best flavour. Regular harvesting encourages more growth. Seed-grown thyme can take a year to be harvestable.

STORING AND COOKING TIPS
The leaves can be used fresh or dried, and the flowers are also edible. Try adding to stews and sauces, herb breads, marinades and salads.

AT A GLANCE:

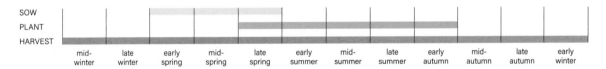

	mid-winter	late winter	early spring	mid-spring	late spring	early summer	mid-summer	late summer	early autumn	mid-autumn	late autumn	early winter
SOW												
PLANT												
HARVEST												

Planting Overview: Ensure this plant does not sit wet; harvest leaves and flowers regularly; useful groundcover plant.

Varieties to Try: 'Silver Queen' (pink flowers, variegated foliage, lemon scent), 'Jekka' (early light pink flowers, excellent taste), Coccineus Group (pink flowers, groundcover), 'Snowdrift' (white flowers, groundcover).

'Jekka'

'Silver Queen'

Ginger

Ginger (*Zingiber officinale*) is a tropical perennial used globally for its aromatic, spicy rhizomes which are used either fresh or dried and powdered. It can be a great family project to grow ginger at home to see how the root is produced. The plant grows up to 1.2m (4ft).

WHAT YOU NEED

Ginger needs warmth, moisture and humidity so is best grown indoors in a sunny spot, such as a conservatory, or in a greenhouse or polytunnel. In summer, ginger plants can be placed outside in a sheltered sunny spot. It thrives in moist, free-draining soil.

SOWING AND PLANTING

Ginger plants or rhizomes can be purchased from reliable suppliers. Supermarket-bought organic rhizomes can also be used for propagation. Use organic rhizomes as these are not sprayed with growth inhibitors and will sprout easily. Plant good-sized, healthy rhizomes about 1–2cm (½–1in) deep in a pot with free-draining compost. For faster establishment, start the rhizomes in a propagator with bottom heat. Move to a bigger container when the plant fills the pot.

HOW TO GROW THE CROP

Keep the plants warm, the compost moist and the air around the plants humid. Ginger will go dormant if temperatures fall below 10°C (50°F) and will not survive frozen soil. Move the plants indoors for the winter. Ideal in containers, as it makes moving plants easier.

WHEN THE CROP IS READY

Harvest 8–10 months after planting, when the leaves die down. Dig the whole plant out, break the rhizomes off, then harvest some and plant some for next season's harvest. If the plant does not establish well, harvest in the second year.

Left: Plant ginger rhizomes just below the soil surface. If grown in containers, the tender ginger plants are easily moved indoors for winter.

Right: If the plants are slow to establish, do not harvest the ginger rhizomes in the first year after planting.

JAPANESE GINGER

Japanese ginger or Myoga (*Zingiber mioga*) is a close relative to true ginger. This attractive hardy perennial is easy to grow and adds an exotic feel to any garden. The variegated varieties such as 'Dancing Crane' or 'Silver Arrow' are particularly ornamental, but slightly less hardy. Myoga is cultivated for its edible flower buds and young shoots and is a popular crop in Japan and Korea. The flower buds and young shoots can be pickled, used raw as garnish, in stir-fries, or made into tempura.

Above: To really thrive, ginger needs tropical conditions.

STORING AND COOKING TIPS

Store ginger in the fridge for a few weeks or freeze for a few months. Freeze rhizomes whole, or peel and cut into slices for easier use. Dry thinly sliced rhizomes on sunny windowsills or in the oven at a low temperature. Dried slices can be powdered or stored whole in airtight containers. Home-dried ginger is more aromatic than anything you can buy. Peeled and cooked rhizomes can be stored in sugar syrup in jars or candied to use in baking, cooking or as a tea. It can also be made into smoothies, syrups and cordials.

Ginger has many medicinal properties – it aids digestion, reduces the symptoms of nausea, and is said to reduce inflammation and fight colds and flu.

AT A GLANCE:

PLANT											
HARVEST											
mid-winter	late winter	early spring	mid-spring	late spring	early summer	mid-summer	late summer	early autumn	mid-autumn	late autumn	early winter

Planting Overview: Propagate by rhizomes; keep plant indoors or out in a warm, humid place, in full sun or partial shade; move indoors for the winter as it will not survive in frozen soil; repot when needed.

Horseradish

Horseradish is a hardy perennial plant from the cabbage family, which resembles common dock. It is mainly cultivated for its spicy root, well known for its ability to clear sinuses.

WHAT YOU NEED
Grow in sun or partial shade in any soil.

SOWING AND PLANTING
Buy young plants or root pieces from reliable suppliers. Plant in spring. Push the root sections vertically into a large pot filled with compost to 5cm (2in) below the surface. Cover the root with compost and water well. Plant three root pieces or one young plant in a 40–50cm (16–20in) diameter pot, or plant in the ground 30cm (12in) apart. Choose the planting position carefully as the plants are persistent once established.

HOW TO GROW THE CROP
Best to grow in pots or raised beds to contain the plant's spreading habit. If grown in pots, water regularly. Mulch in spring. Feed potted plants with a balanced organic fertiliser every four weeks during the growing season.

WHEN THE CROP IS READY
Harvest in autumn or winter; it is best after frost for a more intense flavour. Dig the whole plant out and collect the good-sized roots, then replant at least half of the plant.

STORING AND COOKING TIPS
Store roots in the fridge or a dark cool frost-free place for a couple of months. Use grated with mayonnaise to make horseradish sauce, add to coleslaws and mustards for extra kick, or cook with meat to add a spicy flavour. Horseradish is also used as a wasabi substitute. Leaves are edible and used cooked or raw.

Left: These harvested horseradish roots are ready to use. They can be replanted if more plants are needed.

AT A GLANCE:

PLANT											
HARVEST											
mid-winter	late winter	early spring	mid-spring	late spring	early summer	mid-summer	late summer	early autumn	mid-autumn	late autumn	early winter

Planting Overview: Low maintenance; best grown in pots or in raised beds to contain its spread; if grown in pots, water regularly and feed occasionally.

Black caraway

Also known as black cumin or nigella, *Nigella sativa* is an edible relative of the well-loved garden flower love-in-a-mist. This annual plant, growing up to 40cm (16in) tall, has a long history of use in cooking and medicine. The seeds of black caraway were found in the tomb of the Egyptian pharaoh Tutankhamun. They are used as a spice in a variety of foods and medicinally.

WHAT YOU NEED

Grow the crop in full sun or partial shade in well-drained soil.

SOWING AND PLANTING

Surface-sow seeds directly in the autumn or from early spring. Nigella plants are moderately frost-tolerant, but if sown in the autumn, cover with fleece if hard frost is forecast. Thin the seedlings to 20cm (8in) apart.

HOW TO GROW THE CROP

Black caraway has a relatively short flowering time. Resow a couple more times during the season to ensure a continual supply of seeds. Plants also readily self-seed.

WHEN THE CROP IS READY

Cut stems when the seedpods start to dry and hang upside down in a paper bag. As the seeds finish drying, they will drop into the bag. Separate them from the plant debris.

STORING AND COOKING TIPS

Cleaned seeds are stored in airtight containers in a dark place. The seeds have a spicy fennel aroma and add a peppery nutmeg flavour to food. They are used to season curries, breads and pickles and are popular in Middle Eastern cuisine.

Below: Nigella seedheads are ready to harvest once dry, with their colour changing from green as they dessicate.

AT A GLANCE:

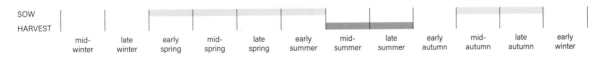

SOW												
HARVEST												
mid-winter	late winter	early spring	mid-spring	late spring	early summer	mid-summer	late summer	early autumn	mid-autumn	late autumn	early winter	

Planting Overview: Best to sow direct; protect from hard frost with horticultural fleece; sow in succession to ensure a continual supply of seeds; self-seeds readily.

Fenugreek

Fenugreek (*Trigonella foenum-graecum*) is a tender annual herb native to the Mediterranean and grown for its aromatic seeds and leaves. The large-leaved type with white flowers is more common, but the small-leaved type, with yellow flowers, is worth seeking out as it can be grown as a cut-and-come-again crop.

WHAT YOU NEED
Grow in a sunny spot in free-draining soil.

SOWING AND PLANTING
Sow directly in late spring in shallow drills after the last frost. Do not move the plants as fenugreek dislikes root disturbance. Thin the seedlings to 15cm (6in) apart.

Below: Fenugreek has been used for thousands of years as a medicine, and adds a pungent nutty flavour to food.

HOW TO GROW THE CROP
Water in hot spells. It is easy to grow in pots. If growing for seeds, pinch the tip of the main stem to make the plants bushier. Sow successively to have a continual supply of leaves and seeds. Fenugreek is also used as a green manure.

WHEN THE CROP IS READY
For the best flavour, harvest the leaves before plants start flowering. Collect the dry seedpods when they change colour to yellow. Finish drying them indoors; the pods will start opening when fully dried. Remove the seeds from the pods and store in an airtight container.

STORING AND COOKING TIPS
Use leaves fresh. Alternatively, freeze or dry for later use. Mild-flavoured fresh leaves are used like spinach in curries or potato dishes. Dried leaves are more aromatic. Seeds are a key ingredient in curry powders and are used frequently in Asian cooking. Fenugreek sprouts are a nutritious addition to salads.

AT A GLANCE:

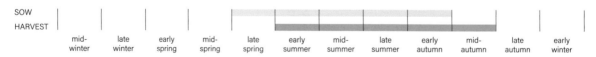

SOW												
HARVEST												
mid-winter	late winter	early spring	mid-spring	late spring	early summer	mid-summer	late summer	early autumn	mid-autumn	late autumn	early winter

Planting Overview: Avoid overwatering; sow directly as plants do not like root disturbance; sow in succession; suitable for growing in pots; also useful as a green manure (see p19).

Chamomile

This aromatic plant works well in wildlife gardens. Roman chamomile (*Chamaemelum nobile*) is perennial with finely divided leaves, while German chamomile (*Matricaria recutita*) is annual with a more upright form.

WHAT YOU NEED
Grow in full sun in free-draining soil.

SOWING AND PLANTING
Sow in mid to late spring, or purchase plants in spring and summer. Named varieties are only available as plants. Chamomile needs light to germinate, so surface-sow outside. Inside, sow into modules, cover lightly with compost or vermiculite, thin to one seedling after germination, then transplant outside in late spring or early summer. Space plants 15–30cm (6–12in) apart.

Above: A pretty garden plant, chamomile is typically used to make herbal tea.

HOW TO GROW THE CROP
This plant is hardy and grows well in containers. Water well until established. Afterwards, try not to let the plants dry out, but ensure they are not waterlogged. Clip back leggy plants, often several times through the season. Both Roman and German chamomile self-seed and the seedlings can be transplanted in late spring or early summer. Named varieties can be divided in autumn or spring. Chamomile likes poor soil so does not need mulching or feeding.

WHEN THE CROP IS READY
Plants flower 10–12 weeks after sowing. Harvest newly opened flowers through the summer. Regular harvests encourage more flowers.

STORING AND COOKING TIPS
Use fresh flowers to make herbal tea. Alternatively, dry flowers by spreading them out and placing somewhere warm, dry and out of direct sun for 1–2 weeks. Store in an airtight jar.

AT A GLANCE:

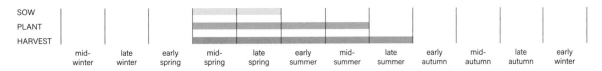

	mid-winter	late winter	early spring	mid-spring	late spring	early summer	mid-summer	late summer	early autumn	mid-autumn	late autumn	early winter
SOW												
PLANT												
HARVEST												

Planting Overview: Named varieties cannot be grown from seed; ensure the plants are not waterlogged over winter; pick flowers regularly to encourage more.

Lavender

This perennial Mediterranean herb is loved by wildlife. The flowers attract insects and the spent flowerheads provide seed for birds. There are many varieties and species available with different growth habits. Some are less hardy to frost than others.

WHAT YOU NEED
Grow in full sun in free-draining soil. Grows well on moderately fertile soil. Ensure the site does not sit wet over winter.

SOWING AND PLANTING
Lavender plants are best bought small. Avoid imported plants as lavender is a high-risk host for the *Xylella* bacterium. Plant in mid to late spring (although they can be planted through to early autumn), spacing at around 45cm (18in).

In heavy soil, plant on a ridge or mound. Propagate via softwood, semi-ripe or hardwood cuttings. Seed can be collected in late summer and sown in spring but plants do not come true to type.

HOW TO GROW THE CROP
Lavender is drought-tolerant, but water well until established. Those in pots need more water and occasional feeds. Prune after flowering in late summer, but do not cut back into old wood. Clip again in early to mid spring. Lavender generally

Below: The simplest way to acquire lavender is to buy plants from a nursery.

Right: Lavender is a must-have herb, and one plant is never enough.

need replacing after several years to keep them at their best. English lavenders are usually hardy but other lavenders, including French, are best moved somewhere frost-free over winter. Remove rosemary beetle when seen to protect your plants.

WHEN THE CROP IS READY

Flowers for cooking are picked just before opening and the buds dried before use.

STORING AND COOKING TIPS

Store dried buds in an airtight container. Lavender flowers are widely used in marinades and baking and are useful as garnishes.

Above: Trim lavender flowerheads and bunch them up for drying – they have many uses.

AT A GLANCE:

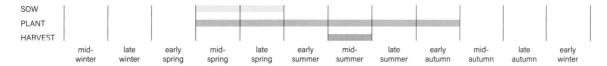

SOW											
PLANT											
HARVEST											
	mid-winter	late winter	early spring	mid-spring	late spring	early summer	mid-summer	late summer	early autumn	mid-autumn	late autumn	early winter

Planting Overview: Ensure plants do not sit wet; flowers are highly attractive to wildlife; protect French lavenders over winter.

Varieties to Try: 'Hidcote' (classic English lavender, purple flowers), 'Olympia' (strongly scented, later flowering than other varieties), 'Arctic Snow' (reliable plant, white flowers), 'Ballerina' (hybrid with French parentage, purple flowers with white bracts).

'Arctic Snow'

'Ballerina'

'Hidcote'

'Olympia'

CHAPTER 9

SAVING AND STORING

Storing and preserving

The food store is very much the key to having year-round veg. There will be lean times, particularly between late winter and mid spring, but at other times you will have gluts when you cannot keep on top of a crop. Many ripe crops can be stored fresh out of the ground, whereas others are better preserved.

STORING

Leeks and parsnips are two of those crops that are best left in the ground to harvest as needed. Others are better harvested and then put away for later use, including winter squash and earthy crops such as celeriac, swede, carrots, beetroot and potatoes, as well as onions and garlic.

When storing crops out of the ground, it is important to first check the produce for damage. Any blemishes can act as entry points for rot, which can then spread to the others in store. Damaged crops will only store for a short while and must always be eaten first. Check the whole store regularly in case rot appears.

Leave winter squash out in the sun to cure (harden the skin) and then store them in a cool location. Other crops do not need curing, but ensure they are dry before storage and brush off some of the soil. Onions and garlic benefit from a few weeks of drying. They can then be packed into breathable hessian sacks and stored somewhere cool, dark and free from frost and rodents to use as needed. The leaves of onions or garlic can also be woven together to make plaits for hanging. The length of storage time will vary between crops and varieties; some produce may go a little soft in storage but remain perfectly good to eat.

PRESERVING

There are many different types of preserves that can be made. While jam is more commonly associated with fruit, many vegetables are also quite sweet and suitable for processing this way, including carrots and beetroot. Mint jelly is more traditional, and pepper jelly also works well. Meanwhile, carrot or runner bean chutneys are worth experimenting with, alongside the more familiar caramelized onion and green tomato chutneys. Some of your courgette glut can also go into making a pickle. There are so many options out there to experiment with, allowing you to experience a whole range of homegrown flavours.

Left: Winter squashes store well in a cool, dry place as long as their skin has been cured in the sun.

Right: Root veg such as carrots and parsnips can be stored in clamps, made by piling soil over the roots to prevent them from drying out.

Dealing with gluts

When a crop is yielding so prolifically that you are struggling to process and deal with what is being produced, you have a glut. This is typical with summer crops, such as beans and courgettes. It is a better problem to have than crops that are not producing adequately, but it still helps to be aware of a few simple steps to stop becoming overwhelmed or to prevent food from going to waste.

AVOIDING GLUTS

The best way to deal with gluts is to avoid them through attention to detail when sowing and planting your crops. Many crops, including lettuce and radish, are best sown in small amounts at multiple points throughout the season. This successional sowing means that the harvests will come in stages, a row of lettuce at a time, in a manageable quantity, instead of loads in one go.

Other crops are not so suitable for successional sowing, either because they are frost-tender so cannot be sown early or late in the season, or because a single plant will crop successionally. Courgettes are the main example of this, but this also applies to climbing beans and fruiting crops such as tomatoes. In these cases, to avoid gluts you need to think carefully about how many plants you will need. If you are going to be able to cope with lots of produce then you may want several plants,

otherwise restraining yourself to just one or two courgette plants is advisable.

Gluts can also be avoided through regular harvesting. Many crops, such as beetroot and courgettes, can be harvested either when young or when they get larger. Picking smaller crops regularly will help to ensure that they never get too large or overwhelming.

PROCESSING A GLUT

However carefully you plan, gluts will occur at some point. When this happens, you will often find friends, neighbours and colleagues are happy to take some produce off your hands.

Gluts can also be preserved or stored for later use. There are several different techniques for achieving this outlined in this chapter. Perhaps try pickling your courgettes, turning your tomatoes into sauce and freezing it, making lettuce soup, or storing your winter squashes for use over the coming months. Many crops can also be made into preserves, such as runner bean chutney.

As a last resort, you can compost any gluts. Home-made compost is a wonderful resource for returning nutrients to the garden. You may not be eating the produce, but it has not gone to waste and the nutrition held within it will help to produce your future harvests.

Left: Avoid courgette gluts by thinking about how many plants you realistically need to grow.

Right: Runner bean gluts are also common: slicing and then freezing them is an option.

Seed saving

If you have never saved your own vegetable seeds, then you should certainly try. It provides a free source of seed and allows you to keep growing varieties that are performing well for you or might be difficult to source. Be aware that it is not worth bothering to save seed from varieties labelled as F1 as their offspring will show too much variation.

CROSS-POLLINATION

When saving seed, you need to consider how easily the crop cross-pollinates. Plants such as tomatoes and peas are straightforward because they tend to self-pollinate and, therefore, there is little risk of varieties crossing, and the saved seed should come true to the parent.

Other crops, including squashes and chillies, cross-pollinate more freely. To get true seed from these crops, they either need to be hand-pollinated, and the flower then covered in fleece or hessian, or individual varieties must be kept a certain distance apart to prevent mixing. For example, French bean varieties should be kept 2–3m (6½–10ft) apart. However, adequate spacing is often impractical. For example, all plants in the beet family, including beetroot and Swiss chard, will cross-pollinate. Since they are wind-pollinated, the isolation distance would need to be about two miles, so only let one type of beet

crop flower at a time. Brassicas also cross-pollinate easily, and the same rule applies.

ANNUALS AND BIENNIALS

Most vegetable crops are annuals, and the seed can be saved the same year. This includes annual classics such as tomatoes, beans and lettuce. Other plants are biennials, including carrots, leeks and beetroot. These will crop in the first year but, if you are looking to save seed, you'll need to leave a few plants in the ground for them to flower and produce seed the following year.

SAVING AND STORAGE

Seed should only be saved from the best specimen of a crop. When the flowers or seedpods turn brown and dry, they can be removed. For peas and beans, the seeds can immediately be removed from the dry pods but other seedheads should be left to fully dry before the seed and chaff are separated. It may be easier to place entire seedheads in labelled paper bags so everything stays together.

With some crops, including tomatoes and peppers, the seed needs to be harvested before the fruit dries out. In these cases, the seeds are scooped out before being dried. Store the seed in labelled paper envelopes in a cool, dark location before sowing the following year.

Left: Chilli seeds are easily extracted from the fruit then left to dry and saved until the following year.

Drying

Removing the moisture from crops through drying is a good way to store them for future use. If correctly dried, many crops will store for months. Some, including onions, garlic and dried beans, simply need to be left somewhere warm to fully dry out, but others require a more involved process. With effort, you can produce your own sun-dried tomatoes or chilli powder.

HOW TO DRY PRODUCE

Dehydrators are machines that circulate hot air evenly and make drying really easy. An oven can also be used. The temperature needed will vary depending on the crop, but vegetables normally dry out best at just above 50°C (120°F), or the lowest setting available on an oven – around 95°C (200°F). The length of time can vary, depending on the size of the items being dried, and the amount of moisture different crops contain. An oven will be quicker than a dehydrator as the temperature will be higher. Finished crops will be totally dry to the touch.

When drying, choose crops that are at peak ripeness, and try to dry soon after harvesting to preserve flavour. Slice the crops thinly and lay them out in a single layer. There is no need to remove the skin. Vegetables you would not normally eat raw, such as beetroot, benefit from being lightly steamed before drying. Seasonings including salt, pepper, herbs and spices can be added at this point, so try experimenting with what flavours suit you. When the drying process is finished, allow to cool, then transfer into airtight containers for storage. Check the containers after a couple of days to ensure that there is no moisture locked inside.

Right: Beans are the perfect crop for drying; they store indefinitely and then are always on hand to make a substantial meal.

GOOD CROPS FOR DRYING

- Cherry tomatoes can simply be cut in half, while larger tomatoes need to be sliced. Dehydrate at 70–95°C (160–200°F) for 4–9 hours, depending on the temperature. Try flavouring with oregano and adding to pasta dishes.
- Dehydrating courgettes can help deal with gluts. These do best at a lower temperature of around 50–55°C (120–130°F) for 9–10 hours but can also be dried in a low oven for 5–6 hours. Ensure that the slices are no thicker than 5mm (¼in). Courgettes work well when they are only lightly seasoned.
- Dry chillies for 4–8 hours at a temperature of 50–95°C (120–200°F). Once dried, grind into powder and use to flavour a range of dishes.
- Other good crops for drying include sweet peppers, aubergines, carrots, sweet potatoes and okra.

Freezing and fermenting

Both freezing and fermenting can help to preserve and store harvests. When done correctly, they can provide nutritious homegrown produce through all months of the year. In both cases, process the produce soon after harvesting to minimize any loss of nutrition or flavour.

FREEZING

Lots of crops can be frozen, although crops with a high water content are best avoided unless they are processed first. For example, a frozen cauliflower can turn rubbery when defrosted but is still delicious if made into soup before it hits the freezer. Tomatoes turned into sauce, lettuce turned into soup and aubergines cooked in a stew all freeze well.

Many other crops, including broad beans, sweetcorn and cabbage, can be frozen virtually

straight from the garden. The preparation needed will vary between vegetables. For example, broad beans should be podded out, French beans topped and tailed, and sweetcorn can be frozen either on or off the cob. Fresh herbs can be frozen into ice cubes. When freezing, try to freeze in meal-sized portions to help when defrosting, and remove as much air as possible from the bag or box to help seal in the produce.

You can blanch before freezing by very briefly boiling the vegetables and then cooling them down fast, preferably in a bowl of iced water. The produce can then be dried and packed for freezing. Theoretically, this process helps to improve the taste of the crops when defrosted, although freezing can also be done without blanching.

FERMENTING

Preserving vegetables using salt works by stimulating *lactobacillus* bacteria to work with the sugars in the raw foods to prevent them from going off, while also producing a distinctive, tangy flavour. Turning cabbage into sauerkraut or kimchi is well known, but there are other options including radish, carrots, cucumbers and French beans.

In order to ferment, clean and finely chop the vegetables before placing in a sterilized jar, adding herbs or spices if desired. Then make a brine using salt and water. The quantity of salt varies according to the vegetable and personal preference, but a rough guide is 2–3 tablespoons of salt in 1 litre (1¾ pints) of water. Pour the brine over the vegetables and gently press down to remove air. Screw the lid on and leave for 72 hours, topping up the brine every day. A room temperature of 15–20°C (59–68°F) is ideal, any warmer and the crop can turn slimy. Once a slight bubbling has started and a sour scent is detectable, seal the jar and place it in the fridge, where it should keep for around a year.

Left: Herbs can be frozen in ice cubes; when needed, the herby ice cubes can then simply be dropped into a cooking pot.

Below: A glut of pickles is easily preserved by fermenting in jars with a sprinkling of salt.

Index

Picture credits

Mitchell Beazley would like to acknowledge and thank the following for supplying images to be used in this book.

Alamy Stock Photo: Alice Holt 217cr, Alison Thompson 195bl, 217cl, Anne Gilbert 114ar, 265l, Antoniya Kadiyska 252, Bailey-Cooper Photography 153, Barry L. Runk/Grant Heilman Photography 164l, Botanic World 75br, 167a, Christian Hütter/imageBROKER 244r, Christopher Burrows 126–127, Christopher Miles 212, Clare Gainey 139br, 159bl, 229bl, Clement Philippe/Arterra Picture Library 21, Danielle Wood/Image Source Limited 148b, Dave Bevan 185br, Deborah Vernon 151bl, 178, 179a, Dorling Kindersley 207l, Dorling Kindersley/Mark Winwood 83, 184, 210l, 234, Fabiano Sodi 237a, FLPA 203c, Frank Hecker 250l, GardenPhotos.com 29r, Garey Lennox 163bl, 194, Gary K Smith 137br, GKSFlorapics 31b, 219br, 226l, Ian Shaw 176, infinity 256, James Davidson 150, joan gravell 196, John Glover 261bl, John Richmond 168br, Julia Thymia/mauritius images 264r, Kim Gagnon/Stockimo 171br, Martin Hughes-Jones 95br, 133br, 193cl, Matthew Taylor 114al, 117a, 118l, 155ar, 202, mediasculp 220, Neil Langan 102, Nigel Cattlin 30, P Tomlins 83bl, 88l, 101br, 163br, 163a, 227r, Peter Moulton 133bl, Photos Horticultural/Avalon.red 179br, 203br, 235, Rachel Husband 203a, Rex May 229br, 244l, Rob Lavers Photography 48, Rob Wilkinson 197, Ruthanna Kuhn 240, thrillerfillerspiller 83br, Tim Gainey 93bl, 100, 215b, 261br, Tomasz Klejdysz 216, Tony Watson 174–175, Washington Imaging 161bl, www.practicalpictures.com 280, Yann Avril/Biosphoto 152l, 152r

Dreamstime.com: Ahird393 123a, Alexander Lebedko 168al, Andreaobzerova 19, Chernetskaya 35ar, Elena Khramova 224, Elizaveta Elesina 73br, Graham Corney 274–275, Gregory Johnston 162r, Hecos255 269, Hel080808 155al, Ivanna Pavliuk 262, Ivgalis 120, Jamaludin Yusup 97l, Jeri Bland 73bl, Josieelias 114 bl, Juan Moyano 169, Kati Finell 205bl, Maksims Grigorjevs 133a, 157bl, Manfred Ruckszio 249, Marian Pentek Digihelion 177, Marsia16 156, Martien Van Gaalen 255cl, Mavririna2017 179 bl, Nadin333 271, Nahhan 265r, Orest Lyzhechka 86l, 143, 268, Paul Maguire 154, 119l, Sahil Ghosh 257, Sahilghosh7777 124, Sarah2 125, Scphoto48 114br, Secrecy Information 106, Serezniy 282, Studiobarcelona 144–145, Supachai Rattanaruengdech 266r, Tchara 170b, Tj876648298 242l, Toni Jardon 170a, 231br, Yorozu Kitamura 231a, Wirestock 159br

GAP Photos: 18, 32, 39b, 68–69, 71, 73a, 78r, 79b, 90, 92b, 94l, 95a, 101a, 183a, 185a, 208, 209a, 209br, 241, 266l, 77al, 108–109, 132, 134, 137a, 189a, 205a, Amy Vonheim 84, Andrea Jones 180, 190r, BBC Magazines Ltd. 36, Carole Drake 210r, Chris Burrows 217br, 221br, Dave Bevan 193bl, 227l, David Tull 248l, Elke Borkowski 135bl, 151br, 172, 181br, Elke Borkowski 264l, FhF Greenmedia 117br, 222r, 225br, 273a, Fiona Lea 191a, Gary Smith 75a, 151a, 272r, 277, Gillian Plummer 72, Hanneke Reijbroek 173a, Heather Edwards 254, Howard Rice 193br, 259 bl, Jacqui Dracup 140, Jacqui Hurst 98, Jo Whitworth 96l, 161br, 182, Jo Whitworth/Design: Nik Williams Ellis 42, Joanna Kossak 185bl, John Glover 15, 35br, 77br, 80ar, 107r, 193cr, John Swithinbank 93a, 191b, 225a, Jonathan Buckley 37, 74, 83cl, 83cr, 89, 94r, 95bl, 97r, 116, 117bl, 136l, 190l, 195a, 204, Jonathan Buckley/Charles Dowding 223, Jonathan Buckley/Design: Marylyn Abbott 58, Jonathan Buckley/Design: Sarah Raven 99, 115, 131br, Jonathan Need 242r, Julia Boulton 226r, Juliette Wade 63, 187a, Lee Avison 16, Maddie Thornhill 122l, Mandy Bradshaw 13, Manuela Goehner 139a, Mark Bolton 131bl, 273cr, Mark Bolton/RHS garden, Rosemoor, Devon 276, Martin Hughes-Jones 12b, 93bl, 101bl, 171bl, 183bl, 187br, 189bl, 195br, 198–199, 213a, 213bl, 217bl, 219bl, 261a, Martin Staffler 121, Maxine Adcock 35bl, 135a, 205br, 207r, Michael Howes 273br, Neil Holmes 77bl, 211br, Nicola Stocken 45, 147, 238–239, 273cl, Nova Photo Graphik 51, 75bl, 87, 131a, 181bl, Pat Tuson 168ar, Perry Mastrovito 103, Rice/Buckland 41, Richard Bloom 80al, 225bl, Robert Mabic 20, 57, 79a, 82, 92a, 107l, 188, 221bl, Sarah Cuttle 136r, Stephen Studd 54, 148a, Stocks and Green 119r, Thomas Alamy 29l, 80bl, 88r, 193a, 211a, 233a, Tim Gainey 142, 149bl, 155bl, 173bl 186l, 186r, 211bl, 248r, Tommy Tonsberg 229a, Visions 130l, 164r, 255cr

Garden World Images: Oscar D'arcy 80br, Trevor Sims 183br, 189br, 209bl, 213br

GardenImage: Frèdèric Didillon 181a, Friedrich Strauss 4, 47a, 77ar, 78l, 85, 91, 112b, 130r, 141, 260l;

iStock: 49pauly 273bl, andreswd 34, BasieB 255br, bgwalker 251, Eileen Groome 40, emer1940 230, eurobanks 253, frank600 246, Jurgute 206, KjellBrynildsen 259a, Kritchai Chaibangyang 245, Michel VIARD 138, Nataliia Sirobaba 122r, nattrass 258r, naturaltexture 105b, NightAndDayImages 259br, Olgaorly 105a, perfectlab 52, Peter Shaw 46, Robert Pavsic 215ar, robertprzybysz 272l, Roman Mykhalchuk 217a, Scharvik 111, septemberlegs 222l, Tetiana Strilchuk 43r, Topaz777 104, Vysochynska 283, y-studio 247

Jason Ingram: 149a, 162l

living4media: Cecilia Möller 157a, Otmar Diez 138r

MMGI: Marianne Majerus 76

RHS: Anna Brockman 255bl, Carol Sheppard 192, Clive Nichols 129, Georgi Mabee 200, 214, Helen Yates 219a, Jason Ingram 10, 24, 43l, 113r, 128, 221a, 279, Julian Weigall 31a, Mark Bolton 113l, Mark Winwood 110, 232, 233bl, 260r, Neil Hepworth 5, 22, 39a, 61, 218, 233br, Nicola Stocken 146, 159a, 255a, Oliver Dixon 8, 9, Sarah Cuttle 55, 215al, Simon Garbutt 236, Tim Sandall 2–3, 35al, 38, 47b, 49, 70, 81, 149br, 157br, 160l, 160r, 161a, 167b, 168bl, 171a, 228, 231bl, 281

Shutterstock: Dajra 243, denise1203 25, effective stock photos 278, Gaston Cerliani 270, greenair 86r, Ian Grainger 112a, JoannaTkaczuk 118r, Joaquin Traverso 263, Konstantin Aksenov 258l, Lilia Solonari 166, LSP EM 96r, M Schoonover 187bl, Neil Gardner 135br, Olga Bondarenko 203 bl, Oporty786 165, Pavel Dobrovsky 267, sanddebeautheil 50, Sound and Vision 155br, Thoha Firdaus 173br, Valentina_G 201, Wirestock Creators 12a

The Garden Collection: FP/Gary Smith 17, FP/Sibylle Pietrek 158, FP/Ursel Borstell 6–7

With thanks to **Chiltern Seeds** (123bl & br), 250r; **Jekka's Herb Farm** (139bl); Quercus Edibles (237b), and **Suttons Seeds** (photo Tozer 137bl)

Further reading

RHS Grow Your Own Crops in Pots by Kay Maguire (Mitchell Beazley, 2022)

Eating to Extinction by Dan Saladino (Jonathan Cape, 2023)

RHS Step-by-Step Veg Patch by Lucy Chamberlain (DK, 2020)

The Self-Sufficiency Garden by Huw Richards and Sam Cooper (DK, 2024)

RHS Half-Hour Allotment by Lia Leendertz (Frances Lincoln, 2019)

Food for Life by Tim Spector (Vintage, 2024)

No Dig by Charles Dowding (DK, 2022)

The Seed Detective by Adam Alexander (Chelsea Green Publishing UK, 2023)

Around the World in 80 Plants by Stephen Barstow (Permanent Publications, 2021)

Creating a Forest Garden by Martin Crawford (Green Books, 2022)

Soil by Matthew Evans (Murdoch Books, 2021)

For the Love of Soil by Nicole Masters (Nicole Masters, 2019)

Root Stem Leaf Flower by Gill Meller (Quadrille, 2020)

River Cottage Veg Everyday by Hugh Fearnley-Whittingstall (Bloomsbury, 2018)

Higgidy Clever with Veg by Camilla Stephens (Mitchell Beazley, 2024)

Mildreds Vegetarian by Daniel Acevedo and Sarah Wasserman (Mitchell Beazley, 2015)

Author biographies

Sheila Das began her edible growing journey via an allotment. After time spent working at Royal Botanic Gardens, Kew, and English Heritage, Sheila is now responsible for education, edibles, seed and wellbeing at RHS Wisley. Sheila is passionate about growing food in sustainable ways to support planetary and human health and cultivates a wide range of vegetables in her home garden and allotment.

Pavlina Kapsalis trained at RHS Wisley and has worked in its Edibles team for a decade. She helped create Wisley's World Food Garden and specializes in unusual crops. She gives podcasts, and is a keen allotment grower who loves cooking and experimenting with homegrown veg.

Paul Kettell leads the Edibles team at RHS Wisley. He trained in organic crop production, ran a vegetable box scheme and looks after a small vineyard. He is enjoying being part of the transformation to more sustainable garden practices at RHS Wisley.

Simon Maughan is a professional gardener and books editor for the RHS. He trained as a botanist at Edinburgh University and is particularly interested in garden design, growing food and the health benefits of gardening.

Elizabeth Mooney works with the Edibles team at RHS Wisley. She began allotment gardening as a teenager, then trained at Wisley before joining Wisley's World Food Garden. She gives talks on edibles and is passionate about no-dig.

Gareth Richards is Associate Editor of *The Garden* magazine and curates the weekly RHS podcast. He trained at Writtle University College and is a keen allotment grower of many kinds of fruit, vegetables and herbs.

Pete Wilson is team leader of the School of Horticulture at RHS Wisley. He grew up on an organic market garden and has grown vegetables most of his life. He studied garden design and horticulture, taught horticulture at Plumpton College, and has an allotment in Brighton, Sussex.